T0398650

POLITICS OF THE PERIPHERY

GLOBAL SUBURBANISMS

Series Editor: Roger Keil, York University

Urbanization is at the core of the global economy today. Yet, crucially, suburbanization now dominates twenty-first-century urban development. This book series is the first to systematically take stock of worldwide developments in suburbanization and suburbanisms today. Drawing on methodological and analytical approaches from political economy, urban political ecology, and social and cultural geography, the series seeks to situate the complex processes of suburbanization as they pose challenges to policymakers, planners, and academics alike.

For a list of the books published in this series, see page 287.

EDITED BY PIERRE HAMEL

Politics of the Periphery

Governing Global Suburbia

UNIVERSITY OF TORONTO PRESS
Toronto Buffalo London

© University of Toronto Press 2024
Toronto Buffalo London
utorontopress.com

ISBN 978-1-4875-4551-2 (cloth)   ISBN 978-1-4875-5003-5 (EPUB)
                                    ISBN 978-1-4875-4709-7 (PDF)

Global Suburbanisms

Library and Archives Canada Cataloguing in Publication

Title: Politics of the periphery : governing global suburbia / edited by Pierre Hamel.
Names: Hamel, Pierre, 1947– editor.
Series: Global suburbanisms.
Description: Series statement: Global suburbanisms | Includes bibliographical
    references and index.
Identifiers: Canadiana (print) 20230521002 | Canadiana (ebook) 2023052107X |
    ISBN 9781487545512 (cloth) | ISBN 9781487550035 (EPUB) |
    ISBN 9781487547097 (PDF)
Subjects: LCSH: City planning – Political aspects – Case studies. |
    LCSH: Suburbs – Political aspects – Case studies. | LCGFT: Case studies.
Classification: LCC HT166 .P62 2024 | DDC 307.74 – dc23 | 307.1/216 – dc23

Cover design: Val Cooke
Cover images: (top) wacomka/iStockphoto; (bottom) *The Battle of Suburbia*, c. 1940
(oil on canvas), by Carel Weight (1908–87) / Leeds Museums and Galleries, UK /
© Estate of Carel Weight. All rights reserved 2022 / Bridgeman Photos

We wish to acknowledge the land on which the University of Toronto Press
operates. This land is the traditional territory of the Wendat, the Anishnaabeg, the
Haudenosaunee, the Métis, and the Mississaugas of the Credit First Nation.

University of Toronto Press acknowledges the financial support of the Government of
Canada, the Canada Council for the Arts, and the Ontario Arts Council, an agency of
the Government of Ontario, for its publishing activities.

Canada Council   Conseil des Arts
for the Arts   du Canada

ONTARIO ARTS COUNCIL
CONSEIL DES ARTS DE L'ONTARIO
an Ontario government agency
un organisme du gouvernement de l'Ontario

Funded by the   Financé par le
Government   gouvernement
of Canada   du Canada

Contents

Figures and Tables

Figures

Tables

Preface

This book brings together eight original case studies of urban regions around the world where suburban governance was experimented under diverse historical and geographical contexts. Recent forms of urbanization in terms of peripheral growth have been modifying the way urban development is nowadays being restructured. Defined as a process involving state, market, and civil society actors, suburban governance is apprehended in the following pages through collective action and considers social conflicts and democratic deliberations at multiple scales. At the outset, the idea was to better understand the challenges that suburbanization entails for the future of metropolitan regions.

These studies are part of the governance perspective that is one of the three categories – the other two being land and infrastructure – defining the pillars under which worldwide suburbanization trends were examined by a network of international scholars brought together under the SSHRC-funded Major Collaborative Research Initiative (MCRI) *Global Suburbanisms: Governance, Land, and Infrastructure in the 21st Century*, managed by Roger Keil.

Defined as a core process of social change, suburbanization requires governance innovation to deal with accelerated problem constellations in rapidly developing peripheral urban settings. For that matter, we examine how suburbanization is planned and managed in diverse metropolitan regions: Toronto and Montreal (Canada), Miami (United States), Frankfurt (Germany), Paris (France), Istanbul (Turkey), Johannesburg (South Africa), and Shanghai (China).

The key questions each chapter is examining are diverse. They are concerned with the definition of the landscape of local suburbanization but also address the issue of city forms and city life resulting from suburban expansion. The clash of interests among diverse categories of inhabitants and/or actors are inevitably at stake. Thus, as a tool for social and economic regulation and as a normative model of coopera-tion, suburban governance faces multiple challenges.

The contributions collected in this volume are part of a collective endeavour aimed at better understanding how governance of suburban retrofitting and expansion has become unavoidable for defining the future of metropolitan regions. It is the result of a joint effort to better understand how and to what extent governing suburbia can improve current urban living conditions.

To conclude, I would like to thank all contributors who have been part of this project. Without their commitment, expertise, and patience, it would not have been possible to complete it with success. I also thank the anonymous reviewers who suggested specific and constructive comments on an earlier version of this volume. Thanks are also due to the acquisition editor at the University of Toronto Press, Jodi Lewchuk, for her professional support and suggestions at different stages of the book completion and to Carolyn Zapf, the book's copy editor, for her meticulousness and efficacy.

Pierre Hamel
Montreal, July 2023

POLITICS OF THE PERIPHERY

1 Introduction: Suburban Governance under Scrutiny – Revisiting Institutional Arrangements and Planning in Metropolitan Regions

PIERRE HAMEL

Focused on sub/urban[1] governance, this book explores the empirical aspects of collective action and planning in eight urban regions around the world. As urban peripheries have grown, they have borrowed elements from the urban landscapes of central cities (for instance, a reliance on density and mobility), while expanding toward and/or absorbing periurban areas. Consequently, relations between the main components of metropolitan regions can no longer be exclusively defined in terms of central cities, a perspective that has traditionally dominated urban and regional studies.

The new urban forms characterizing contemporary metropolises do reflect a certain continuity with the patterns of the past. But they also include unexpected forms of settlement and design that have emerged in response to social and economic needs and/or as a way of leveraging new technologies. The current situation can be compared to the first decades of the Industrial Revolution, when cities had to come to terms with a sudden influx of rural migrants and the increased concentration of the means of production. However, local resources and urban approaches to spatial organization failed to keep pace with changing material conditions. Nowadays, at the scale of metropolitan regions and beyond, sociospatial transformations are forcing cities to cope with disruptions related to new modalities of capital accumulation and social reproduction. Meanwhile, the urban landscape has been marked by a redefinition of historic cities, a process shaped by emergent socio-economic functions and a shift to novel forms of diversified suburban development.

By looking beyond the stereotypes, it becomes possible to appreciate the diversity of suburban forms and/or "multifaceted modes of suburbanism" (Keil & Addie, 2016). Although not entirely new, such an approach calls attention to the multilayered spatial configuration that surrounds central cities and to the governing components involved in planning suburban landscapes. These layers are superposed and intertwined, and together drive the ongoing process of suburbanization. As John Archer, Paul J.P. Sandul, and Katherine Solomonson write, "suburbia is (and always has been) in a constant state of production" (2015, p. viii). Furthermore, the current urbanization process has reached a new level of transformation. Researchers associate this "new era" with a post-suburban reality (Keil, 2018b; Phelps & Wu, 2011), characterized by new forms of urbanization beyond, as well as within, traditionally suburbanized areas.

In addition, this perspective aligns with the concept of "worlding cities" insofar as it requires looking simultaneously backward and forward in order to understand urban experience in the making.[2] Juxtaposing transitory realities can also contribute to a better understanding of the cultural diversity at play on a global scale:

> Any hope we have to grasp the particularity and variability of the great urban transformation demands situated accounts of how urban environments are formed through specific combinations of the past and the future, the postcolonial and the metropolitan, the global and the situated, but is not dominated by any single mechanism or principle. (Ong, 2011, pp. 8–9)

I freely accept the fact that suburbs do not reflect a static mode of peripheral urban settlement. The evolution of the global suburban landscape (Keil, 2013) includes numerous efforts at adapting to diverse historical and geographic contexts. It has led to the emergence of a new regional urban narrative, one that is no longer based on the supremacy of the centre. Rather, it presents suburban areas as increasingly significant components of urban society, prompting new perspectives on the urban question (Lefebvre, 1970; Soja, 2010b).

Suburban diversity, in relation to national and/or local culture, is key – and perhaps *the* key – to understanding the urban as a contextualized reality. In the post-suburban era (Keil, 2018b; Macleod & Jones, 2011; Phelps & Wu, 2011), processes of social and territorial *recomposition* reflect efforts to cope with transformations occurring simultaneously at different scales of governance. In this way, the spatial imaginary of the city (Stevenson, 2013) is directly challenged by uneven development (evident in social inequalities and marginalization) and by emerging forms of solidarity. This process does not mean that consensus has triumphed over conflict as well as over divisions between classes and/or affinity groups. Rather, it suggests that increased attention should be given to the relationship between peripheries and central cities, and to how actors are adapting to and/or transforming sociospatial relations.

Currently, the ability of actors to cope with a multiplicity of interconnected issues is made more difficult by the need to make unexpected adjustments within a reflexive world, which is characterized by new connections between the local and the global (Paasi & Metzger, 2017; Scott, 2019). Even if globalization dynamics can be reinterpreted locally through "glocalisation" (Swyngedouw, 2004), discrepancies in resources and opportunities among actors and across territories continue to limit action, perhaps to a greater extent than before. Within the field of urban politics, these issues need to be further explored in relation to governance and collective action.

Before discussing methodology and providing an overview of the book, I want to set the stage for the individual case studies presented in its chapters. First, I look at the special significance of expanding suburban space for a redefinition of the urban. Second, I examine the theoretical challenges raised by ongoing processes of suburban governance, as understood from the perspective of collective action. Such an approach sheds light on the very nature of governance itself, including its more controversial aspects. Finally, from an analytical perspective, paying greater attention to the theoretical requirements for understanding the urban through the expansion of peripheral territories is a prerequisite for recognizing similarities and differences between suburban governance processes in different sociospatial contexts.

Expanding Suburban Space within Metropolitan Regions

Since the 1990s, urban studies researchers have devoted much attention to metropolitan or city-regional governance (Brenner, 2019; Heinelt, Razin, & Zimmerman, 2011; Jouve & Lefèvre, 2002; Keil et al., 2017; Phares, 2009; Scott, 2001; Soja, 2000). However, their findings have proven ambivalent at best. Governing metropolitan regions appears to be a difficult, if not impossible, task for a number of reasons. Chief among these is the fragmentation of power across local entities. Indeed, throughout the history of cities, this persistent reality has been addressed with varying degrees of success. In nineteenth-century North America – especially in the United States – the preferred solution to fragmentation was simply to enlarge the central city through amalgamation (Frug, 2002). Although not universally adopted (Keil, 2000), this process of annexing neighbouring territories could have positive effects in terms of government efficiency, among other advantages. Meanwhile, citizens seeking lower taxes, better services, and a higher degree of social homogeneity would often fiercely oppose the amalgamation model. This preference for territorial division has nevertheless yielded many negative sociospatial repercussions, including increased spatial inequality, unequal access to services, failed planning outcomes, and an inability to successfully address pressing socio-economic and environmental problems emerging at a regional scale (Gottdiener & Hutchison, 2011; Paasi & Metzger, 2017). Moreover, in terms of conflicts surrounding regional issues, such as the location of an airport or of other regional infrastructure, the political debate has often undermined policymaking at the metropolitan scale (Heinelt & Razin, 2011).

At the same time, metropolitan politics can often appear too abstract for urban residents to care about (Hayden, 2003; Lefèvre & Pinson, 2020). Indeed, the classic dichotomy between city and suburban politics often creates blind spots covering communities that fall somewhere in between. Such communities find themselves represented by neither local nor regional political institutions (Young & Keil, 2014). In addition, policy shortcomings associated with a representation-based approach cannot be entirely overcome through a more participatory and deliberative one (Bevir & Rhodes, 2010; Farias, 2016; Hamel, 2008; Jouve, 2005). But despite these challenges, few would deny the importance of metropolitan regions, suburbs and all, especially in matters of innovation and economic growth (Downs, 1994).

Nonetheless, such challenges do raise issues associated with institutional design, policy responses, and practical choices, given that contemporary cities are characterized by the spatial dispersion of their activities and, in demographic terms, the primacy of the urban periphery over the central city (Bunting & Filion, 2006). Most would argue that these are the key factors behind metropolitan fragmentation and spatial dispersion, leading to "dysfunctional consequences for the larger society" (Dreier et al., 2001, p. 176). From this perspective, fragmentation is synonymous with the increased segregation of social groups, which has fuelled mutual suspicion and exacerbated inequality (Beauregard, 2006).

Based on past experiences, the institutional capacity of metropolitan governments – or administrative authorities that assume supra-local responsibilities – to overcome divisions and conflicts involving actors at a lower territorial scale often depends on legitimacy. At the same time, those responsible for metropolitan governance must reconcile two rather contradictory "registers of legitimization": a capacity to face international competition and an ability to defend territorial values through the promotion of social cohesion within a defined area. But, while mutual agreement in pursuit of these twin tasks remains highly elusive (Lefèvre, 1998, p. 23), it is by no means impossible to achieve (Nelles, 2012).

Of course, the issues associated with metropolitan and suburban governance go far beyond legitimacy and legitimization. In recent decades, the restructuring of urban and/or metropolitan regions has revealed at least three additional dimensions: (1) new types of relationships between centres and peripheries; (2) a redefinition of metropolitan governance, largely in response to the weakening of traditional territorial state politics; and (3) the emergence of a suburban culture on a global scale.

First, although routinized social practices often seem to occur within a proximate and narrow spatial dimension, day-to-day life actually plays out on a regional scale. As Jon C. Teaford (1997) points out, not only are the pace and structure of metropolitanization tied to a process of territorial recomposition, but political culture – and by extension, concepts of planning and management – are as well. Urban settlements can no longer be understood as they were previously. Compared to the industrial era, current patterns of urban regional growth are much more difficult to predict. The development of "multi-nodal metropolitan systems" or "polynucleated city regions" (Soja, 2010a, p. 374) naturally aligns with the emergence of new representations of mixed-use urban patterns. As a result, new actors and innovative planning practices are introduced and promoted (Harrison et al., 2021; Lefèvre et al., 2013).

The second dimension relates to metropolitan governance. Specifically, researchers need to look more closely at the wide range of actors and practices involved in regulating territorial activities at a metropolitan scale. In terms of social diversity and spatial heterogeneity, suburbs play a pivotal role in urban/metropolitan development (Hanlon & Vicino, 2019). From a historical and geographic standpoint, the development of suburban governance can be described in terms of three different models of governing: state, capital, and authoritarian private action (Ekers et al., 2015). As variations in suburban landscapes and environments begin to be assessed globally, careful empirical observations and subtle analyses of local situations are required to better understand the rules underlying suburban governance. This task is precisely what the contributors to this book have taken up through their respective case studies.

The third dimension relates to globalization and the fact that suburbanism – apprehending suburban living as a way of life (Walks, 2013) – is increasingly defined at a global scale (Keil, 2018a). Not only is suburban development an integral component of the "world of cities," but a highly diverse suburban culture has also proven important to the processes driving urban expansion at a global scale (Scott, 2019). Social relations within and between cities are "at the core of the global"

(Stevenson, 2013, p. 174). Suburbs and their contribution to the expansion of metropolitan regions are connected to global networks of information, technology, capital, and immigration. Experiences of suburban living in different cultural and political contexts are constructed in conversation with one another, contributing to the dissemination of a global representation of suburban culture.

That said, the legacy of single-family detached homes has given way to a widespread recognition of suburbia's diverse forms and images. Precarious neighbourhoods, squatter settlements, high-rise areas on the outskirts of central cities, as well as edge cities: these all reflect a city in the making, a reimagined reality. Through their role in metropolitan processes of regulation and governance, the spatial and cultural components of suburbanization and post-suburbanization are challenging, at a global scale, the traditional ways of planning metropolitan regions (Harrison et al., 2021; Phelps & Wu, 2011; Storper, 2014).

Governance and Governing Global Suburbia

Looking at suburbs through the lens of governance provides a decidedly limited perspective. Nonetheless, this approach raises direct and indirect concerns related to democratic decision making that metropolitan regions cannot ignore. Indeed, the state lacks the stability, legitimacy, and resources required to implement viable solutions in the context of the current political crisis – which is rooted in the challenges facing liberal democracy (Bauman & Bordoni, 2014; Crouch, 2004; Eatwell & Goodwin, 2018). As Patrick Le Galès (2021) has observed, amid the restructuring of capitalism and new waves of globalization driven by technological innovation, developments in national politics have paved the way for the "reemergence of local politics" and its redefinition as "urban politics": "The conception of local politics has been undermined especially by critical geographers who work on spatial frames independent of political jurisdictions and whose work implicitly criticizes the reification of the local at a time of general urbanization … a concern heightened by anthropological research that stresses context, micro relations, alternative political orders beyond statehood, and the politics of everyday life" (p. 347). However, this observation does not mean that national policy choices are no longer meaningful, are being forgone in favour of institutional decentralization, or have lost all influence over local and urban policies. Rather, it implies that beyond the limits of political regulation lies a political space where processes of democratization are not only reassessed and reinvented but risk being de-democratized by privileged elites; where discourses and representations, conflicts and struggles, and efforts to reconcile diverse viewpoints shape ongoing adjustments between states and societies.

That said, recognizing the relationship between the crisis of the political and the rise of local politics should not prevent us from addressing the fact that, in certain countries, the local state remains a fragile institution. This fragility is especially true given how reconfigurations associated with globalization – which drives both privatization and devolution – tend to remove decision-making processes from democratic supervision (Judd et al., 2021)

Governance has therefore emerged from the major transformations of the state that have occurred since the 1970s. This new model of public action takes different forms, depending on the nature of the existing state system. Furthermore, it needs to be understood in light of the prevailing relationship between elites, as well as between the state and civil society. Governance involves "a change in the meaning of government" (Rhodes as quoted in Levi-Faur, 2012, p. 7). It refers to *"new* processes of governing; or *changed* conditions of ordered rule; or *new* methods by which society is governed" (p. 7). The resulting ongoing adjustments have naturally raised questions about the changing nature of the state, whose configuration remains subject to pressure from the forces of globalization, including international economic flows and the creation of supranational regulatory authorities: "The resulting complexity and fragmentation are such that the state increasingly depends on other organizations to secure its intentions and deliver its policies" (Bevir & Rhodes, 2010, p. 81). As a result, governance serves to plug the fissures of the state, simultaneously helping to transform the state's modes of functioning and, more fundamentally, to reassess its nationalist culture.

The crisis of the state and the emergence of governance, as defined from a normative and theoretical perspective, must be juxtaposed with the idea that government, implemented according to the "post-Westphalian model," has proven unable to impose indisputable sovereignty – limited and contained by conventional relations with other states – over a given territory. The state has been forced to share the power required to demonstrate its authority in two directions: upward to markets (especially global markets) and transnational networks; and downward to civil society and local authorities. Consequently, relations between different levels of the state – including interactions with local and regional authorities, as well as with international bodies – have come to be better and more commonly understood in terms of governance than in reference to the idea of government (Piattoni, 2010). This new way of thinking is particularly true in the case of local jurisdictions (Jouve, 2005; Kearns & Paddison, 2000).

Today, cities are often seen as a "more concrete space for politics than the nation" (Sassen, 2004, p. 655; see also Le Galès, 2021). Although this notion has, to a certain extent, long been true, the presence of "global circuits and transboundary networks" (Sassen, 2004, p. 655) has fostered exchanges between cities, while also serving to increase their strategic role in politics and policymaking. The impetus for these changes comes from actors in multiple spheres. Voices from Indigenous and new immigrant communities are increasingly being heard alongside those from more established business and professional milieus, civil society organizations, and social movements.

Quite often, local and urban politics depend on non-governmental actors. This situation does not mean that the state is no longer involved, but the state's priorities are different as it deals with the growing presence of non-governmental actors at the local level. According to several researchers, the notion of urban governance can be particularly useful under these circumstances. For instance, it has been argued that "the concept of urban governance makes it possible to account for fragmentation and inconsistency, allowing for greater emphasis on the vertical and horizontal forms of coordination involved in public action. It makes it possible to better account for the strategic capacity of actors, diverse legitimization processes, and the dynamics of negotiations between stakeholders" (Le Galès, 1995, p. 60).[3]

In other words, urban governance provides a new way of thinking about government and of conceptualizing the state. This approach is necessary because the crisis facing the state[4] cannot be resolved by simply reasserting the institutional path dependency paradigm. The individual and collective capacity to cope with a new urbanity that includes post-suburban processes depends on the ability to adjust to both global forces and local demands. Moving forward, suburban governance will need to reconsider the relationship between central cities and urban peripheries as it has evolved since the beginning of the third millennium (Hamel & Keil, 2015; Phelps & Wu, 2011). However, before looking more closely at the issues related to suburban governance, I need to further clarify the very notion of governance.

In the context of the current democratic crisis (Mounk, 2018), scholars in all fields of inquiry, including urban and regional studies, tend to view the transition from government to governance as a paradigm shift (Kazancigil, 2010). Confidence has been lost in the state's capacity to address market failures and renew the social-democratic compromise that gave rise to the welfare state. Granted, there are numerous critiques of the modalities of governance and the normative dimensions associated with the notion, especially in terms of domination and neoliberal ideology (Davies, 2011; Ives, 2015; Offe, 2009). While I will address this criticism, the fact remains that studying urban politics without reference to governance now seems almost unthinkable.

Governance can be understood in any number of ways (Piattoni, 2010). Even if I were to limit myself to the field of urban and regional studies, and focus solely on work completed in recent decades, a comprehensive review of the literature on governance would go well beyond the scope of this project. In line with the objectives set out above, I will limit myself to outlining those perspectives that best contribute to a better understanding of the relationship between centre and periphery with respect to how metropolitan regions are governed.

I will start with the principle that governance implies a process of political rescaling. As the state faces the emergence of a new cognitive framework – wherein it is not immediately accepted as the exclusive hegemonic authority – new actors become involved in making public policy. Although this new context does not make political conflicts vanish, it does alter their form and cause them to be expressed in new terms. As a result, governance is sometimes portrayed as a kind of laboratory (Hamel & Jouve, 2006; Jouve, 2003). Of course, this notion opens a Pandora's box, since it fails to specify either the nature of collaboration among actors or the rules governing conflict resolution. Before going any further, it is therefore necessary to determine how the study of governance relates to state restructuring and, in more practical terms, how actors see the transition from the traditional public model to the governance model.

Governance has emerged alongside renewed questions about the nature of the state. These questions relate to the state's defining historical and cultural characteristics, as well as to the respective roles of civil servants and elected officials in the management of governmental affairs. Other related issues that need to be addressed in order to properly understand governance include representation and legitimacy, the role of elites, and the participation of non-state actors in decision-making processes. The configuration of these elements varies depending on past experiences, contextual features, and the interplay between the intentionality of actors and the contingency of practices: "People act against the backcloth of inherited traditions that influence them. But people can vary these traditions for reasons of their own in response to circumstances, so these traditions do not determine what they come to believe and do" (Bevir & Rhodes, 2010, p. 197).

These remarks reflect an interpretive and historicist approach. Indeed, above all else, Mark Bevir and R.A.W. Rhodes (2010) see the state as a "cultural practice." By moving away from the principle of the sovereign state as a monolithic reality, their comments point back to the notions of governance and governing. Bevir and Rhodes therefore propose to "decentre the state and governance." They make a plea for a "stateless state," replacing an analysis of formal and/or institutional agreements with an analysis of processes, elaborated through practices, beliefs, and actions (p. 98).[5] Defined as a cultural practice, contemporary governance implies paying attention to meanings and how those meanings evolve into "contingent, shifting, and contested practices" (p. 198). Such an understanding of governance is closely aligned with Muller's (2010) theory of change in public action through cognitive frames.

By focusing on confidence between network actors, Bevir and Rhodes (2010) irrevocably break with an essentialist definition of the state. Instead, they offer a vision of a state shaped by restructuring processes (in line with the earlier reference to a "stateless state"). Such an approach certainly has great potential for examining suburban governance in practice. However, like most of the existing research on governance, it fails to address a difficult question concerning how collective action is conceived. In governance theory, as in earlier work on the sociology of organized action, collective action is understood in terms of relationships of confidence based on collaboration, as well as the sharing of resources and knowledge among actors. Since these actors share a common cognitive framework, it is assumed that they can regulate, if not overcome, most conflicts resulting from divergent interests.

Nonetheless, it should be underlined that this understanding of collective action as an inherent trait clashes with the view of politics put forward by various social movement actors since the 1980s. Indeed, researchers in the field of social movement studies tend to agree that collective action is consistently defined not only by conflict but also by domination. In other words, from the perspective of the sociology of social movements, collective action promoted by social actors is disruptive insofar as it challenges the logic of dominance characterizing the sphere of organized action (Snow & Soule, 2010). The capacity of actors to mount such a challenge is a prerequisite in the reformulation of action and testifies to the specificity of the corresponding social movements (Hamel et al., 2012). As a result, there is a clear divide between the definition of collective action associated with governance theory and that put forward by actors and theorists of social movements.

This divergence reflects two related factors: (1) the status of the actors involved; and (2) the assumptions underlying theoretical perspectives. A better understanding of governance depends on determining which conception of collective action is more credible.

The need for collective action in society is obvious, given the clash between individual and general interests, as well as the need to establish public policies (Peters, 2012). Meanwhile, governance as it is understood in urban and regional studies emphasizes the need for a shared framework of understanding in order to facilitate cooperation and negotiation among actors. Nonetheless, governance networks are often limited to organized institutionalized actors, thereby excluding socially disadvantaged groups. In this regard, governance is not necessarily compatible with democracy – and certainly not with more demanding forms of democracy such as those based on broad notions of deliberative and/or participatory democracy.

As Yannis Papadopoulos has emphasized from a normative standpoint, democratic deliberation promotes inclusiveness, since it gives everyone an equal opportunity to take part in the debate:

> Governance networks by contrast are often exclusive, also because the transaction costs for consensus-building – and for bargaining! – increase with the number of actors having a say. Participation in governance networks should not be confused with the requirements of deliberative procedures whose fairness is associated to their openness to all actors claiming to be affected by decisions. Even if some form of unconstrained and reasoned agreement among equals could be achieved within governance networks, in conformity with the requirements of deliberation, it may merely be an agreement that provides self-referential legitimacy by "insiders," so that the condition of inclusiveness is not met. (Papadopoulos, 2002, pp. 7–8)

In fact, the notion of governance networks assumes that all actors share a common background, making differences – including inequalities – easy to overcome and social recognition a given. By contrast, actors in social movements must fight to overcome barriers to recognition and achieve legitimacy (Medearis, 2004). This reality has been observed even in deliberative forms of governance.

Whereas social movements rely on coercive tactics to stimulate debate and critical reflection on democracy, proponents of deliberative governance (Avritzer, 2006; Hajer & Versteeg, 2008) insist that discussions between participants remain non-binding. Furthermore, these differing views regarding collective action mark not only the distinction between governance and deliberative democracy but also that between actors in social movements and promoters of deliberative democracy. Consequently, Iris Marion Young (2001) emphasizes how proponents of deliberative democracy argue that everyone should use reasonable arguments to promote consensus on a given political issue, whereas social activists view the call for deliberation with mistrust. The latter group recognizes that, in the "real world of politics," structural inequalities shape both institutional mechanisms and results, whereas democratic processes established through the implementation of deliberative norms generally favour actors in a position of power.

Notwithstanding some diversity of opinion in the literature (Farias, 2016; Fung & Wright, 2005; Nabatchi et al., 2012), it is generally agreed that assessing deliberative governance requires a recognition of institutional biases rooted in the methods used to implement this model. So how can the advantages enjoyed by dominant actors be counteracted? Is it even possible to empower minorities, the poor, and the marginalized within this framework? Once again, there is a clear divide between two visions of collective action.

There is no obvious way out of this conundrum. Even if the dialogic process inherent in deliberative governance can sometimes be seen as a "means of renewing civic life and enhancing political legitimacy" (Bevir, 2011, p. 468), it is not always the case. Rather, it is necessary to seek a better understanding of the relationship between actors – including social movement actors – and institutions. Indeed, the involvement of social movements in governance networks is often transitory and conditional. Their participation is not an end in itself, but part of a larger mission. In the field of urban and regional studies, as well as that of social movement theory, researchers have begun to examine this phenomenon more closely over the last decade. Some have set out to define the various strategies social actors use to interact within the new public space created by the internet and social media (see Van Haperen et al., 2018). Others have addressed the new conflictual dynamics between social movements and political parties prompted by the unprecedented threats to political stability that followed the 2008 American financial crisis, which spilled over into southern European countries (Della Porta et al., 2017). Still others have examined how green activism has succeeded in placing environmental issues on the political agenda and/or in developing new forms of resistance based on "prefigurative politics" (Schlosberg & Coles, 2016; see also Heyes & King, 2020).

Breaking with the traditional view of the institution "as a marker at the end of a cyclical social movement process" (Lustiger-Thaler et al., 1998, p. 169) can therefore help foster a better understanding of the role of social movement actors in participative processes and their capacity for countering new forms of political inequality. Finding a new perspective on movements and their actors will require recognizing not only the prevailing institutional fragility of contemporary societies

(Bauman, 2000) but also the ambivalence surrounding the aims of the movements themselves.[6]

A parallel can be drawn between, on the one hand, the institutional ambivalence rooted in structural constraints and normative orientations and, on the other hand, the specificity of social movements. Researchers have found the observations made by Robert K. Merton useful in this respect:

> As Merton (1977) argued, allocative and regulative societal mechanisms and institutions cannot avoid the effects of their own ambivalent characteristics, which stem from tensions and contradiction-driven structural elements as well as the pendulum-like reflexes of retreat and participation. This foundational ambivalence, embedded within both structural processes and action's normative orientation, is exacerbated within late modern societies by the constraints and opportunities of globalization. (Hamel et al., 2012, p. 187)

The possibility that social movements can operate within institutions, given both institutional fragility and the weak connection between actors and institutions in late modern societies, fundamentally transforms the prevailing understanding of collective action. It raises the question of whether the notion of "strategic action fields," defined by Neil Fligstein and Doug McAdam (2012, p. 9) as "fundamental units of collective action," could help reconcile the opposing definitions of collective action discussed above. For these authors, what fundamentally matters is the capacity of actors to pursue social change in relation to – and beyond – the structural and normative constraints imposed by societal norms. From this perspective, institutional instability emerges as a key factor for all actors:

> Reproduction of the field may be the norm, but it is always accompanied by routine jockeying for position and incremental changes. As new actors appear and old ones disappear, rules get modified and incumbent/challenger relations are renegotiated. These kinds of piecemeal adjustments are the rule in virtually all fields, even the most stable. (Fligstein & McAdam, 2012, p. 32)

Unfortunately, this reading of social change does not entirely resolve the uncertainty associated with the previously mentioned divergent conceptions of collective action. Participation in network governance and/or deliberative governance is never a given for social movements and their actors. "Strategic action fields," as defined by Fligstein and

McAdam, tend to concentrate on dual relations between challengers and incumbents, too often ignoring "the context of institutions, values, and the broader reach of fractal structures in understanding agency and its consequences" (Goldstone & Useem, 2012, p. 45). If the fundamental claims made by social movements are to be taken seriously, it remains difficult to reconcile the underlying vision of collective action supporting those claims with the one promoted by institutional actors, for whom conflicts can always be overcome or regulated.

From this standpoint, I think that the gap between the two conceptions of collective action should therefore be maintained. Their synthesis is neither possible nor desirable. The contradictions at work remain too strong. However, some degree of reconciliation may be possible on a practical level. For instance, Francesca Poletta (2008) has underscored how "real-world deliberation" (p. 18) can enrich civic and local culture by providing social actors with an opportunity to influence decisions by insisting on "different models of talk or different models of politics" (p. 18). After all, these models correspond to various forms of deliberative civic engagement that residents and/or citizens can adopt in response to shared challenges. It is through practical compromises that social movements are sometimes able to participate in governance and/or deliberative networks and to engage in negotiations with the state and its representatives, as well as with private-sector actors. This actuality is all the more true given the current fragility of institutions. When such opportunities arise, the tension between a radical definition of collective action and an accommodating one can be worked out through practical or empirical compromises. What are the conditions for such compromises (Gourgues et al., 2013)? What place is given to social movement actors in different sociospatial contexts? To what extent is distrust of democracy, in general terms (Rosanvallon, 2006, 2020), transferred to suburban governance issues? These are some of the questions that an empirical analysis of suburban governance must address.

Similarities and Differences in Suburban Governance Processes across Different Sociospatial Contexts

Some additional clarification is needed to establish a comparative framework for understanding suburban governance and its role in redefining urban and/or metropolitan regions. Peripheral urban development is characterized by both its diversity and ubiquity, whereas governance relates to how actors and processes help determine and shape "the planning, design, politics, and economics of suburban spaces and ways of life" (Ekers et al., 2015, p. 19). Suburbanization is therefore producing "qualitatively distinct" ways of living. It follows that the key "modalities" of suburban governance can be associated with specific underlying logics. But what kinds of interactions occur between actors and processes within these modalities? What are the similarities and differences across diverse settlements with regard to these interactions? But before addressing these questions, the centre-periphery relationship requires closer attention.

The hypothesis of "the complete urbanization of society," first put forward by Henri Lefebvre (1970, p. 7) in *La révolution urbaine*, can serve as a starting point for rethinking the centre-periphery relationship. By conceiving of space as the result of the capitalist process of production and by defining it in "global and total" terms (p. 206), Lefebvre reveals new modalities of social relations with regard to space. More helpful still is the historical, social, and cultural critique of cities on which he bases his original theorization of the urban.

The way that Lefebvre (1970) conceptualizes "the urban" is well aligned with more recent theoretical developments (Brenner, 2019; Harvey, 2012; Soja, 2010b). Breaking with a focus on the historical city, the notion of the urban opens up the possibility of addressing social relations with regard to space in an urbanized society. Described as a "pure form," the urban is a "place of encounter," characterized by the idea of simultaneity: "This form has no specific content, but serves as a centre of attraction and life" (Lefebvre, 1970, p. 59).[7]

More importantly, from both an empirical and theoretical perspective, the uniqueness of the urban relates to its "centrality." In general terms, any given point within urban space has the potential to become a core element (Lefebvre, 1970, p. 156).[8] Access to centrality is fundamental to how the urban can transform social spaces, and it is what drives the ongoing "urban revolution." Indeed, for Lefebvre, social justice and "the right to the city" depend on access to centrality. However, access does not reflect a return to traditional cities. Rather, the right to the city refers to a "transformed and renewed" urban life, which itself depends on the power of the urban as such, on its transformative capacity: "The urban brings everything together. As a form, the urban trans-forms what it brings together (concentrates)" (p. 230).[9]

Lefebvre's understanding of urban life and centrality stands as an injunction against continuing to interpret territorial divisions in reference to a traditional reading of industrial urbanization. In other words, peripheries can no longer be merely defined in terms of a hierarchy that subordinates them to central cities. As Stefan Kipfer et al. (2008) explain, "at the regional scale, central functions of city centers can 'implode' socially and economically while cities 'explode' into far-flung metropolitan agglomerations" (p. 292).

It is also important to remember that, in some countries, suburbs have been playing a dynamic role in "urbanization and economic growth" since the early nineteenth century (Hayden, 2003, p. 17). Centrality has therefore not been confined to "crowded centres of cities" but rather spread across regional territories. From an empirical perspective, how can suburban centrality be defined? Is it faced with the same social inequalities that characterize access to centrality in central cities?

In line with Lefebvre's outlook, and in spite of the spatial hierarchies shaped by ongoing realignments, similar contradictions are at play across centres and peripheries, as well as within peripheries. This point is especially important to keep in mind when considering how "the urban revolution" is spreading around the globe. Drawing on Lefebvre's conceptualization, Andy Merrifield directly addresses the consequences of this urban revolution:

> Within this conceptualization we need to dispense with all the old chestnuts between North and South, between developed and underdeveloped worlds, between urban and rural, between urban and regional, between city and suburb, and so forth … From this standpoint, frontier lines don't pass between any North-South or urban-rural divide but reside "within the phenomenon of the urban itself," as Lefebvre says in *The Urban Revolution*. Hence the need to conceptualize and politicize how the globe is no longer demarcated through definitive splits between strict opposites: all demarcations and frontier lines are immanent within urban society, between dominated peripheries and dominating centers that exist all over the planet. (Merrifield, 2012, pp. 3–4)

Researchers in the field of urban studies have once again embraced the notion of "planetary urbanization" in reference to a fully urbanized world – what Lefebvre (1970, p. 223) described as "the prodigious expansion of the 'urban' on a global scale"[10] – as a means of breaking with a centralized reading of urbanity. The result has been a deeper appreciation of the diversity of urban forms present in polynucleated metropolitan regions (Brenner & Schmid, 2015; Keil, 2018b). However, it does not necessarily mean that cities are losing their uniqueness. Again, the specificity of local culture remains strong. As Michael Storper and Allen J. Scott (2016) have highlighted, "despite the fact that in the world system of the 21st century spatial interconnections have attained unprecedented levels of volume and geographic extension, the need for proximity and local interaction has in many ways been bolstered within

the urban land nexus" (p. 1131). From this perspective, planetary urbanization and globalized capitalism do not dissolve attachment to
territorial spaces. In fact, the opposite is true. Territorial differences remain important markers in the construction of individual and social
identities. And thanks to recent waves of capitalist development, the
weight of cities has become the object of renewed attention, generating
competition and conflicts (Lefèvre & Pinson, 2020).

From a practical perspective, these observations on the growing importance of metropolitan issues are not meant to imply that metropolises are "becoming an autonomous political agent of the global space
economy" (Jonas & Ward, 2007, p. 169). Nor does the blurring of traditional boundaries mean that contradictions and inequalities are vanish-
ing. Nonetheless, the emphasis on governance, and more specifically
on suburban governance, introduces a decentred view of metropolitan
growth and issues (Storper, 2014). Such a view can help to examine relations between the multiple components of territoriality from a cultural
and sociopolitical perspective. Beyond a recognition that the problems
faced by suburbs and central cities are "interrelated" (Dreier et al., 2001,
p. 132), an approach to urban politics focused on the "politics of the periphery" allows for a new appreciation of collective action in response
to urban issues, in contrast to the traditional attention given mainly to
central cities (Scott, 2019).

Understanding the restructuring of local-regional and local-global
relations naturally entails considering structural or determining factors –
above all, the capitalist market and the various layers of the state.
But it is the intentionality and agency of social actors that is at play.
Governance poses new challenges to collective action and heightens
the tension between the divergent conceptual definitions given above.
These challenges call for a re-examination of the moral basis of social
inequality in relation to the empirical arrangements that exist in diverse
territorial settings.

Suburban governance involves various categories of actors, regardless of whether it addresses either suburbanization through the expansion of peripheries and the redefinition of territorial networks at a
regional scale or "suburbanisms" characterized by a specific way of life.
Here, I am referring not only to the local state (that is, the various levels
of the state that play a role in managing and planning urban matters)
but also to the business community, professional circles, households,
and social movements. These actors are regularly called upon to play
a rather vital role in suburban governance: How can they resolve ur-
ban/suburban conflicts through governance in different national/local
cultural and economic contexts? To what extent does the regional scale

represent a viable space for building compromise and/or for addressing the multiple issues (separately or simultaneously) faced by centres and peripheries with regard to concerns about the environment, collective mobility, social housing, or inequality across the entire territory of an agglomeration? From a global perspective, does suburban governance engender new forms of governance? What does the future hold for peripheries and central cities, given their "interrelated" destiny?

When it comes to understanding suburban governance, these questions merely scratch the surface. It can be very difficult to grasp how, on a global scale, suburbs and central cities are redefining metropolitan regions in economic and social terms. Indeed, social movement actors have had difficulty implementing strategies at a metropolitan scale. How do they perceive conflicts and/or cooperation between centres and peripheries? In the metropolitan context, how are interactions between state and non-state actors organized? How is it possible to deal with institutions that rarely have a clear mandate to address regional concerns or to provide the required resources?

The wide range of collective actors involved in suburban governance also undermines the definition of collective action provided above. The very form and content of governance therefore need to be reassessed.

It has become necessary to examine suburban governance in relation to empirical realities. Incidentally, I second Jennifer Robinson's (2014) call to put "case studies work into wider conversation" (p. 66), by engaging with the urban studies literature and by adopting a "more critical planetary reading practice," in order to develop "new lines of theorization" (p. 65). Such an approach can also contribute to a better understanding of how suburban governance is implemented at a regional scale and how it is shaped by local culture as well as by global social, economic, and urban trends.

An emphasis on the diversity of urban experimentation sheds light on suburban governance from four different perspectives. The first of these relates to *opportunities for cooperation and conflict between actors involved in suburban governance*. This perspective requires a focus on how the different levels of government involved in providing state services are distributed across the territory and how they adapt to pressures from above and from below. The second perspective involves *assessing the institutional forms taken by suburban governance at different scales of governing*. Indeed, multilevel governance poses a challenge to the very nature of the national state. It is therefore necessary to focus directly on the territorialization of social, economic, and political relations, based on the idea that suburban processes are "no longer focused predominantly upon any single, self-enclosed geographical scale" (Brenner,

2004, p. 47). The third perspective addresses the *political outcomes of suburban governance*. This approach requires examining the strategies implemented by social and political actors, and the results achieved by these strategies in terms of both vested interests and public concerns. Is it possible to stop defining the ideology of governance in terms of "ideals of efficiency and rationality of administration" (Harvey, 2009, p. 71)? Finally, the fourth perspective involves assessing the *impact of suburban governance on civil society actors in relation to metropolitan development*. This viewpoint refers to the capacity of civil society actors to take part in, and influence, decision-making processes pertaining to the future of suburbanization.

Before saying a few words about the methodology and the subsequent chapters, I would like to return very quickly to the themes I have just reviewed regarding the dimensions involved in suburban governance. The literature that I referred to for defining the perspective within which the empirical reality of suburban governance in diverse metropolitan regions around the world has been experienced and documented is at the intersection of three fields of study: urban and regional studies, political analysis concerning the crisis of the state, and social movement studies. When combined, these three fields bring to the fore the theoretical elements required for exploring suburban change in metropolitan regions where the urban periphery is no longer confined to provide housing for the middle classes but is also based on mixed uses, including economic activities and critical connections to global centrality.

The emancipation of suburbs, so to speak, from the core city led scholars of urban studies to change the way they were looking at cities. This development has been examined by a growing number of studies dedicated to better understanding the meaning of planetary urbanization with the emergence of new configurations of urban settings where suburbia is at the forefront for several reasons (Hanlon & Vicino, 2019). From then on, territorial and local values have conflicted with the requirement of an economic competition established more and more at an international scale. It was then difficult to predict how the industrial city was going to be restructured.

At the same time, it was the state, its legitimacy and its definition as an actor and an institution, which was at stake. It was observed that the state had increasingly fewer resources to act in the same top-down manner as before. Its monolithic configuration has been brought to the fore, among other factors, by the rise of neoliberalism from the 1970s onward, contributing to the critique of the welfare state, triggering a real crisis. It is on this background that, in the field of public action, through "urban politics," the discourse and the perspective of governance flourished.

Considering the state defined as a "cultural practice" (Bevir & Rhodes, 2010) brings the notion of governance into a new light, allowing dimensions often overlooked to be brought in. Such is the case with several notions like legitimacy, collective action, and participatory democracy. These notions have been introduced to understand the paradigm shift that goes with governance. In that respect, the sociology of social movements was considered because it helps to make the case for a different understanding of collective action compared to the one utilized in the usual literature on governance, borrowed from the sociology of organizations. If these two definitions of collective action are difficult to reconcile, I think it is possible to maintain the two while exploring some avenues of reconciliation. Finally, when it comes to focusing on suburban governance, and following several researchers, I think it is necessary to put emphasis on a "decentred view" of metropolitan planning and development.

Methodology and Overview

The case studies included in this book are not meant to reflect the full diversity of situations experienced by metropolitan regions worldwide in recent decades. Beyond the established typologies, we know that the trajectories of specific urban regions remain subject to various unique combinations of objective and subjective factors. Although certain common underlying factors do shape collective action, distinct geographic and historic contexts clearly influence the production of suburban forms in relation to the landscape, producing singular results. Here is where the "shifting geographies of global urbanization" (Robinson & Roy, 2016, p. 181) takes on its full meaning.

This book therefore sets out to explore the "politics of the periphery" through suburban governance in diverse contexts in order to better understand how outcomes are shaped by the possibilities and constraints confronting actors. The different case studies feature a diverse range of local actors facing both the specificity of their respective milieus and the broader context of extended urbanization, as metropolitan regions cope with new territorial challenges. Furthermore, the contributors are highly familiar with their respective contexts of study, having extensively researched the corresponding metropolitan regions.

The book's focus on suburban governance provides an opportunity to take a new perspective on governing suburbia. Meanwhile, close attention to the relationship between the local and the global makes it possible to delve deeper into the planning processes of evolving metropolitan regions without ignoring efforts to challenge such processes. Within a *problématique* that defined the urban in reference to theoretical as well as practical concerns and with an awareness of the diverse potential outcomes of collective action, the presence of social actors – especially disadvantaged groups and those facing discrimination – becomes crucial to achieving solidarity and compromise around suburban issues. In this respect, understanding suburban governance requires a more careful examination of collective action. The situation cannot be better conceptualized without the close empirical study of suburban processes, practices, and outcomes within and across metropolitan regions.

In terms of methodology, all the case studies presented in the book are based on two complementary approaches: first, an analysis of official public policy statements released by various levels of the local state with respect to the relationship between different territorial components of the eight urban and/or metropolitan regions under study; and, second, an examination of the positions taken by the main categories of actors, based on data gathered through semi-directive interviews.

The relevance of case study research is well established, not only in urban studies but across the social sciences. Above all, this approach is well suited to context-dependent knowledge, such as that associated with the study of urban agglomerations (Flyvbjerg, 2006). Case study research is particularly useful when it comes to better understanding social practices – their specificity and the circumstances under which they evolve – as well as the various processes involved in formulating public policies (Bartlett & Vavrus, 2016).

When conducting the semi-directive interviews, the contributors relied on a common template covering four key dimensions: (1) the landscape of local urbanization, (2) the role of the state, (3) the role of civil society, and (4) suburban expansion, city form, and city life. The template proposed a series of questions for encouraging interview participants (civil servants, elected officials, social actors) to discuss how suburbanization can be defined in terms of spatial expansion. The interviews were also intended to provide a better understanding of the extent to which this view of suburbanization has informed the actions and choices that have reshaped urban planning on a regional scale and even metropolitan management. Interviewees were encouraged to share their point of view on past and ongoing issues related to governing suburbia. Given the diversity of current urban forms and the fact that their main components are no longer primarily defined in terms of a relationship with a single urban core (that is, the central city), the interviews sought to better understand how and to what extent territorial expansion has been a determining factor in the development of metropolitan regions. While the research presented in the book reflects a shared general perspective on the theme of suburban governance, individual researchers had to adapt the interview template to the specific agglomeration under study and to their own urban *problématique*.

Indeed, the urban and/or metropolitan regions examined in the subsequent chapters have all followed singular paths. Their demographic and economic weights do not have the same significance, whether on a national or a global scale. Nonetheless, local actors have consistently needed to adapt to external constraints, especially those imposed by capitalist restructuring. Although local responses to such forces vary according to multiple structural and conjunctural factors, they always emerge from struggles that occur at the various scales of regulation where political compromises are defined. For example, from one context to the next, the phenomenon described as the "rise of local politics" (Le Galès, 2021) has had an uneven impact on the quality of urban life enjoyed by most residents.

Suburban governance, as it is explored in the different chapters of this book, is embedded in the fabric of metropolitan governance and manifests itself in ways that converge with the latter. In turn, metropolitan governance displays a high degree of heterogeneity, considering the institutional modalities implemented over the last three or four decades. However, this situation does not mean that civil society actors have consistently found themselves marginalized or have lacked any influence in decision-making processes. But, as other researchers have noted, civil society is by no means organized at a metropolitan scale (Lefèvre & Pinson, 2020).

Metropolitan regions, whose modes of governing suburbia are explored in the chapters that follow, belong to a certain extent to the same globalizing world where competitive metropolitan regionalism is being shaped by capitalist restructuring, despite the heterogeneous practices involved. In this context, as new modalities of governing local territories are promoted and revised, strong interdependencies emerge among territorial units and their representatives at several scales (Storper, 2014).

As mentioned previously, the eight case studies presented in this book are not representative of all existing or possible cases of suburban governance. Nevertheless, they do generate contextualized empirical knowledge capable of shedding light on the social, cultural, and political issues that arise through processes of economic and spatial restructuring in metropolitan regions around the world. In that respect, they contribute to a clearer understanding of how extended urbanization is helping redefine cities and urban life amid the increased uncertainty of the early twenty-first century.

The first three case studies address contrasting North American urban agglomerations, including Montreal and Toronto. Even if these two Canadian cities share some characteristics with respect to institutional reforms at the metropolitan scale, they are also quite distinct in terms of their cultural specificity. Meanwhile, Miami increasingly stands out for its social diversity: "it has the highest proportion of foreign-born residents of any major city in the U.S., and the largest proportion of residents that speak another language besides English" (Nijman, 2000, p. 140). The book's focus then shifts to Europe, where the case of Frankfurt is marked by a strong tradition of planning on a regional scale, with that of Paris revealing an original approach to regulation at a metropolitan scale through institutional innovation. The three remaining case studies deal with the urban regions and core cities that have the largest populations in Turkey, South Africa, and China. Over the last two decades, efforts to foster urban and suburban development in Istanbul, Johannesburg, and Shanghai have been subject to pressure from both real estate capital and local initiatives.

Written by Pierre Filion, Roger Keil, and Michael Collens, chapter 2 examines how, in the case of Toronto, patterns of suburban development contrast with those observed in the central city. In particular, some interview participants described a disconnect between "the conventional image of the suburb" and the everyday reality of residents. Recognizing how, in many respects, the Toronto region presents a "subset" of North American suburbs, the authors document the specificity of a suburban landscape characterized by diversity through its population, its built form and infrastructure, as well as its economic profile. In chapter 3, I begin by presenting the main components and issues of suburban development in the Montreal metropolitan region. I go on to investigate the role played in suburban and metropolitan governance by diverse categories of stakeholders. Despite challenges at the metropolitan level, where the actors and interests of the central city have tended to dominate, the political representatives of suburban municipalities have become increasingly assertive. In chapter 4, Fernando Burga considers the issue of segregation in Miami-Dade County, one of the three components of the Miami Metropolitan Statistical Area. He stresses the need to recognize Miami-Dade County as a "majority-minority region, where immigrant, racial, and ethnic minorities represent the majority of residents." The Hispanic population, especially its Cuban component, has become a major actor on the local scene, identifying itself as a distinct ethnic group while increasingly acting as a "dominant stakeholder." Above all, this chapter tells the story of immigrant groups finding empowerment in a context of "authoritarian private governance."

Chapter 5 provides Valentin Meilinger and Jochen Monstadt with an opportunity to explore suburban development in Greater Frankfurt. The authors describe a "sophisticated system of spatial planning" focused on controlling urban sprawl and improving living conditions. Ongoing suburbanization therefore occurs within the context of an "ambitious" land-use planning system. However, this system has often failed to counter the market forces and strong sociospatial polarization prevailing at a regional scale. In chapter 6, Marie-Hélène Bacqué and Éric Charmes analyse two key issues associated with suburban governance in the Paris metropolitan region. Whereas the first concerns the relationship between Paris and its traditional suburbs, the second involves relations with the so-called "periurbs" of "Greater Paris." The institutional authorities responsible for local and regional governance are forced to deal with divisions and conflicts based on complex and often overlapping loyalties. Considering how the metropolitanization of the Paris region has exacerbated social inequality, the authors raise the possibility that the ongoing process of sociospatial fragmentation will only intensify. And given the priorities expressed by the central state so far, it has been difficult for working-class and poorer residents to have their voices heard.

Authored by Murat Üçoğlu and K. Murat Güney, chapter 7 examines the recent history of suburbanization in Istanbul, as well as the corresponding structure of governance at both the local and metropolitan scale. "Unprecedented" population growth that began in the 1980s led the government to create a special agency responsible for housing issues, with the aim of providing affordable housing to middle-class households. In fact, the authoritarian model of governance implemented by the ruling political party – a model that relies on private-sector alliances, including financial investors and construction companies – has prioritized luxury real estate projects in gated communities on the periphery. Meanwhile, the steady growth of social and wealth inequality has only served to aggravate the democratic deficit of both the central city and the metropolitan region. In chapter 8, Margot Rubin, Alison Todes, and Alan Mabin undertake a historical and political analysis of the development of Johannesburg, with an emphasis on the role of "powerful lobbies" and other non-state actors. Since the mid-1990s, institutional reforms have sought to improve land-use planning and better control urban and suburban development through the creation of a metropolitan local government at the scale of the City of Johannesburg (CoJ), the main component of the Gauteng city region – "a polycentric but mostly continuously urbanized area of over 15.4 million people." The chapter focuses on three areas of the CoJ: the township of Soweto, the elite suburb of Emmarentia, and the northwestern periphery of Johannesburg, the site of "new suburban growth." Political initiatives intended to consolidate urban areas within "metropolitan municipalities" have transformed interactions between various categories of actors involved in suburban governance. However, successful planning cannot be taken for granted, since interests groups remain strong and continue to find new means of promoting their projects. The book's final case study is presented in chapter 9, where Fulong Wu analyses how suburban governance has changed in Shanghai over recent years. Previously, territorial expansion and development had taken the form of "urban sprawl driven by residential development adjacent to the core city." Today, the process primarily involves the development of new towns. The author focuses on Lingang, a suburban zone "outside the main built-up area of Shanghai" managed by a "quasi-government agency." This example demonstrates how suburbs are inserted between the city and countryside, as well as how market tools such as development agencies support state entrepreneurialism. Indeed, a new model of governing is emerging as "various social and management innovations" are trying to include local communities into the state's strategic development effort.

In the tenth and final chapter, I conclude the book with a series of lessons that can be drawn from the case studies. In addition to considering the choices made by social and political actors who face diverse issues and general uncertainty with regard to suburbanization processes and suburban governance in their respective metropolitan regions, I also further reflect on the characteristics of the various political regimes where such issues and uncertainty are present.

NOTES

1 Within suburban studies, the written format "sub/urban" emphasizes that the relations between suburbs and city cores have changed fundamentally over the last decades. Suburbs are no longer defined exclusively through their dependency on, and/or as an extension of city centres as was the case during the industrial era of the nineteenth century. The new suburban way of life with its diversity needs to be better understood. In that respect, I can quote Roger Keil (2018b): "The post-suburban in-between city has developed its own logic and dialectics of space, contradictory and productive of

new centre-periphery relationships beyond the old city-suburb binary …
An important insight from this shift beyond the dichotomy is the notion
that, as Bormann says, 'urbanity as a form of life has emancipated itself
from the cities and has long nested in the urban hinterland, even in so-
called rural areas.' We might then speak of the phenomenon of sub/urban-
ity instead" (p. 75). Nonetheless, given that we are dealing with ongoing
transformations still characterized by reminiscences of the past in both representations and through diverse social, political, and planning practices –
but also to avoid certain confusions – I will be using the written format
"suburban" rather than "sub/urban." However, this decision does not
mean that the suburban reality as apprehended in this book aims to restore
a past that is irremediably moving away from us. It's the other way around.

2 As Aihwa Ong explains, "'worlding' is employed here not to signal adherence to a world-historical logic of 'world making,' as in a crude reading of
Marx's conception stages of historical development (cf. Marx and Engels,
1848), but rather to identify the projects and practices that instantiate some
vision of the world in formation" (Ong 2011, p. 11).

3 Author's translation of the following quotation: "Le concept de gouvernance urbaine permet de reconnaître la fragmentation, l'incohérence
et suggère de mettre l'accent sur les formes de coordination verticale et
horizontale de l'action publique. Il permet de mieux prendre en compte la
capacité stratégique des acteurs, la diversité des processus de légitimation,
la dynamique de négociation entre acteurs" (Le Galès, 1995, p. 60).

4 For instance, as Bauman and Bordoni (2014) have mentioned: "We live in a
constant state of crisis, and this crisis also involves the modern state, whose
structure, functionality, effectiveness (including the system of democratic
representation) are no longer suited to the times in which we live" (p. 27).

5 It is worth quoting these authors at greater length: "There is no necessary logical or structural process determining the form of network
governance or the role of the 'central state' in the governance of governance. Patterns of governance, and changes in such patterns, cannot
be explained by any of the intrinsic rationality of markets, the path
dependency of institutions, or the state's new tool kit for managing the
mix of governing structures.

   The third-wave analysis of governance [the first-wave is characterized
by changes in the relation between the state and civil society while the
polity is converging with a 'hollowed-out state,' whereas the second-wave
is driven by a 'return to the state with the idea of metagovernance'] an-
nounces the arrival of the stateless state. It argues that the state arises out of
the diverse actions and practices inspired by varied beliefs and traditions.
The state, or pattern of rule, is the contingent product of diverse actions
and political struggles informed by beliefs of agents rooted in traditions.

Our approach seeks to explain the state by reference to historical meanings infusing the beliefs and practices of individual actors. It encourages political scientists to decentre the state and governance and focus on the social construction of practices" (Bevir & Rhodes, 2010, pp. 98–9).

6 This ambivalence remains at the core of the conception of collective action developed through the theoretical study of social movements. But while recognizing that, "beyond the specter of institutionalization," movements are defined by their ambivalence toward participation and withdrawal, I would argue that institutions are not necessarily an anathema for social movement actors. Indeed, institutions can serve as a starting point for the construction of "personal and social experiences" that movements can provide when they are recognized as legitimate actors (Hamel et al., 2012, p. 188).

7 Author's translation of the following quotation: "Cette forme n'a aucun contenu spécifique, mais tout y vient et y vit" (Lefebvre, 1970, p. 59).

8 This characteristic corresponds to an abstract conception of centrality: "Que n'importe quel point puisse devenir central, c'est le sens de l'espace-temps urbain. La centralité n'est pas indifférente, au contraire, à ce qu'elle rassemble, car il lui faut un contenu. Et cependant ce contenu est quelconque … Tout se passe dans la réalité urbaine comme si tout ce qui la compose pouvait se rapprocher, encore et toujours plus. Ainsi se conçoit l'urbain, ainsi se perçoit-il, ainsi se rêve-t-il, confusément" (Lefebvre, 1970, pp. 156–7).

9 Author's translation of the following quotation: "L'urbain rassemble. L'urbain en tant que forme trans-forme ce qu'il rassemble (concentre)" (Lefebvre, 1970, p. 230).

10 Author's translation of "la prodigieuse extension de 'l'urbain' à la planète" (Lefebvre, 1970, p. 223).

REFERENCES

Archer, J., Sandul, P.J.P, & Solomonson, K. (2015). Introduction: Making, performing, living suburbia. In J. Archer, P.J.P Sandul, & K. Solomonson (Eds.), *Making suburbia: New histories of everyday America* (pp. vii–xxv). University of Minnesota Press.

Avritzer, L. (2006). New public spheres in Brazil: Local democracy and deliberative politics. *International Journal of Urban and Regional Research, 30*(3), 623–37. https://doi.org/10.1111/j.1468-2427.2006.00692.x

Bartlett, L., & Vavrus, F. (2016). *Rethinking case study research: A comparative approach*. Routledge.

Bauman, Z. (2000). *Liquid modernity*. Polity Press.

Bauman, Z., & Bordoni, C. (2014). *State of crisis*. Polity Press.

Beauregard, R.A. (2006). *When America became suburban*. University of Minnesota Press.

Bevir, M. (2011). Governance and governmentality after neoliberalism. *Policy & Politics, 39*(4), 457–71. https://doi.org/10.1332/030557310X550141

Bevir, M., & Rhodes, R.A.W. (2010). *The state as cultural practice.* Oxford University Press.

Brenner, N. (2004). *New state spaces: Urban governance and the rescaling of statehood.* Oxford University Press.

Brenner, N. (2019). *New urban spaces: Urban theory and the scale question.* Oxford University Press.

Brenner, N., & Schmid, C. (2015). Towards a new epistemology of the urban? *City, 19*(2–3), 151–82. https://doi.org/10.1080/13604813.2015.1014712

Bunting, T., & Filion, P. (2006). *Canadian cities in transition: Local through global perspectives.* Oxford University Press.

Crouch, C. (2004). *Post-democracy.* Polity Press.

Davies, J. (2011). *Challenging governance theory: From networks to hegemony.* Policy Press.

Della Porta, D., Fernández, J., Kouki, H., & Mosca, L. (2017). *Movement parties against austerity.* Polity Press.

Downs, A. (1994). *New visions for metropolitan America.* Brookings Institution Press.

Dreier, P., Mollenkopf, J., & Swanstrom, T. (2001). *Place matters: Metropolitics for the twenty-first century.* University Press of Kansas.

Eatwell, R., & Goodwin, M. (2018). *National populism: The revolt against liberal democracy.* Penguin Books.

Ekers, M., Hamel, P., & Keil, R. (2015). Governing suburbia: Modalities and mechanisms of suburban governance. In P. Hamel & R. Keil (Eds), *Suburban governance: A global view* (pp. 19–48). University of Toronto Press.

Farias, I. (2016). Devising hybrid forums: Technical democracy in a dangerous world. *City, 20*(4), 549–62. https://doi.org/10.1080/13604813.2016.1193998

Fligstein, N., & McAdam, D. (2012). *A theory of fields.* Oxford University Press.

Flyvbjerg, B. (2006). Five misunderstandings about case-study research. *Qualitative Inquiry, 12*(2), 219–45. https://doi.org/10.1177/1077800405284363

Frug, G.E. (2002). Beyond regional government. *Harvard Law Review, 115*(7), 1766–1836. https://doi.org/10.2307/1342596

Fung, A., & Wright, E.O. (2005). Le contre-pouvoir dans la démocratie participative et délibérative. In M.-H. Bacqué, H. Rey, & Y. Sintomer (Eds.), *Gestion de proximité et démocratie participative* (pp. 425–52). La Découverte.

Goldstone, J.A., & Useem, B. (2012). Putting values and institutions back into the theory of strategic action fields. *Sociological Theory, 30*(1), 37–47. https://doi.org/10.1177/0735275112437161

Gottdiener, M., & Hutchison, R. (2011). *The new urban sociology.* Westview Press.

Gourgues, G., Rui, S., & Topçu, S. (2013). Gouvernementalité et participation: Lectures critiques. *Participations, 2*(6), 5–33. https://doi.org/10.3917/parti.006.0005

Hajer, M., & Versteeg, W. (2008, 28–31 August). *The limits to deliberative governance* [Paper presentation]. Annual Meeting of the American Political Science Association Conference, Boston, MA.

Hamel, P. (2008). *Ville et débat public: Agir en démocratie*. Les Presses de l'Université Laval.

Hamel, P., & Jouve, B. (2006). *Un modèle québécois? Gouvernance et participation dans la gestion publique*. Presses de l'Université de Montréal.

Hamel, P., & Keil, R. (Eds.). (2015). *Suburban governance: A global view*. University of Toronto Press.

Hamel, P., Lustiger-Thaler, H., & Maheu, L. (2012). Global social movements: Subjectivity and human rights. In A. Sales (Ed.), *Sociology today: Social transformations in a globalizing world* (pp. 171–94). Sage.

Hanlon, B., & Vicino, T.J. (Eds.). (2019). *The Routledge companion to the suburbs*. Routledge.

Harrison, J., Galland, D., & Tewdwr-Jones, M. (2021). Regional planning is dead: Long live planning regional futures. *Regional Studies*, *55*(1), 6–18. https://doi.org/10.1080/00343404.2020.1750580

Harvey, D. (2009). *Cosmopolitanism and the geographies of freedom*. Columbia University Press.

Harvey, D. (2012). *Rebel cities: From the right to the city to the urban revolution*. Verso.

Hayden, D. (2003). *Building suburbia: Green fields and urban growth 1820–2000*. Vintage Books.

Heinelt, H., & Razin, E. (2011). A comparative German-Israeli perspective and summary of the results. In H. Heinelt, E. Razin, & K. Zimmerman (Eds.), *Metropolitan governance: Different paths in contrasting contexts: Germany and Israel* (pp. 322–7). Campus Verlag.

Heinelt, H., Razin, E., & Zimmerman, K. (Eds.). (2011). *Metropolitan governance: Different paths in contrasting contexts*. Campus Verlag.

Heyes, A., & King, B. (2020). Understanding the organization of green activism: Sociological and economic perspectives. *Organization & Environment*, *33*(1), 7–30. https://doi.org/10.1177/1086026618788859

Ives, A. (2015). Neoliberalism and the concept of governance: Renewing with an older liberal tradition to legitimate the power of capital. *Cahiers du MIMMOC*, 14. https://doi.org/10.4000/mimmoc.2263

Jonas, A.E., & Ward, K. (2007). Introduction to a debate on city-regions: New geographies of governance, democracy and social reproduction. *International Journal of Urban and Regional Research*, *31*(1), 169–78. https://doi.org/10.1111/j.1468-2427.2007.00711.x

Jouve, B. (2003). *La gouvernance urbaine en questions*. Elsevier.

Jouve, B. (2005). Metropolitan democracies: From great transformation to grand illusion. In P. Booth & B. Jouve (Eds.), *Metropolitan democracies:*

Transformations of the state and urban policy in Canada, France and Great Britain (pp. 223–49). Ashgate.

Jouve, B., & Lefèvre, C. (Eds.). (2002). *Métropoles ingouvernables*. Elsevier.

Judd, D.R., McKenzie, E., & Alexander, A. (2021). Introduction: Shadow governments and the remaking of the American local state. In D.R. Judd, E. McKenzie, & A. Alexander (Eds.), *Private metropolis: The eclipse of local democratic governance* (pp. 1–17). University of Minnesota Press.

Kazancigil, A. (2010). *La gouvernance: Pour ou contre le politique?* Armand Colin.

Kearns, A., & Paddison, R. (2000). New challenges for urban governance. *Urban Studies, 37*(5–6), 845–50. https://doi.org/10.1080/00420980050011118

Keil, R. (2000). Governance restructuring in Los Angeles and Toronto: Amalgamation or succession. *International Journal of Urban and Regional Research, 24*(4), 758–81. https://doi.org/10.1111/1468-2427.00277

Keil, R. (Ed.). (2013). *Suburban constellations: Governance, land, and infrastructure in the 21st century.* Jovis Verlag.

Keil, R. (2018a). The empty shell of the planetary urbanization: Re-rooting the urban in the experience of the urbanites. *Urban Geography, 39*(10), 1589–1602. https://doi.org/10.1080/02723638.2018.1451018

Keil, R. (2018b). *Suburban planet.* Polity Press.

Keil, R., & Addie, J.-P.D. (2016). "It's not going to be suburban, it's going to be all urban": Assembling post-suburbia in the Toronto and Chicago regions. *International Journal of Urban and Regional Research, 39*(5), 892–911. https://doi.org/10.1111/1468-2427.12303

Keil, R., Hamel, P., Boudreau, J.-A., & Kipfer, S. (Eds.). (2017). *Governing cities through regions: Canadian and European perspectives.* Wilfrid Laurier University Press.

Kipfer, S., Schmid, C., Goonewardena, K., & Milgrom, R. (2008). Globalizing Lefebvre? In K. Goonewardena, S. Kipfer, R. Milgrom, & C. Schmid (Eds.), *Space, difference, and everyday life: Reading Henri Lefebvre* (pp. 285–305). Routledge.

Lefebvre, H. (1970). *La révolution urbaine.* Gallimard.

Lefèvre, C. (1998). Metropolitan government and governance in western countries: A critical review. *International Journal of Urban and Regional Research, 22*(1), 9–25. https://doi.org/10.1111/1468-2427.00120

Lefèvre, C., & Pinson, G. (2020). *Pouvoirs urbains: Ville, politique et globalisation.* Armand Colin.

Lefèvre, C., Roseau, N., & Vitale, T. (2013). Introduction: Les défis de la gouvernance métropolitaine. In C. Lefèvre, N. Roseau, & T. Vitale (Eds.), *De la ville à la métropole: Les défis de la gouvernance* (pp. 21–34). L'œil d'or.

Le Galès, P. (1995). Du gouvernement local à la gouvernance urbaine. *Revue française de science politique, 45*(1), 57–95. https://doi.org/10.3406/rfsp.1995.403502

Le Galès, P. (2021). The rise of local politics: A global view. *Annual Review of Political Science*, *24*, 345–63. https://doi.org/10.1146/annurev-polisci-041719-102158

Levi-Faur, D. (2012). From "big government" to "big governance." In D. Levi-Faur (Ed.), *The Oxford handbook of governance* (pp. 3–18). Oxford University Press.

Lustiger-Thaler, H., Maheu, L., & Hamel, P. (1998). Enjeux institutionnels et action collective. *Sociologie et Sociétés*, *30*(1), 53–73. https://doi.org/10.7202/001456ar

MacLeod, G., & Jones, M. (2011). Renewing urban politics. *Urban Studies*, *48*(12), 2443–72. https://doi.org/10.1177/0042098011415717

Medearis, J. (2004). Social movements and deliberative democratic theory. *British Journal of Political Science*, *35*(1), 53–75. https://doi.org/10.1017/S0007123405000037

Merrifield, A. (2012). Whither urban studies? *Cities@Mancheter blog*. University of Manchester. https://citiesmcr.wordpress.com/2012/12/10/whither-urban-studies/

Merton, R.K. (1977). *Sociological ambivalence and other essays*. Free Press.

Mounk, Y. (2018). *The people vs. democracy: Why our freedom is in danger & how to save it*. Harvard University Press.

Muller, P. (2010). Esquisse d'une théorie du changement dans l'action publique: Structures, acteurs et cadres cognitifs. *Revue française de science politique*, *55*(1), 155–87. https://doi.org/10.3917/rfsp.551.0155

Nabatchi, T., Gastil, J., Leighninger, M., & Weiksner, M.G. (Eds.). (2012). *Democracy in motion: Evaluating the practice and impact of deliberative civic engagement*. Oxford University Press.

Nelles, J. (2012). *Comparative metropolitan policy: Beyond local boundaries in the imagined metropolis*. Routledge.

Nijman, J. (2000). *The paradigmatic city: Annals of the Association of American Geographers*, *90*(1), 133–45. https://doi.org/10.1111/0004-5608.00189

Offe, C. (2009). Governance: An "empty signifier"? *Constellations*, *16*(4), 550–62. https://doi.org/10.1111/j.1467-8675.2009.00570.x

Ong, A. (2011). Introduction: Worlding cities, or the art of being global. In A. Roy & A. Ong (Eds.), *Worlding cities: Asian experiments and the art of being global* (pp. 1–26). Wiley-Blackwell.

Paasi, A., & Metzger, J. (2017). Foregrounding the region. *Regional Studies*, *51*(1), 19–30. https://doi.org/10.1080/00343404.2016.1239818

Papadopoulos, Y. (2002, 22–27 March). *Is "governance" a form of "deliberative democracy?"* (First draft) [Paper presentation]. Workshop: "The Politics of Metropolitan Governance." European Consortium for Political Research (ECPR) Joint Sessions of Workshops, Turin, Italy.

Peters, B.G. (2012). Governance as political theory. In D. Levi-Faur (Ed.), *The Oxford handbook of governance* (pp. 19–32). Oxford University Press.

Phares, D. (Ed.). (2009). *Governing metropolitan regions in the 21st century*. M.E. Sharpe.

Phelps, N., & Wu, F. (Eds). (2011). *International perspectives on suburbanization: A post-suburban world?* Palgrave.

Piattoni, S. (2010). *The theory of multi-level governance: Conceptual, empirical, and normative challenges*. Oxford University Press.

Poletta, F. (2008). Just talk: Deliberation after 9/11. *Journal of Deliberative Democracy*, 4(1), 1–18. https://doi.org/10.16997/jdd.60

Robinson, J. (2014). New geographies of theorizing the urban: Putting comparison to work for global urban studies. In S. Parnell & S. Oldfield (Eds.), *Handbook for cities of the global south* (pp. 57–70). Sage.

Robinson, J., & Roy, A. (2016). Debate on global suburbanisms and the nature of urban theory. *International Journal of Urban and Regional Research*, 40(1), 181–6. https://doi.org/10.1111/1468-2427.12272

Rosanvallon, P. (2006). *La contre-démocratie: La politique à l'âge de la défiance*. Éditions du Seuil.

Rosanvallon, P. (2020). *Le siècle du populisme: Histoire, théorie, critique*. Éditions du Seuil.

Sassen, S. (2004). Local actors in global politics. *Current Sociology*, 52(4), 649–70. https://doi.org/10.1177/0011392104043495

Schlosberg, D., & Coles, R. (2016). The new environmentalism of everyday life: Sustainability, material flows and movements. *Contemporary Political Theory*, 15(2), 160–81. https://doi.org/10.1057/cpt.2015.34

Scott, A.J. (2001). *Global city-regions: Trends, theory, policy*. Oxford University Press.

Scott, A.J. (2019). City-regions reconsidered. *Environment and Planning A: Economy and Space*, 51(3), 554–80. https://doi.org/10.1177/0308518X19831591

Snow, D.A., & Soule, S.A. (2010). *A primer on social movements*. W.W. Norton.

Soja, E.W. (2000). *Postmetropolis: Critical studies of cities and regions*. Blackwell.

Soja, E.W. (2010a). Cities and states in geohistory. *Theory and Society*, 39, 361–76. https://doi.org/10.1007/s11186-010-9113-5

Soja, E.W. (2010b). *Seeking spatial justice*. University of Minnesota Press.

Stevenson, D. (2013). *The city*. Polity Press.

Storper, M. (2014). Governing the large metropolis. *Territory, Politics, Governance*, 2(2), 115–34. https://doi.org/10.1080/21622671.2014.919874

Storper, M., & Scott, A.J. (2016). Current debates in urban theory: A critical assessment. *Urban Studies*, 53(6), 1114–36. https://doi.org/10.1177/0042098016634002

Swyngedouw, E. (2004). "Globalisation or 'glocalisation'? Networks, territories and rescaling." *Cambridge Review of International Affairs*, 17(1), 25–48. https://doi.org/10.1080/0955757042000203632

Teaford, J.C. (1997). *Post-suburbia: Government and politics in the edge cities.* Johns Hopkins University Press.

Van Haperen, S., Nicholls, W., & Uitermark, J. (2018). Building protest online: Engagement with digitally networked #not1more protest campaign on Twitter. *Social Movement Studies, 17*(4), 408–23. https://doi.org/10.1080/14742837.2018.1434499

Walks, A. (2013). Suburbanism as a way of life, slight return. *Urban Studies, 50*(8), 1471–88. https://doi.org/10.1177/0042098012462610

Young, D., & Keil, R. (2014). Locating the urban in-between: Tracking the urban politics of infrastructure in Toronto. *International Journal of Urban and Regional Research, 38*(5), 1589–1608. https://doi.org/10.1111/1468-2427.12146

Young, I.M. (2001). Activist challenges to deliberative democracy. *Political Theory, 29*(5), 670–90. https://doi.org/10.1177/0090591701029005004

2 Negotiating Multiculturalism, Neoliberalism, and Metropolitan Intensification: Suburban Governance in Toronto

PIERRE FILION, ROGER KEIL, AND MICHAEL COLLENS

Introduction

In Toronto, as in most metropolitan regions across the world, talking about suburban governance is talking about the governance of the largest share of the metropolitan region. Even in the core of the region, the City of Toronto, a municipality of close to 3 million with large swathes of peripheral residential and employment lands, it is suburban areas that contain the majority of the population and, thereby, carry most political weight in electoral terms. Yet, in Toronto as elsewhere, the central portion of the metropolitan area is an object of disproportional attention due to its role as the seat of political institutions and its symbolic representation of the entire urban region.

The chapter relies on interviews with people engaged in different types of public-sector and community-based interventions guiding suburbanization and affecting suburbs. Those conversations took place before a provincial election in 2018, which changed political majorities in Ontario. While this more recent development shifted some of the planning priorities and realities in the Toronto region in significant ways that we cannot discuss in detail in this present chapter (see Keil & Üçoğlu, 2021 for a preliminary take), it leaves the analysis presented here mostly intact. The chapter first identifies major governance themes in suburban Toronto and then explores how they relate to the suburban circumstances we have identified and the constraints on governance inherent in these circumstances. To identify the Toronto suburban themes, we interviewed seventeen respondents. They were selected to represent the different levels of government – local, regional, provincial, and federal – as well as non-government agencies dealing directly with suburban issues (such as charity organizations) or commenting and doing research on suburban policy. Activities of respondents involved land-use, transportation, and environmental and social planning, delivered

Table 2.1. Respondents

Function	Agency	Activities	Code Used in Quotes
Researcher and administrator	Independent research organization	Urban research and administration	R-1
Researcher	Independent research organization	Urban research	R-2
Researcher and administrator	University-based research organization	Urban research and administration	R-3
Researcher and administrator	Independent research and lobby organization	Urban research and lobby	R-4
Planner	Municipality	Land-use planning	LPl-1
Planner	Metropolitan environmental planning agency	Environmental planning	EPl-1
Planner	Metropolitan environmental planning agency	Environmental planning	EPl-2
Planner	Metropolitan transportation agency	Transportation planning	TPl-1
Planner and administrator	Regional social planning agency	Social planning	SPl-1
Planner	Regional social planning agency	Social planning	SPl-2
Planner and administrator	Charity organization	Social planning	SPl-3
Planner	Charity organization	Social planning	SPl-4
Politician	Municipality	All aspects of municipal politics	Pol-1
Advisor to a politician	Municipality	All aspects of municipal politics	Pol-2
Administrator	Provincial government	Metropolitan planning	Adm-1
Administrator	Provincial government	Metropolitan planning	Adm-2
Administrator	Public agency	Transportation and urban development	Adm-3

by public-sector agencies or community-based organizations. Other respondents were politicians, administrators, and researchers. Certain respondents engaged in more than one of these functions, but in most instances, they took part in only one of these roles (see Table 2.1).

We asked respondents about their understanding of governance in general and, more specifically, governance in a suburban context. We then inquired about how governance operates in the suburban environments in which they are involved and/or with which they are familiar. We subsequently questioned them about what they considered to be the main suburban governance themes, asking them to provide examples. We closed the interview by inviting respondents to discuss obstacles preventing suburban governance from solving the main problems facing suburban areas. Much of the interview process consisted of prompting respondents to clarify their views regarding governance themes and asking them to expand on their experience of suburban governance.

The chapter's purpose is to understand contemporary suburban governance in Toronto by identifying the themes respondents associate with the governance of the urban periphery, its form, function, and life therein. We build here on related work that sees suburban governance as a process articulating the three modalities of state, market, and private interventions. We also understand that territory, technology, and the discourse of regionalism are important elements of governance in the suburbanizing region (Addie & Keil, 2015; Hamel & Keil, 2015; Keil et al., 2017). Themes that emerge from the interviews reflect present transformations of the social landscape of suburban Toronto. Respondents point to the gap between the conventional image of the suburb and the current suburban reality, and blame this discrepancy for ill-conceived policy responses. Respondents also identify social transformations affecting suburban Toronto and their consequences on suburban life and policymaking. Transformations include rising poverty, a consequence of income polarization, and the growing presence of immigrants, resulting in some cases in their concentration in "ethnoburbs." Other themes relate to the planning of suburbs and, in particular, to their integration into a rapidly growing metropolitan region. One planning theme concerns the transportation problems confronting suburban residents and the solutions, especially public transit investment, proposed to tackle these problems. Another planning theme considers suburban land-use planning within the context of the intensification objectives driving Toronto metropolitan planning. The final theme discussed in the chapter relates to the institutional dimension of governance, especially to how local and regional administrations tackle issues related to the other identified themes.

In this chapter, themes are perceived as stemming from the characteristics of the contemporary suburb and, more specifically, of suburban Toronto: for example, North American suburban planning models, accessibility issues due to the in-between nature of the suburban realm (between the central city and rural areas), and the fragmented administrative structure of suburbs (Keil & Young, 2008). Also relevant to emerging suburban themes are manifestations of global transitions, such as income polarization and the settlement of large contingents of immigrants. Themes raised by respondents mirror efforts at addressing these transitions within the range of possibilities available within the suburban context.

As Hamel points out in chapter 1, his introduction to this volume, one can usefully dissect the *problématique* of regional governance in the suburbanizing region in three steps:

1 acknowledgment of suburban space in the region, which includes shifts in our understanding of what is suburban, who acts in and upon suburban regions, and what lives are lived in those regions;
2 awareness of strategic relationships that make up the capitalist state, which are changing the way we imagine regional governance. This step includes a reliance "on confidence between network actors," rejecting an "essentialist definition of the state," and promoting "a vision of a state shaped by restructuring processes" (researchers have to note the tension between collective agency assumed to attach to a certain territoriality and the problem of fetishizing the region [Paasi and Metzger, 2017]); and
3 recognition of a dialectic of the universality of the regionalization process driven by suburbanization (or extended urbanization) and the simultaneous specificity of "suburban governance processes across different sociospatial contexts."

We are making the assumption at the outset that, while in former decades regional governance in Toronto was built on a distinct differentiation of the core and the periphery – or the city and the suburbs – current forms of regional governance have embraced a more complex spatial imaginary in which suburbanization and suburbanisms are afforded a new role (see Table 2.2). Rather than being merely the outer rim of growth that needs controlling and containing by policies chiefly hatched and implemented in the centre, the suburb has become a contradictory space of agency itself from which demands are placed on how the region is discussed, territorialized, and technologically connected (Addie & Keil, 2015). This shift may, as one of our interviewees told us, be the reason why it appears in international comparison – especially perhaps with the American case – that "Toronto is suburbanizing probably better than most large metros," although the same individual warned that there is "absolutely really no regional coordination driven by the elected officials from the local municipal level" (R-4). With increasing development and diversity across the suburbanizing

Table 2.2. Administrative Units of the Toronto Region

Administrative and Territorial Units	Government Bodies	Main Attributions	Number of Units
GGH (Greater Golden Horseshoe)	Government of Ontario (Ministry of Municipal Affairs and Housing)	Area under the jurisdiction of the Growth Plan, the largest definition of the Toronto region; the government of Ontario has the authority for approving regional governments' (upper tier) and single-tier municipal official plan/official plan amendments that are updated to conform to the Growth Plan	1 (32K km^2, 9.6 million residents)
GTHA (Greater Toronto and Hamilton Area)	The only administrative entity operating at this scale is Metrolinx, the regional public transit agency; over the last years the reach of Metrolinx is more consistent with the GGH than the GTHA	Most usually relied upon definition of the Toronto region, even if it does not refer to a regional administrative entity	1 (8.2K km^2, 7.2 million residents)
Top-tier local governments within the GTHA	Regional governments (upper tier) and single-tier municipal governments	Regional governments are responsible for regional planning and regionally defined services and infrastructure; single-tier municipalities are responsible for both regional and local planning, services, and infrastructure; regional governments have authority for approving the official plan/official plan amendments of lower-tier municipalities	4 regions (Durham, York, Peel, Halton) and 2 single-tier municipalities (Toronto and Hamilton)
Local municipalities within the GTHA	Lower-tier municipalities	Responsible for local planning and services and infrastructure, which are defined as local	26 local municipalities with populations ranging from 11,958 to 746,352

Source: Hemson Consulting Ltd. (2020).

region, the imperative for some form of regional governance in the periphery is clear to this same observer: "the geography on which wealth is created and distributed, competitiveness – economic competitiveness, environmental progress, protection, and a host of other kinds of sort of operational things from policing to water, waste water – can or must in some cases have a degree of regional coordination in order for us to optimize the public policy environment and the competitiveness and prosperity of the region."

The change in what suburbanization and suburban life in the Toronto region means is captured eloquently in this depiction by one of the politicians we interviewed:

> Traditionally, a suburb is an area that is some distance away from where jobs are, in our case Toronto. Toronto used to be the centre of the universe with regards to jobs, but that has changed. Brampton used to be a place where you could afford a house. That was the reason why I moved here, originally, because at the time, the houses were like $59,000. Some are over a million dollars now. Yeah, many, now. It's a challenge to describe suburbanization because it used to be that you lived in one place. This used to be, as my community calls it, the sleeping community because this was the bedroom where you stayed in and you went to work somewhere else. Well, suburbanization has changed in that a lot of the employers are now in the suburbs, so you're not necessarily travelling into the bigger metropolitan area. People are actually travelling to us from downtown Toronto, living in Toronto, and now working in Brampton. I think the definition has changed and evolved quite dramatically. In fact, people are living here and going to suburbs further away, like Waterloo and Kitchener, and Guelph because of the rail lines, because that's changed where the suburb begins and ends. In places that used to be so far away that you couldn't anticipate ever commuting from, people are commuting from every single day. To me, it's kind of, what it looked like when I first moved here in the, I guess, late 80s and what it looks like now are two different animals. (Pol-1)

The chapter opens with reflections on the suburban phenomenon, beginning with an examination of the suburb at a global scale, to then concentrate on its North American manifestation and finally on its Toronto specificities. The consideration of the different scales of the suburban reality brings to light constraints confronting governance in a suburban context. After a brief description of the methodology, we organize the content of the interviews under six themes. The chapter ends by discussing how identified themes illustrate the way suburbs deal with major global trends within constraints inherent in the morphology and dynamics of suburban areas and their institutions.

The interview material on which this chapter is based highlights three main categories of issues relating to the contemporary suburb. The first is the diversification of all aspects of the suburb, including its economy, built environment, and the make-up of its population. The second concerns the difficulty from a governance perspective to deal with this diversity, which is due to maladapted institutional structures and the need to devise novel decision models to address problems unprecedented within the suburban context. The third category of issues pertains to the global nature of many aspects of suburban development, which relate to the difficulties identified by the respondents. In a fashion that is specific to its own historical, institutional, economic, and demographic characteristics, Toronto reflects universal properties of suburbs such as the recent nature of their development, undersupply of infrastructure and services, and their peripheral position relative to centres of political and economic power.

From the Global Suburb to the North American and Toronto Suburb

The present section considers the suburban phenomenon from the general – characteristics shared by all suburbs at a planetary scale – to the specific – features that define Toronto suburbs. Between these two extremes, we identify the characteristics of the North American suburbs, of which suburban Toronto is a subset.

The Global Suburb

We identify five common denominators present in all types of suburbs across the world: distinction from the central city, a scant presence of seats of political and economic power, newness rather than tradition, urban innovation, and urban growth. Everywhere, although in different ways, suburbs present a development pattern contrasting with that of the central city (Stanilov & Scheer, 2004; Vaughan et al., 2009). It is indeed easy on aerial views to distinguish twentieth and twenty-first century suburbs from the central city. In some cases, as for North American and Toronto suburbs, the suburban realm stands out by its automobile orientation and lesser density. In other instances, as where spontaneous development predominates in suburban areas, it is the apparent lack of organized layout that distinguishes suburbs from the older, more orderly, central city. Elsewhere, it is the contrast between high-density and low-density sectors, as well as between functionally specialized areas, that sets suburbs apart from the greater built-form uniformity of central cities. Although they account for most of the population of urban areas and a large share of their economy, suburbs are not generally associated with the seats of political and economic power. It is in the central city that parliaments, ministries, and the main conglomerations of high-rise corporate headquarters and major media and cultural institutions are found. In many parts of the world, it is also in the central city that the economic and cultural elite reside. It is easy, in these circumstances, to understand why suburbs can feel neglected relative to the central city. Given the more recent nature of its development, the built environment of the suburb is new relative to that of the central city. It is in the suburban realm that most new development formulas are introduced. What is more, because the suburb accounts for most urban growth, it often suffers from a lag between a rapidly rising demand for infrastructures and services, and their provision (see, for example, Lucy & Phillips, 2006). As the suburban realm expands, it redefines the understanding of the urban phenomenon (Addie & Keil, 2015).

The North American Suburb

Since the end of the Second World War, all North American suburbs share a similar land-use–transportation dynamic. These suburbs have rapidly evolved, over the fifteen years or so following the war, an urban form that is fully adapted to near universal automobile use: rigid land-use specialization, a predominantly low-density urban form, and dispersion of structuring activities such as employment, retail, and institutions (Hirt, 2014). At the same time, they have become the sites of massive highway investment. The novel suburban car-oriented dispersed model that emerged in the 1950s and early 1960s soon coalesced into a self-perpetuating formula generalized across the North American suburban realm (Filion, 2013; Filion et al., 1999; Marshall, 2000). This depiction is not to imply, however, that these suburban areas have been deprived of innovations since the early 1960s. The adaptation of land uses to the car evolved throughout the period, taking the form of ever larger shopping malls, big box stores, business parks, multiplex cinemas, and so on. Also noteworthy has been the proliferation over the last decades of two new residential formulas – gated communities and, to a lesser extent, new urbanism developments (Jacobs & Lees, 2013) – as well as "retrofitting" measures aimed at rising socio-economic polarization (Poppe & Young, 2015) and sociospatial decline and climate change impacts (Williamson & Dunham-Jones, 2021).

There is a profound disjunction between the perception of autonomy at a personal and municipal level conjured up by the suburb and its intense dependence on large public-sector investments and ongoing government interventions for its infrastructure requirements. Perceived autonomy within the suburb stems from the flexibility inherent in automobile use and reliance on the market, thereby on consumer choice, to fulfil most needs of suburban households. Meanwhile, infrastructure requirements of the suburb are themselves largely a function of its low density and heavy reliance on the automobile, the very features associated with personal autonomy (Burchell et al., 2005). Linked to this apparent autonomy of the North American suburb is its administrative fragmentation, which conveys the vision of a self-governance ideal within small political entities (Filion et al., 2019). Especially in the United States, there is strong attachment to the home-rule principle (Storper, 2014). Although many traditional or emerging suburbs now have hundreds of thousands of residents and workers (as is the case in the Toronto region), much is made in suburban political circles of the democratic advantages of small suburban municipalities, depicted as more responsive to the values and preferences of their residents than are large bureaucratically dominated central city administrations. The comparison is often made between the consumer responsive small-scale suburban administration and large central cities governed by self-interested, insensitive bureaucracies (see, for example, Sancton, 2000).

Notwithstanding their voracious appetite for infrastructure public funding, the long-established administrative fragmentation of North American suburbs foreshadowed the neoliberal transformation of the state by infusing market choice into municipal politics. As observed by Tiebout (1956), households can vote with their feet within the mosaic of suburban jurisdictions, choosing to reside in municipalities where the balance between property taxes and services best suits their preferences (Peck, 2011; Read, 2016). There is, therefore, a market-driven competition between suburban municipalities with the potential of dictating their policy choices (Jimenez, 2014). While in the early phases of post-war suburbanization the opposition was typically between tax- and service-poor central cities and tax- and service-rich middle- and upper-class suburbs, the situation has become more complicated. Some central cities have improved their financial situation and service standards, while the suburban municipal patchwork has become far more diversified, with more distinction between wealthy and poor suburbs. The financial inequity between US suburban municipalities is made worse by reliance on property taxes to pay for education (Sadler & Highsmith, 2016). In Canada, suburban inequality is alleviated to some degree by the presence of larger, more diversified suburban jurisdictions and provincial funding for education.

The Toronto Suburb

While sharing many of the fundamental features of the North American suburb – car orientation, predominance of low density, and functional land-use specialization – Toronto suburbs depart from the continental model in important ways. Toronto suburbs have been more systematically planned at a local and regional scale, and register higher densities and non-automobile modal shares (without challenging the supremacy of the car, however; Sorensen & Hess, 2015; White, 2016). It is important to note that, since Toronto is among the fastest growing North American metropolitan regions, suburban Toronto is growing at a faster pace than most other North American suburban areas – hence the confrontation of Toronto suburbs with issues of metropolitan expansion, such as long commutes due to traffic congestion and the spatial extension of the urban region (Moore, 2017). Toronto suburbs are also distinguished from US suburban home-rule by the presence of large municipalities, regional administrations, and a provincial government that readily intervenes in urban matters (Frisken, 2007). In Canada, municipalities are constitutionally defined as "creatures of the provinces," therefore subjected to provincially induced territorial and administrative reorganization (Young & Leuprecht, 2004).

Toronto suburbs are presently undergoing two major transitions. The first involves a rapid diversification of their population. These suburbs have long broken with the stereotypical middle-class bedroom community of the 1950s and 1960s targeted at middle-class families with children. Suburbs have since witnessed a considerable mixture of age and income groups as well as household types. But over recent decades, the main transformation altering Toronto suburbs has been a large-scale settlement of immigrants. Whereas in the past the inner city constituted the point of entry for immigrants in the Toronto urban region, suburbs now play this role (Fong, 2016; Zhuang & Chen, 2017). While the proportion of immigrants is high throughout the suburban realm, some large districts are taken over by specific ethnic groups. At the same time, income polarization translates into growing poverty, a social phenomenon that used to be mostly associated with the inner city (Hulchanski, 2010).

The second transition concerns the planning and development of Toronto suburbs, especially their densification and the improvement of their public transit services. This transformation is driven by the provincial government Growth Plan, which attempts to tackle worsening traffic congestion, urban sprawl, and infrastructure costs in the face of accelerated growth while improving quality of life (Ontario, 2006/2017). The Growth Plan, which was given force of law in 2006, covers a vast Toronto-focused yet polycentric region (the Greater Golden Horseshoe, GGH). These policies, along with market trends driven by stagnating incomes and high housing costs, have contributed to raise public transit modal shares and residential density.

Increasing poverty is one of the most serious issues confronting Toronto suburbs. Rising poverty levels stem from income polarization and the difficulties for some immigrants to integrate into the employment market. A social phenomenon traditionally associated with the inner city is now taking a suburban face. Poverty is especially prevalent in the older ring of suburbs, those within the City of Toronto, but is now spreading into newer suburbs. A related issue is the growing social gap between the inner city and suburbs. The inner city is increasingly populated by well-to-do small, often young, households. Virtually the entire inner city is now in the grips of gentrification. As the inner city becomes more socially homogenous, suburbs are diversifying (Harris, 2015). Other gaps are also opening between the inner city and the suburbs. There is a political distinction, the inner city voting more to the left than the suburbs do, and a lifestyle contrast, reflected by much higher public transit use, walking, and cycling in the inner city (Walks, 2006). In the Toronto region, there is little street life outside the inner city. Rob Ford, as a candidate for the Toronto mayoralty and mayor from 2010 to 2014, politically exploited the rift between prosperous inner-city constituencies (which he labelled the "downtown elite") and economically struggling suburban areas within the City of Toronto (Cunningham, 2014). A major problem, presently felt in all parts of the metropolitan region, is the high cost of housing. There is a debate raging about reasons for the escalation of residential real estate prices. Some blame speculation fuelled by foreigners and local buyers alike (Ferguson & Benzie, 2017). Others refer to the style of housing being built, in particular the dearth of middle-density housing, which is neither a single-family home nor a high-rise condo unit. Finally, pro-market advocates zero in on the effects of restricted supply caused by Growth Plan–driven growth management policies, especially the Green Belt and the channelling of development within delineated built boundaries (BILD, 2017). Since our interviews took place in 2017, and especially since the onset of the pandemic, the housing crisis has been exacerbated and can be seen in direct relationship to the suburban-based growth regime that drives the Southern Ontario economy (Üçoğlu et al., 2021).

Constraints to Suburban Governance in Toronto

Before engaging in the exploration of Toronto suburban governance themes, we consider constraints facing actors involved in this governance. Our reflection is informed by the prior discussion on the suburban phenomenon in its global, North American, and Toronto manifestations. It is intended to help understand the context in which our respondents operate and, therefore, reasons for the themes they have selected.

An obvious constraint on suburban governance concerns the jurisdictional scope and intervention capacity of suburban political institutions. Suburban local and regional municipalities (first and second tier) must operate within their provincially set field of responsibilities. They are also restricted by the financial resources they can tap. Within the Toronto context, financial restrictions make it impossible for these administrations to engage in major infrastructure projects (such as light rail transit [LRT] or expressways) without funding assistance from senior governments. Suburban areas also suffer from the absence of an overarching elected administration that could represent the collective interests of the suburban realm and campaign for it. True, thanks to their demographic weight, suburbs can have a considerable impact on provincial and national politics. How the Toronto suburban belt votes is, indeed, a major factor determining which party is victorious at these two levels. But the attention provincial and national parties give to suburban values does not necessarily translate into urban interventions reflecting the preferences of suburbanites. This disconnect is because urban and suburban matters are watered down by the maelstrom of provincial and federal political priorities. The suburban realm possesses sufficient shared features to be considered as a territorial entity in its own right, but it lacks the institutional framework to operate as such an entity (Paasi & Metzger, 2017).

Another constraint facing suburban governance is the impact of the suburban development cycle on municipal revenues, which compels municipalities to first develop their entire territory and then promote its densification. The need to heed sources of municipal revenues has the effect of a "growth machine," which dictates land-use policies. During its initial growth phase, a municipality benefits from substantial income originating from development charges, which allow it to proceed with infrastructure investments without incurring resistance from incumbent residents apprehending rising property taxes. But once their territory is fully built, municipalities must rely primarily on tax revenues to maintain and replace aging infrastructure, which increases the property tax burden. Meanwhile, some built-out municipalities run the risk of incurring filtering down, as they compete with more up-to-date developments. The coupling of a stagnating or even declining property tax base with rising demands on tax revenues makes for perilous financial circumstances. The option for such municipalities is to densify through redevelopment, hence re-establishing a development charge cash flow and broadening their property tax base.

A third constraint pertains to the land-use–transportation dynamics inherent in North American car-oriented suburban development, which has prevailed for seventy years. Powerful path dependencies make it difficult to depart from, on the one hand, a functionally segregated, decentralized, and generally low-density pattern of development and, on the other, an overwhelming prevalence of the automobile (Metzger, 2013). These path dependencies are maintained by the existence of mutual reinforcement mechanisms between this form of land use and car reliance. With so much public and private capital sunk in this morphology and transportation system, and given the role both play in setting the way the economy functions and people organize their lives, breaking from these land-use–transportation dynamics is a tall order. It requires a well-coordinated and well-financed planning strategy involving a simultaneous shift to public transportation and large-scale densification accompanied with multifunctional development. But such an approach is especially vulnerable to transportation funding restraints and not-in-my-backyard (NIMBY) resistance to changes in land-use development patterns.

Related to efforts at shifting suburban development patterns are unintended consequences of regional planning strategies. For example, we have noted the existence of debates around the link between built boundaries and escalating housing costs. Proponents of Growth Plan strategies argue that there is sufficient available land to meet demand until 2031; hence, in their view, insufficient land supply cannot be blamed for rising housing costs (Neptis, 2015) – which is true from a pure land supply and demand perspective. Such a perspective does not, however, account for the impact the concentration of land ownership can have on housing prices. In Toronto, as in many other metropolitan regions, land available for development is in the hands of a small number of large development companies. The setting of designated greenfield areas, land outside the built boundaries where municipalities are required to identify the land that will accommodate new urban developments, advantages large landowners because they already are in possession of the best-located tracks of land, those within these boundaries. Meanwhile, small developers who could have competed with large developers by launching cheaper residential projects outside

Table 2.3. Themes Raised by the Respondents

Respondents' Codes	Theme 1: Image of the Suburb	Theme 2: Poverty	Theme 3: Ethnoburbs	Theme 4: Mobility	Theme 5: Planning	Theme 6: Institutions
R-1				X	X	X
R-2				X	X	X
R-3	X			X	X	X
R-4				X	X	X
LPI-1				X	X	X
EPI-1					X	
EPI-2					X	X
TPI-1		X	X	X	X	X
SPI-1		X	X			
SPI-2		X	X			X
SPI-3	X	X	X	X		X
SPI-4	X	X	X	X		
Pol-1	X	X	X	X	X	X
Pol-2	X	X	X	X	X	X
Adm-1	X		X	X	X	X
Adm-2				X	X	
Adm-3				X	X	X

the perimeter of the land owned by large development companies are prevented to do so.

Emerging Suburban Governance Themes

From the interview material, we have identified six themes pertaining to suburban governance (see Table 2.3). These themes can be grouped in two categories. The first three themes relate to suburban social change, while the last three themes concern planning and institutional issues.

Theme 1: The Growing Gap between the Traditional Image of the Suburb and the Contemporary Suburban Reality

A theme raised by six respondents is the enduring prevalence of the perception of the suburb as middle-class and suited to traditional family values. Such an image also depicts the suburban realm as an appendage of the central city, economically and culturally dependent on the central parts of the metropolitan region. There is a strong belief among respondents that such a perception is obsolete and does not do justice to the increasing social and economic diversity of the suburb.

> You can't tell a book just by the cover. I think that in some ways we've used the notion of suburb and suburbia as a seal beyond which we don't bother looking into to see what's actually going on in there. (Adm-1)

> The biggest difference between suburbia and [the City of] Toronto is that suburban is the name you take before you become a metropolis. (Pol-2)

Respondents present many examples of the contemporary suburban reality that clash with the stereotypical image of the suburb. The suburb is no longer a middle-class haven. All social indices point to its advancing diversification. Most suburbanites work in the suburbs, and there is evidence of reverse commuting from the central city. In fact, many suburbanites interact minimally, if at all, with the central city. All these changes are to be expected as the suburban realm (comprising sectors built since 1946) now accounts for about four-fifths of the residents of the Toronto urban region and probably close to that economic activity level (Gordon & Janzen, 2013).

Some respondents complain that policymaking directed at the suburbs, especially when originating from senior governments, is often informed by these outmoded stereotypes – hence the importance of updating the perception of suburbs.

> We have what we've called for the longest time our fair share issue, fair share [for our region]. And that really has to do with the incredible growth that we've had as a community since the 1980s. The funding that we get for the region has really not kept pace on a per capita level, primarily from the provincial government, but also from the federal government. And we have been advocating for recognition of that growth and the complexity of issues here. We've had some successes. But it has not been seen in some circles as a priority, and there is a lack of understanding of the issues. (SPl-3)

This first theme intersects with several subsequent themes.

Theme 2: Economic Decline and Poverty in the Suburbs

The second theme is mentioned by seven respondents. In direct opposition with the outdated middle-class stereotype of the suburb are emerging pockets of poverty within the Toronto suburban realm. Toronto suburbs were always socially mixed to an extent, the outcome of a policy intended to assure that what are now City of Toronto suburbs would host their fair share of public housing. Such a policy was not implemented with as much fervour in outer suburbs, the ones beyond City of Toronto boundaries, however. Income polarization and the difficulty for many immigrants to integrate into the employment market fuel poverty within the suburban realm. It is not that unemployment levels are high in suburban Toronto; rather, it is that many of the available jobs pay minimum wage, or close to minimum wage, and are temporary and/or part time. It is especially difficult for young people to find jobs corresponding to their qualifications. Immigrants whose credentials are not recognized face similar circumstances. Many immigrants arrive with financial assets, which are depleted as they struggle to find employment commensurate with their education and experience.

> You see a decline in [immigrants'] financial assets because many of them are coming in with a significant amount of financial assets, and that declines. It's a very important question. (SPl-3)

Another factor of income decline, especially prevalent in older suburbs, is the loss of their industrial base. In places such as the Golden Mile in Scarborough, well-paid industrial employment has been replaced by a much fewer number of low-income retailing jobs, largely in big box stores.

Poverty is not as visible in the suburbs as it is downtown and in the inner city. Rarely do we see homeless people sleeping on the streets or even panhandling in the suburbs, common sights in central parts of Toronto. Still, homelessness, if largely hidden, does exist in the suburbs, often taking the form of households sharing a house or apartment, or of people living in their car.

> [Poverty is] very hidden. It's not seen in the same way as in other communities like Toronto or Hamilton or Windsor … The other reason why we have started to learn about hidden poverty, and particularly homelessness, is that we've become aware that people because of a loss of job or family breakdown, whatever the case may be, are living in their cars. Because they're no longer able to afford their home, they've lost the home. They've lost perhaps their family. But they keep the car because they're still working, and they can get to work, but they are not able to afford a home. And so they are sleeping in their cars, and we've become more and more aware of that over the last several years. (SPl-3)

> But if you were to ask most of the people [living in suburban areas], they wouldn't know that people live in poverty. So we have that perception

problem about poverty. So we have moved from this suburban area that was considered wealthy. And, yes, there are pockets of poverty, but it's totally invisible if you're not necessarily working in this area like we're doing. (SPl-4)

To make matters worse, the suburbs provide fewer services for the poor than the central city does, which is especially evident in the case of social housing and homeless shelters. I think in the past it was always, "Go to Toronto and get the services you need," and just kind of rid ourselves of the problem. (SPl-2)

And we know of several stories where people who were on the waiting list did not get access to housing. And so they've gone to Hamilton, for example, and within a matter of two years they could access subsidized housing. I know this one family. [The mother] was able to get access to subsidized housing in Hamilton. Whereas, here, she would still be waiting – her child would be grown up and working, and she still would not have anything. (SPl-3)

Theme 3: "Ethnoburbs"

Perhaps the main social change that has affected Toronto suburbs over the last decades is the concentration therein of recent immigrants and – given the changing nature of Canadian immigration in the last generation – therefore of largely non-European ethnic groups. Eight respondents mentioned immigration. It is to be expected that, in an urban region that absorbs four out of ten immigrants landing in Canada and where suburbanites constitute a large majority of the population, suburbs would become immigrant gateways, and the presence of immigrants in these areas would grow as flows of immigrants entering the country increase. In 2016, the proportion of immigrants in the Toronto census metropolitan area was 46.1 per cent and varied in suburban municipalities from 12.4 to 58.7 per cent.

While Toronto suburbs have long been a magnet for European settlers and immigrants, mostly in the second generation of settlement, more recently they have become the destination of new immigrants of non-European origin. This demographic change is notably apparent in the Chinese concentration in Scarborough and Markham, and the strong presence of South Asians in Brampton. As these ethnic groupings are a matter of choice and cover large sectors offering a variety of housing types, suited to different income categories, they are referred to as ethnic enclaves rather than ghettos (see Walks & Bourne, 2006). There is an absence of correspondence between this ethnic spatial convergence and low incomes, as is classically assumed in immigration and settlement studies. The Toronto suburban realm is experiencing two parallel and possibly antithetical processes regarding the presence of ethnic groups: a process of assimilation and one of ethnic expression.

> [Immigration] is the GTA's [Greater Toronto Area's] issue. It's a subconscious, hidden debate. (Pol-2)

Immigration poses a challenge for social planners, in particular, as they are learning to adjust to issues of diversity in the suburban environment.

> We're a really growing, diversified area. There's so many languages, people from different parts of the world settling here and choosing to settle. It's their decision to settle here. So those are some of the things. So we have to try and keep up with the population growth, and the infrastructure isn't always there to do that. (SPl-4)

The conjunction of an important presence of immigrants in suburbs and a limited supply of social services is a source of problems when new immigrants face difficulties integrating into society. There is also the tendency for some immigrants to rely on family resources rather than on social or medical services. While such self-sufficiency can be useful to immigrants and perceived as an exemplary way of reducing reliance on social services, consequences can be dire, as when mental health is involved.

> We are aware of the cultural barrier to accessing services, and we see that in the case of mental health. So we did a research piece on mental health a couple of years ago with a lens on the South Asian, Chinese, and Black community. And each of those have their own cultural nuances on mental health and also their own sort of stigma about mental health and accessing supports, because that's a Western notion to go somewhere and get help and seek help and treatment. Whereas, in some of those cultures, it's more about you've done something wrong, and so now you're being punished, or if you just pray hard enough, you will overcome it. Or this is a matter for the family, and the family will tell you how to deal with it, and they'll support you with that. (SPl-3)

From a governance perspective, there is a lag effect between the presence of immigrants and their political representation. The delay in political representation can be explained by the time it takes to acquire Canadian citizenship, and therefore be able to vote and run for office, and the need for immigrants to integrate into the economy, leaving little time for politics. Such circumstances explain why immigrants tend to enjoy less political influence than their demographic weight would suggest. It is also worth mentioning that the very notion of political representation of and by immigrant communities is perennially subject to change and divergence along lines of class differences, date of arrival, and other factors (Bascaramurty, 2021).

Theme 4: Mobility Issues

Theme 4 is the first theme to fall under the planning and institutional issues category. This theme, raised by thirteen respondents, concerns the transportation problems Toronto suburbs experience. Suburbs have been planned with near universal reliance on the automobile in mind.

> There's no pedestrian environment here. So, all of the things that Metrolinx has pointed out that are challenges to increased transit and mobility are the very things that could start to be addressed by planning in a different way. (Adm-3)

The farther out suburbs extend and the longer car journeys are, the more congested highways become. The solution advanced by the provincial Growth Plan is to increase density and rely more on non-automobile modes, especially public transit. Such a solution confronts deep-seated path dependencies supportive of automobile use. For example, the suggestion by the mayor of Toronto to set tolls on municipally owned expressways, which are mostly used by outer suburban motorists, raised the ire of suburban politicians. Flying in the face of the intent of this measure, which purported to fund public transit in harmony with the provincial transportation strategy, was the politically motivated opposition of the province to City of Toronto expressway tolling. The provincial government reaction was driven by fears of an electoral backlash from suburban voters (Benzie, 2017).

Overall, respondents agree that we are in a catching-up phase regarding suburban public transit. But some raise doubts about the possibility of providing effective conventional public transit services in the low-density, functionally specialized suburban landscape. And current suburban land-use planning may not be improving the potential for public transit.

> I still don't understand why we enable the problem to keep getting bigger, and why nobody has said that above a certain threshold we should not be building large trip generators [that are not accessible by public transit] ...

So, as long as we continue adding such trip generators to this area, we just keep making the problem bigger. (TPl-1)

There is also concern about the provincial (and, to a degree, federal) government's capacity to fund the massive public transit investments required to alter suburban modal shares and about the possibility of coordinating densification with transit investment to assure that a large proportion of residents are served by public transit lines.

> Quite frankly, there's simply not enough money to go around. It's just something where there's not enough money to pay for the infrastructure. (Adm-2)

> We're spending $32 billion building regional transit. If you really look at it, it's not going to serve that many people. Our biggest infrastructure investment should be retrofitting the infrastructure necessary to accommodate intensification around those transit lines. So, we're leaving it up to the developers and the municipalities to be able to build affordable homes there. So, consequently, you end up with low density around transit lines. (R-3)

Finally, suburbanites may mobilize against improved transit because of the cost it represents and the disruption it can cause, especially in the case of surface rail transit. The rejection by Brampton City Council of a fully provincially funded north-south light rail line was due to its anticipated disruption of Downtown Brampton and adjacent residential areas, and preference on the part of citizens for an east-west line.

> The argument was we don't want it in our downtown. It'll be disruptive to our historic downtown. I would venture to guess that ours is not historic. If you compare it with any other downtown, in like Rome, or Israel, I think they're pretty old and they manage to get by with LRTs. (Pol-1)

Theme 5: Planning Issues and Regional Coordination

Issues related to theme 5 were mentioned by thirteen respondents. Since the adoption of the provincial Growth Plan in 2006, planning within Toronto suburbs is mandated to promote densification and increase reliance on public transit. Most Toronto suburban local and regional municipalities have bought into the principles of the Growth Plan, which has not, however, prevented them from maintaining much of the car-dependent business-as-usual suburban development trajectory. So, while they are advancing aspects of the Growth Plan, local and regional administrations are, at the same time, pursuing conventional car-oriented suburban growth.

Local and regional government support for densification and public transit is not only driven by Growth Plan prescriptions. In the case of densification, it is also a response to market trends, as more people opt for condos and apartments owing to rising housing costs and lifestyle preferences. In addition, it dovetails with the interest of municipalities in creating centres that combine retailing, employment, and public institutions. Such centres are perceived as a means of keeping these activities within their boundaries and widening the municipal assessment base. They also provide an opportunity to create urban-type settings within suburban areas.

> So I think, you know, everyone was very captured by policies [concerning the development of the new municipal centre]. We're in the same league as Toronto now, you know? And you could see whenever you were in a meeting with [the consultants], they kept referring to what they had done in Toronto. They were always giving examples. (LPl-1)

Likewise, local and regional governments react to increasing public transportation patronage, fed by the combined effect of higher suburban density and stagnating, if not falling, income. There are also problems with the implementation of the Growth Plan. While the Growth Plan imposes density thresholds on local and regional administrations, implementing them – how to reach the density objectives – is left largely to the interpretation of these administrations. This reality explains why local and regional planning has performed much better regarding the achievement of densification than of multifunctionality. Multifunctionality is more difficult to implement than densification because it entails more fine-grain forms of planning.

> So, that notion of mixing, I think, it's going to be very hard to get complete communities where everyone lives, works, plays in the exact same areas, essentially. (R-1)

> All density is not good density ... If we don't plan for the broad range of activities ... lifestyle considerations, walkable, livable, all the different things that we would consider to be the elements that together create complete communities, then you're going to undermine your policies. (Adm-2)

Densification faces obstacles, largely in the form of NIMBY reactions. While suburban residents do not generally object to strip retail development and heavily trafficked arterials, they show little tolerance for high-rise development. It is then difficult to coordinate density with public transit, a condition for the creation of density hubs around public transit stations.

> We're being crammed and jammed by legislation that says you must have accessory units, which I believe we should have, but I got a population that says we don't want those people living here. We don't want the density. (Pol-1)

> Now, if someone proposes townhouses, that's great. Everyone loves them. But if you propose a high-rise, then 400 people show up. (LPl-1)

> [Municipalities] thought, this is going to be wonderful, we're going to have our own multi-use development, it's going to be great, it's going to build our identity, and so on. These parts went well. The other parts didn't go so well … This is where the system breaks down. It's because of a councillor responding to the local demands [against density], one demand after the other, but those demands are not set within the big picture frame. (R-2)

Perhaps the perceived main threat to the Growth Plan strategy was the possible outcome of the provincial election in 2018, very much on our interviewees' minds as we talked to them (as discussed above, see Keil & Üçoğlu, 2021 for a preliminary assessment of the effects of this outcome on planning). As interest groups blaming skyrocketing housing costs on Growth Plan sprawl containment policies chime increasingly loud in planning debates, these policies were considered an important factor in that and future electoral campaigns.

> The "sprawlers" are winning the affordability message. They're winning the narrative … People think we're bumping against the greenbelt, and they think we're not building another single detached house, which is totally untrue. (R-3)

If provincial planning priorities were to shift away from those of the Growth Plan, there is doubt about the extent to which local and regional administrations would maintain their engagement with the principles of that plan. The formulation and implementation of the Growth Plan are characterized by a top-down process, whereby local and regional administrations are expected to comply with provincial directives.

> Explaining and engaging with the public around – the Growth Plan is creative but it was dropped like a hot potato, and there was no real champion

from the provincial level to remind people of that regional vision. It was all through regulation, and regulation can only get you so far. (R-1)

There is insufficient public buy-in to the principles advanced by the Growth Plan, in large part because it is difficult for most to visualize the range of compact development that can yield the densification dictated by the plan.

But at the same time, we don't have a vision in society – between the population, the development industry, the building industry, the planners – of what it looks like to have compact, efficient family housing. So, you have what we see in Liberty Village [condo towers with small units] and you have subdivisions, and then the rest just feels like kind of a squashed version of what we already know. (TPl-1)

I think we're seeing the weakness of having a benevolent provincial government that's doing the right things. We're so reliant on a benevolent right-minded provincial government ... and that's the vulnerability that I really fear. And so, I do believe a government with a different point of view could significantly erase whatever progress we think we've made. (R-4)

Present planning and development trends are criticized for a lack of new middle-range affordable housing, which is neither single-family homes, whose prices are beyond the reach of most households, nor high-rise condos, which are too small for families.

I think the most important thing is dealing with this affordability crisis while implementing the Growth Plan. But just implementing the Growth Plan isn't going to change anything. All those policies to make missing middle housing affordable throughout the region and urban centres along transit lines, we've got to do that. Or else we're just going to keep along our trajectory of sprawl, and unaffordability, and this bifurcation of suburb and sprawl and high-rise ... Kind of soulless high-rises, right? (R-3)

In a similar vein, local administrations are requesting an adaptation of the Growth Plan directives, especially those concerning intensification, to the specific circumstances of their municipalities.

There was, there still is, a fair amount of tension in the periphery about driving the kind of growth with similar policies for them as we have in place for the GTA. There's apprehension out there about that. Politically,

I think they feel that they are different, that people live in those communities because they are not as dense as some of the growing urban areas. They're less comfortable with significant policies around intensification. (Adm-2)

Theme 6: Local and Regional Administrations

The last theme concerns the institutional dimension of suburban governance by focusing on suburban issues as seen through the lens of the jurisdictional boundaries and the interests of local and regional municipalities. These institutional considerations were raised by thirteen respondents. Multilayered administrations are a source of friction, each administration arguing for the predominance of its role in terms of policymaking. For example, local governments stress their proximity to residents when complaining about what they see as infringements on their sphere of competence by other levels of government. They also note the lack of identification of residents with the regional tier.

> Many residents in the suburbs don't necessarily identify with that upper-tier structure. And so, that upper-tier structure has quite a number of powers, and particularly when you're looking at the Growth Plan, that's how everything is implemented. Residents not identifying with that upper tier becomes an issue. (R-1)

Meanwhile, regional administrations emphasize their capacity to coordinate infrastructures and services across municipal boundaries. And there is resentment on the part of local and regional governments toward provincial directives. If local and regional administrations generally subscribe to the principles of the Growth Plan, they take exception to the strict density thresholds imposed by the provincial government.

Local democracy in suburban Toronto is impeded by an inadequately informed public, due to a lack of suburban news coverage in the main metropolitan media outlets and the loss of autonomy of local suburban newspapers.

> I think the biggest structural challenge is we certainly have the *Globe and Mail*, the *Toronto Star*, the *National Post*, they can cover the Toronto issues. The local media is often owned by Metroland, which is the *Toronto Star*. We're seeing less local coverage. So, I think it's difficult to get people to follow local politics here and advocate for their own communities. (SPl-2)

The self-interest of local administrations is also shaped by their need to raise sufficient revenue to provide infrastructures and services – hence their reliance on enlarging the property tax base through fiscal zoning and the development of their entire territory, and after this, its densification. In their efforts to widen their fiscal base, municipalities are in competition with each other, a consequence of the administrative fragmentation of the suburban realm. The impact of this financially motivated inter-municipal competition on land-use planning is a dispersion of fiscally lucrative activities throughout suburban areas rather than their strategic concentration in places apt to fuel multifunctionality and public transit use. Some respondents point to the role a metropolitan-wide administration could play in terms of planning coordination and advocacy for the common interests of suburbs and of the metropolitan region as a whole. Such an administration would counterbalance the tendency for localities to focus exclusively on their own needs.

> [There] is the case that needs to be made for regional governance, a new level of regional governance. On top of the municipal, upper-tier regions, I think that's worth exploring or at least considering. Could there be like a Metro Vancouver type of government agency that could help do that coordination or convening across municipal governments? (EPl-2)

The need for a larger coordinating institutional governance vision was felt particularly, as some of our interlocutors noted, because the current capacity among local politicians and planners often was insufficiently matched to the challenges ahead. Many suburban councillors continue to submit to their anti-urban and anti-regional reflexes, and politicians at the municipal level obstruct the introduction of better regional suburban governance arrangements (Pol-1; R-4).

Global Tendencies Meet the Toronto Suburban Reality

Themes raised by respondents illustrate the forms that the meeting of global trends take in a suburban context. They have shown how these tendencies are shaped by the prevailing suburban reality and how they also modify this reality. These themes point to a mutual adaptation between global trends and suburban Toronto, and illustrate how this adaptation is negotiated within the suburban political institutional and civil society organizational ecosystem (Hamel & Keil, 2015). Adaptation can refer to institutional learning (as suburban municipalities here are looking for best practices elsewhere), economic relationship building (as happens often through channels opened by diaspora communities in Toronto's ethnoburbs), or simply serendipitous or accidental learning as one municipal planner told us in an interview.

> So, my staff, they're constantly going on vacation somewhere, they're constantly seeing these new formats for stores and taking pictures. So eventually you're not going to see these free-standing big developments like that. (LP-1)

The mutual adaptation observed in Toronto happens in many other metropolitan regions across the world, with variances according to their specific circumstances. The suburban realm best reflects the effects of global trends on the urban phenomenon, in large part because it is where most urban residents live and work. As urban regions have become primarily suburban, it is, as expected, in suburbs that the main forces transforming the urban phenomenon are at work.

Four themes raised by respondents mirror global transformative tendencies. *Economic decline and poverty in the suburbs* are, in large part, local manifestations of the globalization of the economy and adherence to a neoliberal agenda, which has itself achieved worldwide influence (Soederberg et al., 2005). The withering of the middle class and its replacement by wealth and poverty extremes are indeed consequences of globalization and neoliberalism. As we have seen, this social transformation clashes with the suburban middle-class stereotype and draws attention to insufficient service availability therein for people in need. A second theme is that of *ethnoburbs*, driven by international population flows made possible by a Canadian immigration policy, leading to a considerable increase in the number of immigrants from different parts of the world. From 1971, the adoption of the federal multiculturalism policy encouraged immigrants to express their cultural distinctions. The other global trend, the influence of environmentalism, is reflected by two more themes raised by the respondents: *mobility issues* and *planning issues and regional coordination.* These two themes chronicle attempts at introducing environmentally sensitive ways of dealing with the transportation needs and land-use planning of a rapidly expanding suburban realm.

The content of the interviews has documented how these global trends have unfolded in the Toronto suburban context. They have had to adapt to the form and dynamics of the Toronto suburbs, which explains, for example, why it is in the retail and services occupying car-oriented strip malls that cultural diversity finds its upmost expression. Likewise, when confronted by poverty, suburbanites will let go most of their other possessions before doing away with their car, for without it they are unable to function in a suburban environment, including accessing a job. In the case of attempts to make Toronto suburbs conform to environmental principles, enhanced public transit services and intensification, while of an unprecedented scale for the Toronto suburban realm, have not substantially modified suburban land-use–transportation dynamics. The way identified global trends have deployed in suburban Toronto has also been a function of the institutional make-up of the suburban realm. Interviews have illustrated how inter-municipal competition and the jurisdictional hierarchy between levels of government have impeded the possibility for suburban administrations to address the consequences of transitions brought on by global trends. The picture emerges of a suburban realm that is ill-equipped to provide sufficient services capable of dealing with rising poverty and the integration needs of immigrants. As regards the achievement of a more environmentally benign suburban form, there are doubts about the financial capacity of governments to provide the public transit services needed to sustain large-scale suburban intensification and about the durability of the provincial commitment to the Growth Plan agenda.

The interviews have also demonstrated, on the other hand, that there is growing sophistication in how Toronto's suburbs meet the specific challenges of a maturing suburban environment that is increasingly diverse in population and economic make-up, in built form and infra-structure. Some of this diversity is expressed in the ascent of a new generation of mayors in places like Brampton and Mississauga who embrace the challenges of the new suburban municipalities actively and aggressively. Southern Ontario's suburban decision makers are not anymore the boosters of bedroom communities at the peripheral fringe. They shape their destiny actively through individual municipal policy initiatives and concerted efforts among mayors, planners, and activists across various sectors. These agents of suburban governance do not react passively to pressures and trends visited upon them by the global economy, provincial policy, or the hegemony of Toronto. They attempt to chart an independent course when it comes to policy and planning decisions affecting their communities (including municipal-ities that will soon have up to a million inhabitants, such as Bramp-ton and Mississauga, west of the core city). In that, decision makers in the suburbanizing region are keenly aware of Toronto's hegemonic position in the region and the constraints and opportunities of regional governance as noted above. Regional governance across the suburban expanse of Toronto remains a mix of state, market, and private initia-tives, of institutional and informal arrangements and processes.

The suburbanizing region continues to produce its own "real existing regionalism" (Addie & Keil, 2015), where a home-grown regime has spearheaded a particular and endogenous "suburban–financial nexus on which the Ontario economy depends" (Üçoğlu et al., 2021) while perpetuating a suburban growth machine that appears to skate uneasily along the reality and perception of corruption and government favouritism (Buist et al., 2021). Yet, we have seen, as hypothesized at the opening of this chapter with reference to Hamel's (chapter 1, this volume) classification, that the notion of what is suburban has shifted in Toronto. Accordingly, we have seen changes in the institutional make-up and the governmentality of the regional state and its institutions (through planning and policy documents in particular), although many of the traditional challenges of the suburban reality remain or become more accentuated in an age of climate change and economic globalization. And lastly, the dialectic of universal extended urbanization and specific conditions under which that process takes place has been well illustrated for the Toronto case. The Toronto periphery displays contradictory dynamics between the ostensibly fixed nature of the suburbs (their built, social, and institutional environment) and the tendency for accelerating and often disquieting social, cultural, economic, and technological change.

REFERENCES

Addie, J-P.D., & Keil, R. (2015). Real existing regionalism: The region between talk, territory and technology. *International Journal of Urban and Regional Research, 39*(2), 407–17. https://doi.org/10.1111/1468-2427.12179

Bascaramurty, D. (2021, 16 September). In Brampton, federal campaign pledges to boost immigration are creating friction among classes and generations. *Globe and Mail.* https://www.theglobeandmail.com/canada/article-for-brampton-voters-campaign-pledges-to-boost-immigration-raise-hard/

Benzie, R. (2017, 26 January). Kathleen Wynne stopping John Tory's plan for tolls on DVP, Gardiner. *Toronto Star.* https://www.thestar.com/news/queenspark/2017/01/26/kathleen-wynne-stopping-john-torys-plan-for-tolls-on-dvp-gardiner.html

BILD (Building Industry and Land Development Association). (2017, 4 May). Demand for new homes continues to outpace supply and drives prices in the GTA [Press release]. https://web.archive.org/web/20170924201306/https://www.bildgta.ca/news/newsreleases/demand-for-new-homes-continues-to-outpace-supply-and-drive-prices-in-the-GTA/

Buist, S., Javed, N., & McIntosh, E. (2021, 3 April). Friends with benefits? An inside look at the money, power and influence behind the Ford

government's push to build Highway 413. *Toronto Star*. https://www
.thestar.com/news/investigations/2021/04/03/ford-friends-with-benefits
-an-inside-look-at-the-money-power-and-influence-behind-the-push-to
-build-highway-413.html

Burchell, R.W., Downs, A., McCann, B., & Mukherji, S. (2005). *Sprawl costs:
Economic impacts of unchecked development*. Island Press.

Cunningham, F. (2014, 24 July). What Rob Ford can teach us about populism
in Canada and some strategies to counter it. *Spacing*. https://spacing
.ca/national/2014/07/24/rob-ford-can-teach-us-populism-canada
-strategies-counter/

Ferguson, R., & Benzie, R. (2017, 12 April). Real estate speculators driving up
prices to be target of reforms, Sousa says. *Toronto Star*. https://www.thestar
.com/news/queenspark/2017/04/12/wynne-wants-to-cool-frantic-greater
-toronto-real-estate-market.html

Filion, P. (2013). Automobiles, highways, and suburban dispersion. In R. Keil
(Ed.), *Suburban constellations: Governance, land, and infrastructure in the 21st
century* (pp. 79–84). Jovis.

Filion, P., Bunting, T., & Warriner, K. (1999). The entrenchment of urban
dispersion: Residential preferences and location patterns in the dispersed
city. *Urban Studies*, 36(8), 1317–47. https://doi.org/10.1080/0042098993015

Filion, P., Keil, R., & Pulver, N. (2019). Introduction: The scope and scales of
suburban infrastructures. In P. Filion & N. Pulver (Eds.), *Critical perspectives
on suburban infrastructures: Contemporary international cases* (pp. 3–41).
University of Toronto Press.

Fong, E. (2016). Immigration and its impacts on Canadian cities. In G.B.
Prato (Ed.), *Beyond multiculturalism: Views from anthropology* (pp. 39–55).
Routledge.

Frisken, F. (2007). *Metropolis: The political dynamics of urban expansion in the
Toronto region, 1924–2003*. Canadian Scholars' Press.

Gordon, D.L.A., & Janzen, M. (2013). Suburban nation? Estimating the size of
Canada's suburban population. *Journal of Architectural and Planning Research*,
30(3), 197–220. https://www.jstor.org/stable/43031005

Hamel, P., & Keil, R. (2015). Introduction: Governance in a suburban world.
In P. Hamel & R. Keil (Eds.), *Suburban governance: A global view* (pp. 3–16).
University of Toronto Press.

Harris, R. (2015). Using Toronto to explore three suburban stereotypes, and
vice versa. *Environment and Planning A: Economy and Space*, 47(1), 30–49.
https://doi.org/10.1068/a46298

Hemson Consulting Ltd. (2020). *Greater Golden Horseshoe: Growth forecasts to
2051*. Ontario Ministry of Municipal Affairs and Housing. https://www
.hemson.com/wp-content/uploads/2020/08/HEMSON-GGH-Growth
-Outlook-Report-26Aug20.pdf

Hirt, S.A. (2014). *Zoned in the USA: The origins and implications of American land-use regulations*. Cornell University Press.

Hulchanski, J.D. (2010). *The three cities within Toronto: Income polarization among Toronto's neighbourhoods, 1970–2005*. Cities Centre Press, University of Toronto.

Jacobs, J.M., & Lees, L. (2013). Defensible space on the move: Revisiting the urban geography of Alice Coleman. *International Journal of Urban and Regional Research*, 37(5), 1559–83. https://doi.org/10.1111/1468-2427.12047

Jimenez, B.S. (2014). Separate, unequal, and ignored? Interjurisdictional competition and the budgetary choices of poor and affluent municipalities. *Public Administration Review*, 74(2), 246–57. https://doi.org/10.1111/puar.12186

Keil, R., Hamel, P., Boudreau, J.-A., & Kipfer, S. (Eds.). (2017). *Governing cities through regions: Canadian and European perspectives*. Wilfrid Laurier University Press.

Keil, R., & Üçoğlu, M. (2021). Beyond sprawl? Regulating growth in southern Ontario: Spotlight on Brampton. *disP – The Planning Review*, 57(3), 100–18. https://doi.org/10.1080/02513625.2021.2026678

Keil, R., & Young, D. (2008). Transportation: The bottleneck of regional competitiveness in Toronto. *Environment and Planning C: Government and Policy*, 26(4), 728–51. https://doi.org/10.1068/c68m

Lucy, W.H., & Phillips, D.L. (2006). *Tomorrow's cities, tomorrow's suburbs*. American Planning Association.

Marshall, A. (2000). *How cities work: Suburbs, sprawl, and the roads not taken*. University of Texas Press.

Metzger, J. (2013). Raising the regional leviathan: A relational-materialist conceptualization of regions-in-becoming as politics-in-stabilization. *International Journal of Urban and Regional Research*, 37(4), 1368–95. https://doi.org/10.1111/1468-2427.12038

Moore, O. (2017, 3 February). As Toronto home prices soar, commuters will feel the pain. *Globe and Mail*. https://beta.theglobeandmail.com/news/toronto/torontos-rocketing-home-prices-could-be-a-nightmare-for-commuters/article33898872/

Neptis. (2015). *Understanding the fundamentals of the Growth Plan*. The Neptis Foundation. https://neptis.org/sites/default/files/gp_primer/understanding_the_fundamentals_of_the_growth_plan_march20_0.pdf

Ontario (Government of Ontario, Ministry of Municipal Affairs). (2017). *Growth Plan for the Greater Golden Horseshoe*. Queen's Printer for Ontario. (Original work published 2006)

Paasi, A., & Metzger, J. (2017). Foregrounding the region. *Regional Studies*, 51(1), 19–30. https://doi.org/10.1080/00343404.2016.1239818

66   Pierre Filion, Roger Keil, and Michael Collens

Peck, J. (2011). Neoliberal suburbanism: Frontier space. *Urban Geography*, 32(6), 884–919. https://doi.org/10.2747/0272-3638.32.6.884

Poppe, W., & Young, D. (2015). The politics of place: Place-making versus densification in Toronto's tower neighbourhoods. *International Journal of Urban and Regional Research*, 39(3), 613–21. https://doi.org/10.1111/1468-2427.12196

Read, C. (2016). *The public financiers: Ricardo, George, Clark, Ramsey, Mirrlees, Vickrey, Wicksell, Musgrave, Buchanan, Tiebout, and Stiglitz*. Palgrave Macmillan Secaucus.

Sadler, R.C., & Highsmith, A.R. (2016). Rethinking Tiebout: The contribution of political fragmentation and racial/economic segregation of the Flint water crisis. *Environmental Justice*, 9(5), 143–51. https://doi.org/10.1089/env.2016.0015

Sancton, A. (2000). *Merger mania: The assault on local government*. McGill-Queen's University Press.

Soederberg, S., Menz, G., & Cerny, P.G. (Eds.). (2005). *Internalizing globalization: The rise of neoliberalism and the decline of national varieties of capitalism*. Palgrave Macmillan.

Sorensen, A., & Hess, P. (2015). Building suburbs, Toronto-style: Land development regimes, institutions, critical junctures and path dependence. *Town Planning Review*, 86(4), 411–36. https://doi.org/10.3828/tpr.2015.26

Stanilov, K., & Scheer, B.C. (2004). *Suburban form: An international perspective*. Routledge.

Storper, M. (2014). Governing the large metropolis. *Territory, Politics, Governance*, 2(2), 115–34. https://doi.org/10.1080/21622671.2014.919874

Tiebout, C. (1956). A pure theory of local expenditures. *Journal of Political Economy*, 64(5), 416–24. http://www.jstor.org/stable/1826343

Üçoğlu, M., Keil, R., & Tomar, S. (2021). Contagion in the markets? COVID-19 and housing in the Greater Toronto Area. *Built Environment*, 47(3), 355–66. https://doi.org/10.2148/benv.47.3.355

Vaughan, L., Griffiths, S., Haklay, M., & Jones, C.E. (2009). Do the suburbs exist? Discovering complexity and specificity in suburban built form. *Transactions of the Institute of British Geographers*, 34(4), 475–88. https://doi.org/10.1111/j.1475-5661.2009.00358.x

Walks, R.A. (2006). The causes of city-suburban political polarization? A Canadian case study. *Annals of the Association of American Geographers*, 96(2), 390–414. https://doi.org/10.1111/j.1467-8306.2006.00483.x

Walks, R.A., & Bourne, L.S. (2006). Ghettoes in Canada's cities? Racial segregation, ethnic enclaves and poverty concentrations in Canadian urban areas. *Canadian Geographer*, 50(3), 273–97. https://doi.org/10.1111/j.1541-0064.2006.00142.x

White, R. (2016). *Planning Toronto: The planners, the plans, their legacies, 1940–1980*. UBC Press.

Williamson, J., & Dunham-Jones, E. (2021). *Case studies in retrofitting suburbia: Urban design strategies for urgent challenges*. Wiley.

Young, R., & Leuprecht, C. (2004). *Canada: The state and the federation, 2004: Municipal-federal-provincial relations in Canada*. McGill-Queen's University Press.

Zhuang, Z.C., & Chen, A.X. (2017). The role of ethnic retailing in retrofitting suburbia: Case studies from Toronto, Canada. *Journal of Urbanism, 10*(3), 275–95. https://doi.org/10.1080/17549175.2016.1254671

3 Institutional Reform and the Reconfiguration of Power: Greater Montreal's Experience with Suburban Governance

PIERRE HAMEL

Since the end of the Second World War, the redistribution of key economic, social, cultural, and political activities within cities has caused a clear break with pre-war patterns of urbanization. Cities can no longer be studied in the same way. Granted, on a symbolic level, the central core or central city continues to play an important role in defining the identity and uniqueness of a metropolitan area. However, the future of such regions cannot be accurately understood without also examining the development of suburban communities. In recent decades, the collective demographic weight of communities on the so-called periphery has surpassed that of the central city. Meanwhile, as suburban communities take on roles that are no longer entirely dependent on the vitality of the central city, the latter's importance for a metropolitan area's growth has declined in various ways (Teaford, 2006). Everyday representations of the city and of urban space have changed accordingly. In many ways, this change is true of Greater Montreal.

By examining "suburban governance"[1] as it has been practised both formally and informally in Montreal in recent decades, my primary goal is to understand the political dimension of the process. How can the ways that suburbanization has been implemented best be described? What degree of flexibility do local stakeholders enjoy? To what extent are they able to adapt to the constraints or requirements inherent to – or even specific to – suburban governance?

In order to answer these questions, I draw on interviews conducted with various categories of suburban governance stakeholders, while considering structural reforms and interventions undertaken by the government of Quebec since the turn of the twenty-first century. The chapter is divided into three parts. I begin by quickly reviewing the key characteristics of Greater Montreal, with a focus on specific features in terms of suburban governance. Next, I explore the constraints and opportunities that shape cooperation among local stakeholders. Finally, the third part of the chapter analyses the positions held by different political actors. My goal is therefore to provide a better understanding of how suburban governance relates to the redefinition of power relations and how this process affects the planning and structure of urban life.

Urban and Suburban Governance in Greater Montreal

Both the potential for and the structure of social action at a metropolitan scale remain hotly debated topics (Metzger, 2013; Paasi & Metzger, 2017; Savini, 2016). These debates also address planning models and urban forms, as well as various components of the local state (municipalities, regional authorities, higher levels of government). Ultimately, it is a matter of expressing, guiding, or implementing collective choices. Moreover, the issue of "metropolitan solidarity" – why and how to promote it – lies at the heart of the controversy.

Urban development has long had a regional dimension. Marc V. Levine (1998) provides the following summary of the arguments put forward by the new regionalists, who claim that the central city and the suburbs should cooperate for the benefit of both areas: (1) the decline of central cities has negative impacts on living conditions in the suburbs; (2) some services, including transportation networks, can be better managed at the regional level; (3) a "regional economic development strategy" provides a better basis for competing in the global economy (p. 113).

Without reviewing all the objections raised against the new regionalism, I would point out that it offers few opportunities for understanding "metropolitan governance" from a political perspective (Ghorra-Gobin, 2015). In particular, Levine (1998) has criticized the new regionalists for being "too abstract and technocratic." Indeed, they remain largely silent on the question of suburban governance.

Like cities, metropolitan areas are not bound by a predetermined destiny. Rather, political choices profoundly shape their development. Urban studies research going back to the 1980s has clearly demonstrated this fact,[2] despite a general focus on central cities (Cox, 2011). The same studies show the extent to which urban development, through support for certain growth regimes or through resistance to the new geography of global capitalism, has highlighted certain power dynamics that reflect class conflict, ethnic discrimination, and cultural identities (Keil et al., 2017). Reflections on the relationship between politics and urban space have addressed the topic from a variety of perspectives (Beveridge & Koch, 2017; Kipfer, 2018; Rodgers et al., 2014). Here, I will focus on regional or metropolitan governance.

Two conflicting theories have emerged from this scholarship. I am referring, on the one hand, to the idea that metropolises are essentially ungovernable, given the difficulty of structuring collective action across such a vast territory (Jouve & Lefèvre, 2002); and, on the other hand, to the argument that the fragmented nature of metropolitan regions, which can be divided along so many different lines, provides opportunities for tinkering with institutional structures (Storper, 2014). In fact, these two interpretations are not as divergent as they might appear at first glance. They both recognize how the state and political life have been transformed as metropolises become "the new framework for regulating contemporary society" (Jouve & Lefèvre, 2002, p. 17). Furthermore, they both see governance as a problem to be solved, given the divisions that need to be overcome and the uncertainty arising from a "reassignment of the territorial reference point from the city to the metropolis" (p. 19). Meanwhile, addressing questions of efficiency, power, and justice at the metropolitan level can provide new insights into the relationship between the various components of local administration. Finally, both theories recognize that a fully satisfactory model of metropolitan governance has yet to be developed.[3] Not only are the proposed solutions to metropolitan challenges highly dependent on specific national contexts and their respective political traditions – which define both constraints and opportunities – but prospects for action further depend on the overall culture of cooperation and solidarity present in local communities.

The approaches advocated by the two theories outlined above may reflect differing intentions and distinct normative sensibilities. However, they both seek to better understand the challenge of local democracy in light of suburban development and/or metropolitanization, as well as new forms of governance advocated by social and political actors.

In Montreal, political and institutional observations on urban, suburban, and metropolitan governance are made in the context of a slow process of economic and urban restructuring that affects the entire urban area. Looking back to the late nineteenth century, Montreal was once a vibrant commercial, industrial, and financial centre, not to mention Canada's undisputed metropolis. At the same time, it remained a "colonial city in the economic sense of the term," given that its economy was controlled by an "ethnic minority" that identified with the mother country. The primary role of turn-of-the-twentieth-century Montreal was therefore to "facilitate the extraction (and export) of the resources found in its vast hinterland" (Polèse, 2012, p. 961).

Although Montreal had previously boasted a thriving economy, the city's elites struggled to adjust to the rapid pace of structural change following the Great Depression of the 1930s (Higgins, 1986). Granted, the city experienced a strong economic recovery during the Second World War and over the following two decades. However, it never fully regained its lost vitality.

I will refrain from listing either the city's economic failings or the many attempts that have been made to address them over the years. Instead, I will simply point to the bleak picture painted by an Organisation for Economic Co-operation and Development (OECD) report (Organisation de coopération et de développement économiques [OCDE], 2016) that aims to provide an action plan for boosting innovation. The report compares Montreal to nineteen other metropolises with similar characteristics, including Barcelona, Lyon, Dublin, and Stockholm. Montreal ranks eighteenth in terms of per capita gross domestic product (GDP) growth, in part because worker productivity remained very low between 2001 and 2012. Other indicators, including a low overall university graduation rate and high unemployment among newcomers, also reflect a lack of economic vitality. As some observers have noted in response to the OECD report, the problem is not that Montreal lacks significant assets – for instance, it boasts a dynamic university network and impressive growth in cutting edge industries like aerospace and artificial intelligence – but that it is not "the engine it could be" (Corriveau, 2016). Simply put, there is concern regarding the urban area's failure to convert "its assets into results" (Dubuc, 2016).

Amid increasing economic globalization, urban governments are redefining their modes of intervention. Where they once restricted themselves to managing infrastructure, equipment, urban services, and urban planning, they are now also engaged in matters of economic development (Pinson, 2006). In addition, they are more than willing to rescale their territories in order to better respond to heightened competition (Savitch, 2007). In the case of Montreal, political elites, along with some segments of the business community and the labour movement, began demonstrating a willingness to pursue economic restructuring as early as the 1970s. Granted, moving from an industrial paradigm to a service economy has proven difficult. But the political class became more committed to change around the turn of the twenty-first century, when the provincial government initiated a major overhaul of local government institutions that affected all communities in Greater Montreal. Municipalities were amalgamated, while certain administrative responsibilities, including the management of local services for residents, were devolved to the borough level. The reform also created

Table 3.1. Administrative Units of the Montreal Metropolitan Region

Administrative and Territorial Units	Governing Bodies	Main Responsibilities	Scope and Composition
Montreal Metropolitan Region	Montreal Metropolitan Community (MMC)	Plan, coordinate, and finance projects advancing the region's strategic and territorial development	Single unit covering 4,374 km^2 and with a population of 4.099 million in 2016 (encompasses the 82 municipalities located within the territory of Statistics Canada's Montreal Census Metropolitan Area)
Agglomerations of Montreal, Longueuil, and Laval; outer suburbs on the South Shore and North Shore	According to provincial legislation, the municipalities located within these zones share common interests based on either their inclusion within one of the 11 regional county municipalities (RCMs) on the territory of the MMC or their status as an agglomeration (Laval is both an agglomeration and an RCM)	Within each zone, coordinate municipal activities related to territorial planning and management	Five zones on the territory of the MMC (covering a total of 4,374 km^2 and with a total population of 4.099 million in 2016)
Municipalities defined in reference to general purpose and governing responsibilities with the power of taxation	Local municipalities in charge of planning and management of a territory according to the provincial jurisdiction	Municipalities have the legitimacy for local planning and managing infrastructure and services considered local	82 municipalities are recognized as being part of the MMC, even though their influence is largely related to their demographic weight
Boroughs and districts subordinated to municipalities with decentralized powers	Lower tier of municipalities	Responsible for managing local services and infrastructure, which are defined as local in cooperation with the municipality	The number of units regarding boroughs and districts are variating a great deal; the municipality of Montreal has 19 boroughs – each one being under the responsibility of a mayor and a council – while Longueuil is divided into 3 boroughs; Laval does not have any borough, but has 21 districts

Sources: Adapted from Hamel (2006); CMM website, https://cmm.qc.ca/.

the Montreal Metropolitan Community (MMC), a body responsible for consultation, coordination, and planning across the entire metropolitan area (Hamel, 2006). In this institutional context, both elected officials and local managers are required to coordinate and cooperate at multiple levels (see Table 3.1). This situation has produced unpredictable changes in the urban governance system, leading to increased uncertainty surrounding modes of cooperation and destabilizing existing models of action.

Constraints and Opportunities that Shape Cooperation among Local Stakeholders

The coordination of collective action at the regional or metropolitan level is not at all straightforward. By introducing a new forum for political dialogue at the regional level,[4] the creation of the MMC established new rules governing relations between communities, including not only relations between the central city and the periphery but also those involving regional county municipalities (RCMs). The latter are subregional consultation bodies established by the Quebec government in 1979, with the aim of modernizing municipal management.

The MMC's first step in meeting its responsibility to coordinate public policy across Greater Montreal was to define a "strategic vision" (CMM, 2002) for guiding the creation of a metropolitan development framework (CMM, 2005). However, not all Greater Montreal municipalities ended up endorsing this vision. Some of them objected to the imposition of a consultation model that swept aside modes of collaboration and planning practices that had been established through the creation of RCMs (Douay & Roy-Baillargeon, 2015). This resistance prompted a second attempt at defining a shared vision, leading to the adoption of a Metropolitan Planning and Development Plan (MPDP; CMM, 2012) for the entire region. In adopting the MPDP, the MMC embraced transit-oriented development (TOD), to be achieved by promoting denser development around public transit infrastructure (Metro, commuter train, and bus stations).[5]

Several outer suburban municipalities were reluctant to accept the planning restrictions and constraints laid out in the metropolitan plan. But they ultimately accepted the urban development model put forward by the MMC after the latter "relaxed" the requirements associated with the implementation of TOD: "Watering down the MPDP in this way was essential to its acceptance, because the changes placated elected representatives from the outer suburbs on the North Shore and South Shore, and dispelled their fears that they would no longer be able to develop their municipalities. Negotiating the changes also allowed them to reaffirm their role as political decision-makers" (Roy-Baillargeon, 2017, p. 58).

However, the compromise failed to resolve the MMC's challenges in terms of not only bolstering regional solidarity but also building a common vision based on priorities shared by all stakeholders. As one university researcher I spoke with pointed out regarding the development of the MPDP, the metropolitan body failed to propose development options that would not only allow for consensus but also inspire strong support from all municipalities:

> In short, the plan failed to identify any priorities. Although one of its aims was to prioritize public transit, the plan essentially ended up providing a laundry list of projects that were all assigned the same importance, whether it was a bus line serving 2,000 people or the Metro's Blue Line.
>
> The MMC did not fulfil its duty ... Every community still has the idea that it needs to pursue growth, that it is required to pursue growth, but nobody really knows why. It is as if municipalities need to grow, to increase their population, as a sign of "good health," whereas this connection has never been proved. (R-1)[6]

In light of these observations, it is important to remember that the regional planning process carried out by the MMC failed to forge a metropolitan identity capable of appropriately acknowledging the commitment of all local stakeholders to a common project. It also failed to rank projects or establish regional development priorities. In fact, the MPDP identified no fewer than 155 TOD zones: "All communities are treated equally. Each one is entitled to its own TOD, whereas the total number of TODs should have been no higher than 30" (R-1).

This outcome cannot be blamed on the vague desires of policymakers, managers, or planners. Choices made by citizens, based on their preferences and the options available to them, must also be taken into account.

Some argue that the decision to live in the central city is based on values that are diametrically opposed to those that underlie the decision to live on the periphery (TLP-1). The rise of a "suburbanism" defined in terms of a specific suburban way of life and associated with suburban forms of land use – strict separation of uses and reliance on the automobile as the primary and preferred means of transportation, leading to lower density than in Toronto or Vancouver – reflects a choice perceived or even affirmed as legitimate. Of course, suburban culture is characterized by hybrid and diverse patterns that are aligned with social and cultural norms specific to the suburban lifestyle (Ekers et al., 2012). Even if recent events have unfolded in a context that could be described as post-suburban – a context where "classical suburban expansion is just one in a range of ways in which cities' peripheries are being reformed and rearranged" (Keil, 2018, p. 14) – the old dichotomy between low- and high-density development persists.

> One thing is for sure, I won't be moving to Blainville. That wouldn't fit with my personal values. I have no desire to spend two-and-a-half hours in the car every day. At the same time, I really understand why someone would want to live in Blainville and suffer through a two-and-a-half-hour daily commute so they can have a pool in their yard. I'm not going to judge them. We simply have different values. It's also a matter of income. Some people have no choice. They live where they can afford to live. But yes, people have different values. (LP-1)

To some extent, according to an urban planner working for the central city, these words evoke traditional representations of the difference between life in the central city and life in the suburbs. But these representations are not exclusively or even chiefly cultural. Rather, they are based on material realities, starting with the infrastructure that supports each way of life.

> In terms of accessibility, of the modes of transportation associated with different lifestyles, there is most certainly a divide between the two worlds. For instance, new forms of mobility – Uber, mobile apps, demand-responsive transportation, bicycle sharing, car sharing – are all pervasive in the central city, in densely populated neighbourhoods, because these areas provide the mass of users necessary to make such services cost effective. But as soon as you leave Montreal's dense urban core, you start to find classic mobility behaviour focused on automobile use … As soon as you start moving away [from the urban core], even on the Island of Montreal, you immediately start to see travel patterns based primarily on the car, with a rapid decrease in the modal share of public transit and far less change over the years. Things are much more static, likely because the land has been developed in a way that tends to limit the possibilities for change. (TLP-1)

It is important to nuance these observations. Many suburban Montreal communities have been growing at a rapid pace for several years. Although their density is not comparable to that of the central city's urban core, they have nevertheless embraced new modes of development, including the densification of certain areas. An elected representative from a northern suburb made a passing reference to these developments while describing his municipality's changing role:

> We have changed from being a bedroom community, a suburb with little in the way of commercial development, to a community with a diverse economy and an active cultural life, whose population is growing faster than the Quebec average, and that is emerging as a preferred destination for immigrants. (Pol-1)

For geographical and historical reasons, Montreal was built on an island. The city's port, which provides access to the entire North American continent,[7] has played a strategic role in the development of the larger urban area. The relationship between the central city and the periphery has therefore developed in a highly symbiotic fashion, despite recent technological changes that have altered consumption patterns and transformed how goods are distributed. As one private sector manager working in the field of transportation infrastructure pointed out, compared to other cities, Montreal has not seen as many distribution centres relocate to the periphery. This situation has benefited the urban core.

> Montreal's island location, its history, the fact that its transportation system initially developed on the island – this all helps explain why the relationship is not so dichotomous as in other metropolitan areas. In particular, I am thinking about cities that were not built around a port, where many businesses have relocated to the periphery, and where the suburbs have come to dominate the relationship with the central city. By contrast, in Montreal, the central city still dominates the relationship with the suburbs. (Adm-1)

This historical reality has certainly helped to limit the centrifugal forces that have largely driven suburban development in recent decades. From this perspective, the role and vitality of the urban core have helped discourage and possibly reduce the flight of middle-class households to the periphery, a trend that began in the 1960s (Poitras, 2012).

Moreover, beyond the old dichotomies that have traditionally structured not only representations of the urban centre and periphery but also the relationship between the two, the issue of the quality of suburban life has gained greater significance. Whether they live in the suburbs or in the central city, residents are looking for quality of life.

Essentially, people moving to the suburbs are trying to escape urban constraints, which may be defined in terms of housing and transportation
costs, noise, or even crime. Whatever the case, they are looking for some
degree of peace and tranquility. This may be reflected in different expectations regarding the territory and its amenities. Suburban residents want
the fewest possible restrictions on access to the urban centre, whereas inhabitants of central neighbourhoods favour a greener and less congested
city. Ultimately, although these two populations share a similar discourse,
they are discussing distinct spaces and territories. As a result, they don't
always understand each other, even if they are both basically aspiring to a
better quality of life. (R-2)

By reconciling the centre and the periphery in this way, that is to say
through a focus on the fundamental aspirations of their inhabitants,
some stakeholders not only see the potential for identifying values
shared by local populations across the metropolitan area, but they also
emphasize how processes of suburbanization can increasingly be defined in reference to urban space. In other words, whether they live on
the periphery or in the central city, residents face similar urban problems, despite lifestyle differences. This finding is particularly true with
regard to the quality of services provided. Ultimately, these considerations call into question the very principle of centrality as it has historically been defined in reference to a hierarchical – and dominant – urban
space. As a result, the traditional understanding of the periphery and of
the relationship between centre and periphery needs to be reassessed.

The term "periphery" may no longer be appropriate. You can go back to the
late 1970s, when the government of Quebec produced its *Preferred Development Option for the Region of Montreal*, which aimed to fight urban sprawl.
We now realize that this was little more than wishful thinking … Urban
sprawl continued unabated, and even picked up pace in the years that followed, in such a way that it is now completely redefining the city. (LP-2)

These remarks reinforce the idea that key suburban components have
either converged or been made obsolete (Keil, 2018). However, they fail
to address the political choices that underlie the governance of these
components on a metropolitan or regional scale. It is one thing to recognize that suburban expansion has reconfigured urban space and the
issues associated with it, and quite another to shed light on the policy
choices and political arrangements that will determine future directions for the entire metropolitan area. And that is precisely what I will
address next.

Political Actors and Suburban Governance

Suburban governance involves many players, including local authorities and their partners. It also engages civil society and higher levels of government, both of which have come to see cities primarily as partners (Ghorra-Gobin, 2015). This situation stems from a context of globalization, in which the most recent forms of metropolitanization have taken shape, enhancing the role of local authorities (Boudreau et al., 2007).

In matters of metropolitan management, institutional reforms cannot immediately provide a sustainable means of reconciling the economic and social functions required for urban development. This reality is due to several factors, starting with the territorial expansion inherent in metropolitanization processes. Decision-making bodies tend to be poorly matched or out of sync with networks, functions, and realities on the ground (Halbert et al., 2021). At the same time, local elected officials are often focused on maintaining their existing status and prerogatives (Tomas, 2012).

Nevertheless, certain studies (OCDE, 2001) have highlighted how crucial it is for public authorities to invest in urban infrastructure in order to foster innovation and thereby increase the competitiveness of metropolitan regions. The underlying assumption is that improvements to the built environment and to living conditions lead to better economic performance by local and metropolitan areas. This expectation makes metropolitan-level governance, including suburban governance, a necessity, despite the many challenges faced by stakeholders: How can social and geographic inequalities be reduced? Is it possible to share resources more equitably across the region's population centres? What measures can be taken to promote new forms of cooperation at the metropolitan level (Gilli, 2013; Storper, 2014)?

As I suggested at the start of the chapter, a change of perspective is required to properly address the issue of suburban governance. We can no longer understand metropolitan integration solely from the viewpoint of the central city. An analysis of my interviews with stakeholders from Greater Montreal (Table 3.2) points to the same conclusion.

To begin with, I should note that many local stakeholders recognize the importance of regional governance, especially in matters related to transportation and the environment. For instance, as one independent researcher affiliated with a community organization explained:

> Here, we are trying to foster awareness at the metropolitan level on common issues such as air quality and transportation, as well as water conservation. (R-2)

Table 3.2. Respondents

N°	Function	Agency	Activities	Code Used in Quotes
1	Planner and administrator	Municipality	Local planning	LP-1
2	Planner and administrator	Regional planning agency	Transport and land-use planning	TLP-1
3	Planner and administrator	Provincial government	Metropolitan planning	ADM-1
4	Independent planner	Self-employed	Local planning	LP-2
5	Politician	Municipality	Municipal politics	Pol-1
6	Politician	Municipality	Municipal politics	Pol-2
7	Politician	Municipality	Municipal politics	Pol-3
8	Researcher and community organizer	Community organizing	Urban and environmental research and mobilization	R-2
9	Researcher and planner	University-based research organization	Urban research	R-1
10	Administrator	Consultative and coordination council	Transportation and logistic	Adm-1

This view is shared by other stakeholders, including elected officials, as well as by representatives of civil society and the business community. Furthermore, it is the very basis of the MMC's legitimacy, which therefore naturally works to promote it. But to date, it has not been enough to build a strong, shared vision of the metropolitan area's identity.

In the MMC's defence, resistance to such a vision is in no way specific to Greater Montreal. The obstacles to forging a metropolitan identity are inherent in how powers, levels of authority, and allegiances are divided. The diversity of interests also makes it difficult to develop a concerted strategy that all stakeholders can embrace (Horak, 2012). Moreover, territorial and administrative fragmentation is largely the result of previous initiatives and political choices that reflect the preferences expressed by the full range of social and political actors (Storper, 2014). We therefore need to better understand the configuration of the forces at work.

In creating the MMC, the Quebec government initially expressed vague but ambitious objectives: "Ensure the competitiveness and attractiveness of the metropolitan territory with a view to encouraging sustainable development" (CMM, 2018, p. 4). Above all, this goal meant working to coordinate or at least harmonize the key components of a fragmented territory. But it also meant overcoming the social and economic challenges facing the region.

As some have pointed out (Pol-1), although local elected officials may focus on the need for cooperation, they carry out their work in a context marked by political divisions deeply rooted in the region's development and the ethnolinguistic distribution of the electorate. This context has consequences for electoral influence in terms of the prevailing balance of power between the central city and the periphery. At least that is how one City of Montreal borough councillor sees things:

> It's easy to understand. Montreal is not at play in provincial elections, not at all. Parties don't take or lose power in Quebec because of Montreal (that is to say the Island or City of Montreal). Whatever the results in Montreal, elections aren't won here. They're won in the 450.[8] (Pol-2)

This reading of electoral dynamics implies that the Quebec government tends to overlook the needs, priorities, and expectations expressed by citizens and elected officials from the City of Montreal. It also has implications for the balance of political power, since the voters in the metropolitan area's five main population centres fit distinct social and cultural profiles. This demography needs to be considered in order to better understand resistance and/or alliances at the level of the MMC. Indeed, expectations, demands, and issues vary greatly from one population centre to the next. And the nature of opposition to the approaches and projects put forward by the MMC varies accordingly. It should therefore not be surprising if the strongest resistance to the MMC initially came from elected officials representing the outer suburbs on the North Shore. One of my interviewees explained:

> We mustn't forget that the outer suburbs on the South Shore are older and face problems that are much more urban – revitalizing old town centres, revitalizing infrastructure … The outer suburbs on the North Shore face issues that have more to do with development, since apart from a few resort communities, everything is all very new. In such a context, local elected officials still see some advantages to acting like the "emperors" of their respective communities. Of course, this will play itself out in a few years, when they realize that their communities need to address issues related to adapting, revitalizing, and maintaining infrastructure. At that point, they will find themselves in the same situation as South Shore communities, and I

think they'll become much more open to the idea of the Metropolitan Community. They will see it as providing an opportunity to act on two fronts: they can influence government policy at the provincial level … but they can also operate at the metropolitan level. So, in short, I don't think the MMC has been such a bad thing for suburban communities. There was some initial fear – which persists in some quarters – that they would be "swallowed up" by the City of Montreal. But the MMC has actually provided them with a new avenue for better negotiating with other levels of government. (R-1)

These observations suggest that, despite appearances and the City of Montreal's influence within the MMC, the latter has generally been favourable to the suburbs. This interpretation reflects not only the evolution of metropolitan planning but also a change in attitude on the part of some municipalities, including some outer suburbs on the North Shore that ultimately endorsed the MPDP.

This interpretation may also explain the reservations expressed by some elected officials from Montreal regarding the MMC. While recognizing that the central city makes up only part of a larger metropolitan area, they argue that its uniqueness needs to be reaffirmed. In light of trends shaping suburban development off the Island of Montreal, these elected officials point out that suburban expansion is being pursued at the expense of the central city. For them, even if cooperation with suburban municipalities is necessary – if not inevitable, given trends in urban development – it must not be allowed to "compromise" Montreal's boroughs. For instance, they argue that the fiscal burden currently shouldered by the central city alone should be shared more broadly by transportation infrastructure users. Here is how the Montreal borough representative cited above put it:

I think about the number of cars entering the city, about the cost of infrastructure repair, compared to how little is invested in public transit, whether on the island or for reaching the island. Meanwhile, Montreal finds itself solely responsible for the fiscal burden associated with maintaining and refurbishing this infrastructure. We have the data to prove it. Most streets, some three-quarters of them, are used by people who don't live in the borough. How can we make it so all road users contribute to infrastructure repair and maintenance? How can we reduce Montrealers' tax burden? … We need to take this question seriously because the road network is in a terrible state. We're forced to raise tax rates, and Montrealers inevitably move away, saying: "I pay too much tax in Montreal." We risk ending up like Detroit. We're headed for the "doughnut effect" if we don't change course. (Pol-2)

Fiscal issues are therefore closely related to mobility issues, as the same elected official went on to explain:

> Today, when a company considers setting up shop in a community, the first thing it looks at is how much time it will take its employees to get to work. Because every minute spent in traffic has a negative impact on productivity. You could even say that an employee's quality of life and happiness are directly tied to their mobility. If the mobility issues of workers and city residents are not addressed, we will continue to lose both businesses and people. We often hear companies say: "You know what? I'm going to move my business to Laval. Not because it's nicer there or because it's a better location, but because most of my employees live on the periphery. It will take them less time to get to work if I move there. They'll automatically be less stressed, less tired, less exhausted" … If Montreal is aiming for economic prosperity and competitiveness, it needs to be able to attract businesses. And to do that, it needs to improve mobility. Currently, workers in Montreal do not enjoy quality mobility. As a result, businesses think twice about coming here. (Pol-2)

But residents of the Island of Montreal, especially those living in the urban core, are not solely concerned with mobility and its impact on tax rates. Without dismissing the issue of mobility, we should at least explore the possibility that the quality of urban life also depends on other factors. The quality of social and cultural life and access to urban services are two specific elements that come to mind. From this broader perspective, it seems less appropriate to draw a clear distinction between residents of the central city and residents of the outer suburbs. As another Montreal borough representative pointed out, the region's administrative boundaries start to lose their importance where social issues are concerned:

> We cannot turn in on ourselves. We know that Montreal is left to deal with a lot of social issues. The problems the city inherits come from all across the metropolitan area. But I'm not looking for a reason to lay blame … Ultimately, someone who has difficulty finding housing, who faces homelessness, will end up in Montreal, if only because of the range of services offered here. We want these people to be taken care of, to find the support that they need, but we clearly shouldn't think of these problems as just city issues. We definitely need to address them within a larger context and to find solutions together. (Pol-3)

Urban environments are at the crossroads of a whole series of processes that extend, to varying degrees, across the entire metropolitan area. The MMC sought to take this fact into account from the moment it was established. However, communities located within the borders of the MMC, like all Quebec municipalities, are subject to provincial regulations. And the government of Quebec adopted "policy guidelines that apply to RCMs, whether they are located in the Montreal region or elsewhere" (Adm-1). This issue reflects the constitutional status of Canadian municipalities as creatures of the provinces: "The Canadian Constitution, provincial laws, and political culture all place limits on the ability of the country's municipalities to act autonomously or as major players within the Canadian federal system" (Turgeon, 2006, p. 405).

However, it is important to also recognize the growing influence of metropolitan areas as social, economic, and political actors. Indeed, notwithstanding jurisdictional constraints, cities and metropolitan areas have emerged as key actors on the political scene, a fact reflected in the economic and demographic changes of recent years (Hiller, 2014a, 2014b). Furthermore, the vitality and leadership qualities demonstrated by local stakeholders need to be recognized, as they are often what makes it possible to overcome administrative and institutional constraints.

That said, the MMC's powers remain limited. Its failings in terms of metropolitan planning are already widely recognized (Lafortune & Collin, 2011; Sancton, 2009). On the political scene, its role is limited both by the lack of public resources at its disposal and by administrative constraints. Moreover, we need to remember that MMC representatives are not directly elected by the population. Rather, they are appointed based on the offices they hold within their respective municipalities and within the corresponding population centre.

Can the quality of leadership really make a difference? The comments of elected officials, planning professionals, and other stakeholders interested in the future of the metropolitan area reveal some residual tension between the central city and the periphery, despite the role of suburban governance in changing attitudes. The dichotomy between the realities of the central city and those of the suburbs has not been entirely relegated to the past. Even though changes in recent decades have altered social relationships with urban space, some players continue to convey perceptions that have fallen out of sync with reality. Nevertheless, suburban governance has clearly fostered cooperation among local stakeholders, something that political leaders at the provincial level – as well as within the region's main population centres – have sought to either encourage or impede, depending on the circumstances. Many of the issues of identity and legitimacy that have been addressed were simply not anticipated by existing legislation and regulations. Stakeholders have therefore had to rely on the frameworks and the trust developed through their various projects.

Concluding Remarks

From a political standpoint, the study of suburban governance in Montreal requires a fresh analysis of local authorities across the entire metropolitan area. Experimenting with the regionalization of urban space by way of institutional reforms, such as those initiated through the creation of the MMC, brings to light social, cultural, and political divisions that simply cannot be ignored.

Meanwhile, suburban governance makes it possible to see both the challenges rooted in Montreal's history and old planning practices in a new light. This new perspective presents an opportunity for better understanding the tensions looming behind the clash between "hierarchical" and "networked" understandings of urban space (Hatuka & Bar, 2018). By further asserting their presence in metropolitan space, suburban communities – including the outer suburbs – help define suburban governance. This development can be understood by adopting an approach that locates both political and governance processes in relation to "changing geographical logics of authority and rule that must be interpreted in terms of discourses and practices" (Agnew, 2013, p. 1).

In the political arena, the nature of alliances between leaders from the central city and those from the periphery has changed in the wake of the reforms introduced at the turn of the twenty-first century. For instance, when the expanded City of Montreal held its first elections in November 2001, mayoral candidate Gérald Tremblay was swept to power in part because of his openness to suburban communities on the Island of Montreal. The same holds true for Denis Coderre, who was elected in 2013. In fact, he went even further by campaigning on the idea of solidarity across the entire metropolitan area, including the outer suburbs on the North Shore and South Shore.

However, in the course of his mandate, Coderre managed to secure a new status from the Quebec government, one that recognized the City of Montreal itself as a metropolis, as opposed to the larger metropolitan area. This change was reflected in the framework agreement titled "Réflexe Montréal" (Gouvernement du Québec, 2016), which was signed by the City of Montreal and the government of Quebec in December 2016, as well as in Bill 121 – An Act to increase the autonomy and powers of Ville de Montréal, the metropolis of Québec[9] – which received royal assent on 21 September 2017.

Even if some find that this legislation "rings a bit false" (R-1), it still reflects, if only on a symbolic level, a step back from the desire to establish a metropolitan sphere that covers the entire region. The results of my interviews clearly show that suburban governance has not entirely extinguished either the values conflict or the tensions between the urban core and the periphery. Looking at the context and components of urban development in broader terms, including their connection to an emerging metropolitan sphere, suburban governance nevertheless raises the issue of cooperation between stakeholders in a more appropriate manner (Guay & Hamel, 2015). This observation is reflected in the significant influence of suburban communities within the MMC, as well as in the adoption of the MPDP, despite its limited scope for guiding urban development. More extensive analysis of projects undertaken at the metropolitan level, especially transportation projects, would further address the issue.

At the metropolitan scale – but also at the city, borough, or neighbourhood level – there is no one optimal solution to the problem of defining collective preferences or social and political choices (Lefèvre, 2009; Storper, 2014). It should therefore not be surprising that improvisation is a key aspect of governance and that the latter can fail when it comes to implementing forms or modes of cooperation favoured by local actors.

As other chapters of this book point out, there are many aspects to suburban governance. Key themes include the environment, transportation infrastructure, mobility, international promotion, public funding for social housing, fiscal imbalances, and the integration of newcomers. As for the individuals I interviewed, they raised issues related to transportation, mobility, the environment, taxation, and social relations.

Meanwhile, models based exclusively on institutional analysis tend to focus on the role of the state and to consider urban issues solely from the perspective of the central city. In this chapter, I have proposed an alternative understanding of urban space and urban planning, one that supports a more nuanced analysis of urban issues. It would also allow for a reassessment of the accepted definition of urban space itself.

NOTES

1 In addressing these topics, I adopt the definition of "suburban governance" put forward by Ekers et al. (2012): "the constellation of public and private processes, actors, and institutions that determine and shape the planning, design, politics, and economics of suburban spaces and everyday behaviour" (p. 406).

2 "In the late 1980s a series of important publications signalled the formation of a very productive period of work in urban political economy, urban political studies, and urban geography on the nature of power and politics in cities under the challenge of accelerated restructuring. The publication of Logan and Molotch's *Urban Fortune* (1987), Clarence Stone's *Regime Politics* (1989), Harvey's extended essay on the subject in his *The Urban Experience* (1989) ... and Stone and Sanders's (1989) *The Politics of Urban Development* amounted to a strong starting point for a new generation of debate on the urban political question" (Keil et al., 2017, pp. 10–11).

3 Michael Storper (2014) emphasizes this point: "All metropolitan areas share underlying needs to govern themselves, which stem from the strong interdependencies and externalities generated by urbanization; but all such regions have fragmented political geographies for addressing these problems. This is why some version of the same basic mishmash is found in countries whose political and administrative systems are otherwise quite different" (p. 118).

4 The MMC encompasses eighty-two municipalities in Greater Montreal, covering a territory that essentially corresponds to Statistics Canada's Montreal Census Metropolitan Area (CMA). However, it should be noted that, at the time the MMC was created, ten municipalities in the Montreal CMA were excluded from the new metropolitan institution because they had relatively low rates of commuting to the urban core of Montreal. The MMC contains three major population centres: the central city (Montreal); Longueuil, on the south shore of the St. Lawrence River; and Laval, located on Île Jésus, just north of the central city. Completing the picture are the outer suburbs on both the North Shore and South Shore, which are home to municipalities with varying demographic weights. That makes for a grand total of five geographic zones, which are intended to provide a foundation for regional governance. The new management system that has been put in place reflects the region's geographic segmentation and administrative divisions: "The [MMC] is managed by a council of twenty-eight members: the mayor of Montreal and thirteen councillors appointed by the Montreal Agglomeration Council, the mayor of Laval and two councillors appointed by the council of Laval, the mayor of Longueuil and two councillors appointed by the agglomeration council of Longueuil, four mayors designated by the municipalities of the North Shore of Montreal, and four other mayors designated by those of the South Shore of Montreal" (Lafortune & Collin, 2011, p. 405).

5 One respondent explained: "TOD can be seen as a means of achieving densification. It reshapes development in the outer suburbs by promoting densification around transportation hubs. In practical terms, this requires changes to planning by-laws in order to allow for the construction of taller buildings and higher densities" (R-1).

6 For the list of respondents and their respective roles and responsibilities, see Table 3.2.

7 "Montreal's major competitive advantage is its fluidity, the fact that the St. Lawrence provides access to markets 1,200 kilometres inland. The great advantage of the Port of Montreal is that containers that are unloaded can immediately be loaded onto trains. The rail network makes it possible for a container to reach Chicago in less than 36 hours" (Adm-1).

8 The number 450 is the telephone area code associated with the Montreal suburbs, as opposed to the 514 area code, which is more prevalent within the borders of the central city.

9 This legislation specifies the new prerogatives enjoyed by the City of Montreal: "The Government intends to establish the 'Montréal Reflex,' that is, to add a 'Montréal chapter' in all policies affecting the metropolis, and to ensure that the characteristics specific to Ville de Montréal due to its special metropolis status are taken into account in the drafting of laws, regulations, programs, policies and directives that concern the metropolis, and as the Government intends to consult the city in a timely manner for that purpose."

REFERENCES

Agnew, J.A. (2013). Editorial: Territory, politics, governance. *Territory, Politics, Governance*, 1(1), 1–4. https://doi.org/10.1080/21622671.2013.765754

Beveridge, R., & Koch, P. (2017). The post-political trap? Reflections on politics, agency and the city. *Urban Studies*, 54(1), 31–43. https://doi.org/10.1177/0042098016671477

Boudreau, J.-A., Hamel, P., Jouve, B., & Keil, R. (2007). New state spaces in Canada: Metropolitanization in Montreal and Toronto compared. *Urban Geography*, 28(1), 30–53. https://doi.org/10.2747/0272-3638.28.1.30

CMM (Communauté Métropolitaine de Montréal). (2002). *Vision stratégique: Document déclencheur*. CMM.

CMM (Communauté Métropolitaine de Montréal). (2005). *Cap sur le monde – Pour une région métropolitaine de Montréal attractive: Projet de schéma métropolitain d'aménagement et de développement*. CMM.

CMM (Communauté Métropolitaine de Montréal). (2012). *Un Grand Montréal attractif, compétitif et durable: Plan métropolitain d'aménagement et de développement*. CMM.

CMM (Communauté Métropolitaine de Montréal). (2018). *Cahiers Métropolitains, no 7*. CMM.

Corriveau, J. (2016, 15 juin). Montréal n'est pas le moteur qu'elle pourrait être. *Le Devoir*, A 5. https://www.ledevoir.com/non-classe/473460/etude-de-l-ocde-montreal-n-est-pas-le-moteur-qu-elle-pourrait-etre

Cox, K.R. (2011). Commentary: From new urban politics to the "new" metropolitan politics. *Urban Studies, 48*(12), 2661–7. https://doi.org/10.1177/0042098011413947

Douay, N., & Roy-Baillargeon, O. (2015). Le *Transit-Oriented Development* (TOD), vecteur ou mirage des transformations de la planification et de la gouvernance métropolitaines du Grand Montréal? *Flux, 3–4*(101–2), 29–41. https://doi.org/10.3917/flux.101.0029

Dubuc, A. (2016, 23 juin). Le mystère de Montréal. *La Presse.* https://www.lapresse.ca/debats/201606/20/01-4993787-le-mystere-de-montreal.php

Ekers, M., Hamel, P., & Keil, R. (2012). Governing suburbia: Modalities and mechanisms of suburban governance. *Regional Studies, 46*(3), 405–22. https://doi.org/10.1080/00343404.2012.658036

Ghorra-Gobin, C. (2015). *La métropolisation en question.* PUF.

Gilli, F. (2013). Postface: Comment la métropolisation recompose les pouvoirs locaux. In C. Lefèvre, N. Roseau, & T. Vitale (Eds.), *De la ville à la métropole, les défis de la gouvernance* (pp. 355–64). Éditions L'œil d'Or.

Gouvernement du Québec. (2016). *Le "Réflexe Montréal": Entente-cadre sur les engagements du Gouvernement du Québec et de la Ville de Montréal pour la reconnaissance du statut particulier de la métropole.* Gouvernement du Québec.

Guay, L., & Hamel, P. (2015). The environmental governance of Canadian city-regions: Problems, actions and challenges. In K.E. Jones, A. Lord, & R. Shields (Eds.), *City-regions in prospect? Exploring points between place and practice* (pp. 213–36). McGill-Queen's University Press.

Halbert, L., Pinson, G., & Sala Pala, V. (2021). Contester la métropole. *Métropoles, 28*, 1–29. https://doi.org/10.4000/metropoles.7769

Hamel, P. (2006). Institutional changes and metropolitan governance: Can de-amalgamation be amalgamation? The case of Montreal. In E. Razin & P.J. Smith (Eds.), *Metropolitan governing: Canadian cases, comparative lessons* (pp. 95–120). The Hebrew University Magnes Press.

Hatuka, T., & Bar, R. (2018). The city-region and the challenge of its representation: The hierarchical network of newly built neighborhoods in the Tel Aviv Metropolitan Area. *Environment and Planning A: Economy and Space, 50*(4), 869–94. https://doi.org/10.1177/0308518X18754535

Higgins, B. (1986). *The rise and fall? of Montreal: A case study of urban growth, regional economic expansion and national development.* Canadian Institute for Research on Regional Development.

Hiller, H.H. (2014a). Canadian urbanization in historical and global perspective. In H.H. Hiller (Ed.), *Urban Canada* (3rd ed.; pp. 1–18). Oxford University Press.

Hiller, H.H. (2014b). The dynamics of Canadian urbanization. In H.H. Hiller (Ed.), *Urban Canada* (3rd ed.; pp. 19–42). Oxford University Press.

Horak, M. (2012). Conclusion: Understanding multilevel governance in Canada's cities. In M. Horak & R. Young (Eds.), *Sites of governance: Multilevel governance and policy making in Canada's big cities* (pp. 339–70). McGill-Queen's University Press.

Jouve, B., & Lefèvre, C. (2002). Le nouvel âge d'or des villes européennes? In B. Jouve & C. Lefèvre (Eds.), *Métropoles ingouvernables* (pp. 13–37). Elsevier.

Keil, R. (2018). *Suburban planet*. Polity Press.

Keil, R., Hamel, P., Boudreau, J.-A., Kipfer, S., & Allahwala, A. (2017). Regional governance revisited: Political space, collective agency, and identity. In R. Keil, P. Hamel, J.-A. Boudreau, & S. Kipfer (Eds.), *Governing cities through regions: Canadian and European perspectives* (pp. 3–26). Wilfrid Laurier University Press.

Kipfer, S. (2018). Pushing the limits of urban research: Urbanization, pipelines and counter-colonial politics. *Environment and Planning D: Society and Space*, *36*(3), 474–93. https://doi.org/10.1177/0263775818758328

Lafortune, M.-È., & Collin, J.-P. (2011). Building metropolitan governance capacity: The case of the Communauté métropolitaine de Montréal. *Canadian Public Administration/Administration publique du Canada*, *54*(3), 339–420. https://doi.org/10.1111/j.1754-7121.2011.00182.x

Lefèvre, C. (2009). *Gouverner les métropoles*. L.G.D.J.

Levine, M.V. (1998). Montréal et les nouveaux enjeux métropolitains. In Y. Bélanger, R. Comeau, & F. Desrochers (Eds.), *La CUM et la région métropolitaine: L'avenir d'une communauté* (pp. 110–16). Presses de l'Université du Québec.

Metzger, J. (2013). Raising the regional leviathan: A relational-materialist conceptualization of regions-in-becoming as publics-in-stabilization. *International Journal of Urban and Regional Research*, *37*(4), 1368–95. https://doi.org/10.1111/1468-2427.12038

OCDE (Organisation de coopération et de développement économiques). (2001). *Mieux vivre dans la ville: Le rôle de la gouvernance métropolitaine*. OCDE.

OCDE (Organisation de coopération et de développement économiques). (2016). *Montréal, métropole de talent: Pistes d'action pour améliorer l'emploi, l'innovation et les compétences*. OCDE.

Paasi, A., & Metzger, J. (2017). Foregrounding the region. *Regional Studies*, *51*(1), 19–30. https://doi.org/10.1080/00343404.2016.1239818

Pinson, G. (2006). Projets de ville et gouvernance urbaine. *Revue française de science politique*, *56*(4), 619–51. https://doi.org/10.3917/rfsp.564.0619

Poitras, C. (2012). Les banlieues résidentielles planifiées dans la région de Montréal après la Seconde Guerre mondiale: Un modèle en redéfinition? In D. Fougères (Ed.), *Histoire de Montréal et de sa région: Tome 2. De 1930 à nos jours* (pp. 899–924). Les Presses de l'Université Laval.

Polèse, M. (2012). Montréal économique: De 1930 à nos jours: Récit d'une transition inachevée. In D. Fougères (Ed.), *Histoire de Montréal et de sa région: Tome 2. De 1930 à nos jours* (pp. 959–60). Les Presses de l'Université Laval.

Rodgers, S., Barnett, C., & Cochrane, A. (2014). Where is urban politics? *International Journal of Urban and Regional Research, 38*(5), 1551–60. https://doi.org/10.1111/1468-2427.12143

Roy-Baillargeon, O. (2017). La symbiose de la planification et de la gouvernance territoriales: Le cas du Grand Montréal. *Canadian Journal of Urban Research, 26*(1), 52–63. https://cjur.uwinnipeg.ca/index.php/cjur/article/view/65

Sancton, A. (2009). A review of Canadian metropolitan regions: Governance and government. In D. Phares (Ed.), *Governing metropolitan regions in the 21st century* (pp. 221–36). M.E. Sharpe.

Savini, F. (2016). Self-organization and urban development: Disaggregating the city-region, deconstructing urbanity in Amsterdam. *International Journal of Urban and Regional Research, 40*(6), 1152–69. https://doi.org/10.1111/1468-2427.12469

Savitch, H.V. (2007). Globalisation et changement d'échelle dans le gouvernement urbain. *Métropoles, 2*, 132–66. https://doi.org/10.4000/metropoles.652

Storper, M. (2014). Governing the large metropolis. *Territory, Politics, Governance, 2*(2), 115–34. https://doi.org/10.1080/21622671.2014.919874

Teaford, J. (2006). *The metropolitan revolution: The rise of post-urban America.* Columbia University Press.

Tomas, M. (2012). *Penser métropolitain? La bataille politique du Grand Montréal.* Presses de l'Université du Québec.

Turgeon, L. (2006). Les villes dans le système intergouvernemental canadien. In A.-G. Gagnon (Ed.), *Le fédéralisme canadien contemporain: Fondements, traditions, institutions* (pp. 403–33). Les Presses de l'Université de Montréal.

4 Suburban Governance in Miami-Dade County: Immigrant Empowerment and the Rebellion of Municipal Incorporations

FERNANDO BURGA

This chapter addresses the modalities of suburban governance by delving into the history of Miami-Dade County, the region colloquially known as "Miami." By charting the city's history and focusing on the period from the early 1990s to the mid-2000s, it explores a rebellion of municipal incorporations that arose in order to consider secessionism against the backdrop of immigrant empowerment. During a period of fourteen years, nine new cities were forged in Miami-Dade County's suburban unincorporated areas following the election of Cuban American leaders to political positions in municipal and county government. *Communities of interest* – racially and economically homogeneous groups composed of white affluent residents – mobilized grassroot efforts that put county commissioners, urban planners, and community groups in conflict by separating from "Metro," Miami-Dade County's government.[1]

The chapter begins with an exposition of Miami's context. It describes the region's governance structures, demographic indicators, and physical characteristics before shifting into key aspects of its early urban history. Attention is placed on the challenges of decentralization and the introduction of Miami-Dade County's government. The chapter continues by chronicling the rebellion of municipal incorporations and concludes by evaluating the municipalities' development in relation to the three modalities of suburban governance: the role of the state, capital accumulation, and authoritative private governance. Recounting this case shows how the state evolves through time to manage decentralization and how the political empowerment of immigrants transforms suburban governance into a field of revanchist politics.

Miami-Dade County in Context

"Miami" is a world-renowned destination. The region is globally known for its amenable weather, idyllic tropical landscape, tourist attractions, and vibrant multicultural life. These characteristics under-line its uniqueness in relation to other American cities. According to Nijman and Clery (2015), the region's suburbanization did not follow the same development logic as other American cities. Miami is a young metropolis with an urban footprint that started late in the nineteenth century. Unlike other American cities, it did not experience the waves of heavy industrialization that drove urbanization. Similarly, Miami did not undergo the settlement of an expanding middle class, which pushed suburban expansion in the mid-twentieth century. Rather, Miami exemplifies a Sunbelt post-war metropolis. Most of its growth took place during the latter half of the twentieth century. The settlement of immigrants from Latin America and the Caribbean, particularly from Cuba, fuelled the engine of decentralization.

"Miami" encompasses the geographic region formally known as Miami-Dade County. It includes the City of Miami, thirty-three other municipalities, and suburban unincorporated areas in the southeastern tip of the State of Florida, United States. Miami-Dade County is an administrative unit of governance functioning at the regional level. Table 4.1 synthesizes the different scales and characteristics that comprise the governance structure of Miami. In the United States, the county stands as a layer of government below the federal and state governments but above the local municipal government. Unincorporated areas comprise urban and suburban territories without local governance because they are not in a municipality. Instead, they are usually governed by the county until they are either annexed by municipalities or community groups choose to incorporate into their own city.

Together with the Palm Beach and Broward Counties to its immediate north, Miami-Dade County comprises the Miami Metropolitan Statistical Area. This US census-designated area is the eighth most populated metropolitan area in the United States, with an estimated population of 6,166,488 in 2019. In July 2022, Miami-Dade County was projected to have almost half of the tri-county population shed with 2,673,837 residents. The racial breakdown of this statistic demonstrates the political power that Hispanic groups – particularly Cuban Americans – and African Americans have in South Florida.[2] In 2022, Hispanics made up 69.1 per cent of the population, compared to African Americans at 17.1 per cent and white "Anglos" at 13.8 per cent.

Miami-Dade County, therefore, is a majority-minority region, where immigrant, racial, and ethnic minorities represent the majority of residents. This factor translates into social, economic, and political influence. It is estimated that 35.7 per cent of the Hispanic population is of Cuban origin, making this particular ethnic group a dominant stakeholder

Table 4.1. Administrative Units of the Miami Metropolitan Area as of 2020

Administrative and Territorial Units	Government Bodies	Main Attributions	Number of Units
Miami Metropolitan Area	3 counties composed of 107 municipalities and unincorporated areas	Regional planning, transportation	3 (6.1 million inhabitants)
Miami-Dade County	Metropolitan government headed by 13 elected county-wide commissioners – Board of County Commissioners	*Upper Tier of Government:* emergency management, airport and seaport operations, public housing and health-care services, transportation, environmental services, solid waste disposal, comprehensive planning	1 (2.7 million inhabitants)
(Miami-Dade County Incorporated Areas) Municipality, Town, Village, or City	City Council, composed of single-member elected city commissioners	*Lower Tier of Government:* police and fire protection, zoning and code enforcement	34 (City of Miami has 442,241 inhabitants)
(Miami-Dade County Incorporated Areas) Single-member District	Elected city commissioner	Oversees and runs local government, enacts policies and ordinances, identifies local issues, decides on municipal budget	5 in the City of Miami (number of inhabitants vary according to district boundaries)
(Miami-Dade County Unincorporated Areas) Unincorporated Municipal Service Area (UMSA)	Community councils composed of elected representatives	Everyday operations, management, and services; coordination of planning, funding, etc.	10 (44% of inhabitants from total Miami-Dade County population)
(Miami-Dade County Unincorporated Areas) Community Councils	6 elected residents from unincorporated areas and 1 member appointed by the County Commisssion	Zoning decisions, local planning decisions; communications and budgeting; makes recommendations to the Board of County Commissioners	n/a

Sources: Synthesized from Wikipedia.org (Miami Metropolitan Area, Miami-Dade County, Miami); Miami-Dade County (https://www.miamidade.gov/zoning/community-councils.asp).

within the majority-minority. The City of Miami, which is Miami-Dade County's most recognized municipality and the region's political, economic, and cultural hub, has a population of about 454,000 residents. More than 80 per cent of Miami-Dade County's population lives in surrounding municipalities and suburban unincorporated areas. This distribution signals a historical trend regarding the concentration of ethnic voting power in suburban unincorporated areas in Miami-Dade County.

Miami-Dade County's territory comprises a surface area of approximately 1,946 square miles, with an average population density of 1,419 residents per square mile. This density is distributed by geographic features, making the estimate spread throughout the region. Only half of the territory is settled. The other half comprises preserved land and water areas under the jurisdictions of the Everglades and Biscayne Bay National Parks. These federally designated territories function as another layer of governance next to county and municipal governments. They influence decentralization, particularly where jurisdictional boundaries meet. The coordination between municipal, county, state, and federal mandates are required at these locations.

The conservation of South Florida's natural environment dictates Miami-Dade County's suburban expansion. The region lies on the southeastern edge of Florida along a twenty-mile-wide swath of oolitic limestone emerging as a coastline for hundreds of miles along Florida's eastern edge. Miami-Dade County is the penultimate link in a vast linear metropole connecting Palm Beach and Broward Counties to the Florida Keys archipelago, the southernmost point in the United States. The configuration of urban settlement in southeastern Florida is determined by this geologic feature. Urban agglomerations are located along the US 1 and I-95 corridors, two parallel corridors spanning the whole American Eastern Seaboard. Historically, decentralization grew from these north-south axes through secondary corridors extending westward into Florida's subtropical wilderness. In this way, Miami-Dade County's urban footprint is defined by the constraints of geography, natural resources, and population growth.

Miami-Dade County's urban footprint started at the mouth of the Miami River, a tributary flowing from the Florida Everglades into Biscayne Bay, as a Tequesta Native American settlement. In the early nineteenth century, a military outpost was established on the site. The location eventually became a railroad station that grew into a frontier town. The settlement was officially incorporated as the City of Miami in 1896 through the efforts of railroad barons, city boosters, and African American labourers, who were included as signatories in the city's charter to increase population numbers.

Early in its history, speculative development drove Miami's decentralization through the development of uncontrolled subdivisions. This pattern was exemplified by communities that remained racially segregated according to shifting municipal boundaries and fragmented unincorporated areas. Sprawl and segregation were exacerbated by the incorporation of twenty-six municipalities from the early twentieth century to the mid-1940s. Miami's estimated rate of demographic growth up to 1935 led civic leaders to forecast that the city's population would increase to one million residents. As Miami expanded westward, it became a prime destination for residents from different backgrounds arriving at the city in order to access its construction industries as well as its service and tourist economies. The new arrivals included northern transplants of Anglo and Jewish origin, African Americans from the American South, descendants of Bahamian settlers, and Puerto Rican residents, who inhabited the city's most recognizable ethnic enclaves at the time.

Miami-Dade County and the Birth of Metro

Miami's demographic forecasts and suburban growth became major concerns for civic leaders during the mid-twentieth century. The municipal incorporations that characterized the region's early process of decentralization brought forth new challenges at the local and regional levels.

While some municipalities governed speculative growth according to master-planned visions determining urban design and built-form guidelines, unincorporated areas grew without local representation, land-use planning, or the provision of public services. The county existed as a territory, but it did not embody a government or a formal governance structure that could give it a mandate. The budding metropolis was a mosaic of governed and ungoverned territories. Given the rate of demographic growth and the need to control speculative development and address the management of transportation systems, public works, and traffic congestion, the establishment of a county government became a prescient issue.

In 1957, the Dade County Home Rule Charter was adopted following a referendum authorizing the formation of a Dade County government (Sofen, 1961). The charter established a central government – Metro – with the authority to govern regionally at the county level and locally in suburban unincorporated areas. From this point onward, a large bureaucracy was set in motion to deal with Miami's decentralization challenges and to plan for future demographic growth. The establishment of Metro introduced a new form of government: a county commission composed of nine districts with representatives who were elected through county-wide elections. In this way, the charter entrenched a "two-tier" system of governance that still exists today, composed of a central government – Metro – and autonomous governments – municipalities. The county is responsible for the "upper" first tier of regional governance concerning provisions such as emergency services, airport and seaport management, public housing, health care, transportation, environmental services, and solid waste disposal. Municipalities provide a "lower" second tier of services such as police, fire, zoning, land-use regulations, and building code enforcement. The two-tier system aimed to establish a second "lower" tier of governance in suburban unincorporated areas by charging the county with the mandate of local representation and service delivery.

Comprehensive planning emerges with the inception of Metro as one of its new departments to address decentralization in the fast-growing, fragmented city. Metro impacted the traditional way municipal incorporations were carried out. The formation of new cities was traditionally governed by state law and involved the lobby of developers in Florida's capital, Tallahassee. The two-tier system was set in place to balance county and municipal interests but also to halt local political corruption.

Metro and the Crisis of Legitimacy

Metro's bureaucracy grew in size and manpower to become a large public-sector apparatus during the second half of the twentieth century. In the last decades of the twentieth century, however, Metro faced a rebellion of municipal incorporations challenging the legitimacy of its mandate as a central government. The rebellion arose as a result of three powerful tensions that coalesced at the start of the 1990s: (1) Metro's failure to establish a second "lower" tier of local governance in suburban unincorporated areas; (2) Metro's growing budget and fiscal crisis; and (3) the demographic transformation of Miami-Dade County and the resulting empowerment of Cuban Americans.

Since the formation of Miami-Dade County and the birth of Metro, county commissioners and urban planners sought to establish local representation and basic services for residents in suburban unincorporated areas (Citizens Charter Review Committee, 1986; Dade County Charter Review Committee, 1982; Dade County Metropolitan Study Commission, 1971; Hertz, 1984; Touche Ross & Co., 1978). However, as the first upper tier of regional governance became established throughout the

1960s, 1970s, and 1980s, its expansion took precedence over the second lower tier of local representation and service delivery in suburban unincorporated areas.

Suburban governance remained an unfulfilled promise. This failure led to disparities in the distribution of public services across Miami-Dade County's territory. The lack of basic service provisions at the local level – such as fire and police protection, waste disposal, and land-use and zoning controls – became critical. Moreover, residents living in suburban unincorporated areas did not have a decision-making body to advocate for their needs. Instead, they depended for political representation on county commissioners who lived far from them. This situation led to a political calculus in county politics. County commission candidates courted voters from existing municipalities and affluent suburban unincorporated areas to mobilize county-wide voting blocs during elections, awarding the residents in these areas a privileged political status.

The need to maintain a solvent budget and the efficient delivery of services across Miami-Dade County's vast territory stood out as another unresolved tension in Metro's development. As Metro's bureaucracy grew in size and organizational capacity, its expansion paralleled decentralization and Dade County's population increase due to immigration. The bureaucracy's growth, coupled with the need to service existing and new residents, led to more expenditures and tax revenues. To solve this problem, county commissioners and urban planners balanced the tax revenues of *donor communities* – areas generating revenue greater than their service expenditures – with those of *recipient communities* – areas with less revenue than their service expenditures. In essence, Metro subsidized the services of poor communities in suburban unincorporated areas with the surplus of more affluent communities. This redistributive approach caused disaffection among residents in donor communities, who felt burdened by a top-down subsidy uplifting poor, immigrant, and racial communities that did not pay their share of the fiscal burden.

The last tension fuelling Metro's crisis of legitimacy concerned demographic change and the empowerment of Miami's Cuban American community. County commissioners and urban planners never envisioned how immigrant influx would reshape the city's politics. In the late 1950s, suburban unincorporated areas had a population of 109,860 inhabitants – 22 per cent of the total population of Miami-Dade County at the inception of Metro. By 1990, the county's total population reached 1,937,000 inhabitants, with the population of suburban unincorporated areas at 1,037,000 inhabitants – 54 per cent of the total population. Between 1980 and 1990 alone, 76 per cent of Dade County's population growth occurred in suburban unincorporated areas, bringing new de-centralization challenges, residents, and votes to bear on county com-mission elections (Dade County Metropolitan Study Commission, Citizens Advisory Committee, 1992).

Two additional developments emphasized the reconfiguration of po-litical power in Miami-Dade County and its municipalities. The election of Xavier Suarez to the City of Miami in 1985 – the city's first Cuban American mayor – and the election of Cuban American leaders in other municipalities and county positions signalled the growing political power of Miami's Cuban American community. Similarly, the outcome of the *Meek v. Metropolitan Dade County* civil rights lawsuit changed the county commission's electoral map from nine county-wide districts to thirteen single-member districts. This new political geography meant that political power would align with demographic concentrations in the county, benefitting ethnic and racial minorities. Both the election of Cuban American leaders and the outcomes of *Meek* intensified the perception among white affluent residents in suburban unincorporated areas that the status they traditionally held over county and munici-pal politics was gone. Metro's power balance had shifted to minority groups. The following accounts detailing the stages of the rebellion of municipal incorporations challenging the legitimacy of Metro's man-date as a central government are based on information from interviews with Miami-Dade County urban planners active during this period, as well as on various studies by the cited authors.

The Formative Wave of the Rebellion of Municipal Incorporations (1985–94): Key Biscayne Incorporates, Coconut Grove and Kendall Ally for Independence

From 1991 to 2005, a number of communities of interest comprised of affluent, white residents led secessionist agendas in the aftermath of Metro's failed promises.[3] Through oral histories gathered from urban planners active during this period in Metro's history, several themes that defined this period emerge. Below, the localist ideology inciting the waves of secessionism resulting in nine new municipalities becomes evident.

> There was clearly a movement for communities to break away from Dade County and secede. They would say: "We don't want to be part of the greater Miami-Dade government. We want to have our own municipal-ities." People envied municipalities because they had more control over local decisions, including zoning and land use. They asked: "Why should

those decisions be made by someone who doesn't live in my community?" (Account drawn from Miami-Dade County urban planner interview)

In the first "formative" wave, Key Biscayne was the only community that successful seceded from Metro, while two other communities, Coconut Grove and Kendall, failed. This wave was characterized by the singularity of Key Biscayne's geographic context and the attempts of mainland communities to follow suit. The incorporation of Key Biscayne was the catalyst for other communities to pursue secession as it provided strategies and tactics that could be used to mobilize support for incorporation.

Key Biscayne is an island located in Biscayne Bay. The community's incorporation efforts arose from the fear that urban development pressures were going to alter the island's small-town environment. In 1985, the opening of the Rickenbacker Causeway Bridge brought traffic and tourism to the island (Tomb, 1985). A local group of homeowners conducted an analysis on secession leading to the unofficial election of a "village" council. The rebel council called on Metro to stop high-density development on the island, but the request was ignored because the council was unofficial (Biddulph, 1989). The council reacted by holding and winning another unofficial election calling for the island's secession from Miami-Dade County (Ycaza, 1989). Faced with the steadfastness of Key Biscayners, county commissioners voted in 1990 to allow incorporation (Petchell, 1990; Shukovsky, 1990). In 1991, Key Biscayne became a municipality, marking the first time in more than thirty years in Metro's history that a new city was formed (Faiola, 1991).

Across the bay, Coconut Grove, the City of Miami's wealthiest district, followed Key Biscayne's lead. In 1991, a citizen committee formed and proposed a referendum on secession (Martin, 1991; Tanfani, 1991a, 1991b). The mandate passed, and elections for a village council were held. However, the City of Miami's City Council needed to authorize a city-wide vote on secession for it to be official. This condition placed Groveites in direct confrontation with the City of Miami's Cuban American leadership. Groveites by-passed the authority of the city council by taking their proposal directly to the county commission, where it was accepted (Filkins, 1992; Tanfani, 1992a).

Cuban American leaders, advocates, and businesses countered the county vote by organizing a county-wide anti-secession campaign. The City of Miami City Council voted against the county resolution. Groveites regrouped by placing the measure on county election ballots (Filkins & Strouse, 1992). Coconut Grove secession seemed certain until 24 August 1992, when Hurricane Andrew derailed the vote (Tanfani, 1992b).

With their initial petition drive unfulfilled, Groveites joined the Kendall Homeowners Association – a community group in Miami-Dade County's western suburbs – in a final attempt for a combined county referendum measure in 1994. The measure called for the secession of Coconut Grove and the establishment of eight local councils providing local political representation for suburban unincorporated areas in Miami-Dade County. Ultimately, the measure was repudiated by county commissioners who received campaign contributions from the Latin Builders Association, South Florida's most powerful Cuban American construction guild. With this final defeat, Coconut Grove and Kendall's secessionist efforts ended. In Andrew's aftermath, Metro's central role in post-hurricane recovery efforts dissipated further efforts.

The Main Wave (1995–7): Aventura, Sunny Isles Beach, and Pinecrest Incorporate; Destiny Fails

The second "main" wave of municipal incorporations began in 1995 with Aventura separating from Miami-Dade County. Named after a regional mall, Aventura lies on the intercoastal shores of northeast Miami-Dade County. The area was well known by county commissioners and urban planners for its social networks of northeastern retirees (Filkins, 1994). Aventura was the richest donor community in suburban unincorporated areas and represented a coveted voting bloc for politicians seeking election or county commissioners seeking re-election. As the testimony of urban planners show, its drive for secession emerged from the perception that residents lost political clout over the county commission following the election of Cuban Americans and the outcome of the *Meek v. Metropolitan Dade County* civil rights lawsuit.

> In 1992, the commission's geography changed. There was enormous nostalgia for at-large districts. The good government argument maintained that the commission kept the interest of the county at large, but the reality had changed: everybody was looking out for themselves. (Account drawn from Miami-Dade County urban planner interview)

Aventura's incorporation began when a coalition of homeowner associations called for a referendum on secession, advocating the need for local police presence, land-use controls, and fiscal responsibility. County commissioners voted against the action, and the coalition proceeded to file a federal lawsuit against Metro. That tactic forced county commissioners to allow the referendum. Secession won. After the experience of Key Biscayne and Aventura, Metro introduced stringent controls over municipal incorporations. Their goal was to slow the potential revenue loss resulting from fleeting tax bases (Dade County Metropolitan Study Commission, 1995; Hartman, 1995). The effort included the passage of ordinances formalizing the process of incorporation according to new financial requirements and operational criteria (Filkins, 1995).

Like Aventura, Pinecrest's incorporation took place in 1996 after residents threatened to pursue a federal lawsuit against Metro for halting a referendum. Pinecrest is a wealthy suburb in southeastern Miami-Dade County, home to historic mansions and the original site of the famous Parrot Jungle attraction, one of Miami's most recognized touristic landmarks. Pinecrest's secessionist drive focused on police safety. The fear of crime that drove secession was due to the perception of local residents regarding the area's proximity to neighbourhoods in adjoining suburban unincorporated areas where African American populations resided. As the voices of urban planners involved in the process of Pinecrest's incorporation illustrate, Pinecrest's incorporation was accentuated by the legacies of segregation and racism that combined with the loss of political power to inform the mobilizations of small local communities of interest.

> There was a racial ethnic component to it; white affluent areas were pulling out. There was a perceived loss of power and clout, historically and politically, in Miami. You had cases in which a small group created an issue which would lead to a long-term jurisdiction. (Account drawn from Miami-Dade County urban planner interview)

The incorporation of Sunny Isles Beach followed in 1997. Sunny Isles Beach is a strip of coastal land in northeast Dade County. Its residents originally sought to become part of Aventura, but Aventura's residents prevented their annexation based on concerns regarding traffic congestion and tourism overwhelming their municipality. Sunny Isles residents mobilized for incorporation after Aventura residents withdrew support for their annexation. The area's location as a key on the Atlantic coast made its case comparable to Key Biscayne. The argument that the community was a self-contained geographical entity with a small fiscal base separated from the mainland swayed Metro to allow the area's incorporation. Following its incorporation, the small municipality took advantage of land-use controls to bring high-density development and make the area a competing destination next to Aventura.

While Aventura, Pinecrest, and Sunny Isles Beach represented communities of interest that were predominantly white and affluent, the case of Destiny introduced a new dynamic in the evolution of the rebellion: Could a community of interest composed of residents who are not affluent and white secede from Dade County? Destiny's case challenged the notion that all communities could secede.

The story of Destiny precedes the rebellion of municipal incorporations and was central to the *Meek v. Metropolitan Dade County* lawsuit. This prelude involved efforts by African American activists who organized in the mid-1980s against the construction of Hard Rock Stadium (formerly known as Joe Robbie Stadium). The site selection, development, and planning of the stadium was sanctioned by a vote of county commissioners composed of eight white members – out of nine in total – in the mid-1980s. Faced with the top-down imposition of a megastructure in their community, the activists launched the lawsuit against Metro, claiming that the commission's decision violated their civil rights because the at-large voting system diluted the African American electoral power in the county. After several years of court battles, the courts favoured their claim. Following the *Meek v. Metropolitan Dade County* decision, the judge ordered Metro to reconfigure its political map and the number of its commission seats. This decision was one of the reasons that provoked the mobilization of white affluent communities, but the reconfiguration of Miami-Dade County's political map did not automatically translate into political clout for African American communities.

Years later, the experience of the stadium's construction catalyzed African American activists to organize for incorporation. Their fiscal strategy consisted of forming a municipality with boundaries around the stadium to absorb its property value and adopt its tax base as a source of revenue. However, the plan faced unsurmountable challenges. Destiny's activists confronted a $100,000 anti-incorporation campaign by the stadium's owner (May, 1996). Moreover, county commissioners and urban planners stood with the stadium's owners, arguing that, if Destiny incorporated, it would not have a strong property tax base to pay for local services. Metro feared that Destiny's incorporation would provoke a domino effect driving donor communities to opt out of servicing recipient communities. Once again, Destiny's advocates accused Metro of racial bias, arguing that white affluent communities of interest were able to incorporate based on the high revenue of their taxes, a structural difference that was insurmountable. In the eyes of Destiny's advocates, the economic logic meant that such communities would always have an upper hand in seceding, while poor communities would not since they could not achieve those financial thresholds. Destiny's efforts were halted, but its memory informed the incorporation of Miami Gardens during the final wave of municipal incorporations after Metro's moratorium.

Metro's Moratorium and the Introduction of Community Councils
(1997–2000)

The previous waves of municipal incorporations led county commis-sioners and urban planners to enact a moratorium in order to allow them to evaluate how Metro's fiscal disparities could be solved (Fine-frock, 1996). The realization that secessionism was rapidly expanding caused the introduction of twelve community councils in suburban un-incorporated areas of Miami-Dade County (Tanfani, 1996). According to urban planners, community councils were introduced to alleviate the problem of political under-representation at the local level, which had historically plagued Metro's two-tier system of government.

> We were trying to give some power away. By inventing community coun-cils, the commission could legally give away some of its powers. It was in part a way of saying: "You don't have to go all the way towards incor-poration. We will give you this" … There was an effort to give a certain level of control to communities. Give them budgets, authority over zoning decisions, recommendations over land-use decisions, and a way to meet to discuss community issues. (Account drawn from Miami-Dade County urban planner interview)

The councils were established as a unit of local governance providing residents with decision-making power over a range of issues including zoning requests; preparing annual profiles of community needs; rec-ommending comprehensive planning measures, expenditure priorities, and revenue needs; and disseminating information about community and county organizations. Their operational capacity was comple-mented by the introduction of "Team Metro" offices: six sites through-out suburban unincorporated areas where residents could be in direct contact with Metro staff concerning local needs in their commission district (Cauvin, 1995; Charles, 1995; Metro-Dade County Boundaries Commission, 1996). The vision of community councils had been enter-tained for years within Metro, but it wasn't until the threat of municipal incorporations became evident that they were deployed as a suburban governance strategy.

While community councils were established to deal with the failure of the second tier of governance and to halt the fever of secessionism, they also functioned as incubators for political power. The practices modelled in community council meetings gave emergent political lead-ers in suburbia, including the mayors of future municipalities, members of future municipal councils, state representatives, and even members of the Dade County School Board, a space to perform local leadership and gain constituents. The councils functioned until the mid-2000s, when budgetary constraints forced Metro to end them. Over their decade-long trajectory, however, they became spaces where municipal incorporation efforts germinated through the indirect support of Metro's staff. They were implemented to slow down secessionism, but paradoxically, they became sites where community groups organized for secession and emergent politicians seeking election or re-election to the county commission interacted with a suburban public to campaign for votes. County commissioners realized that community councils held valuable political capital. Secessionism was a challenge to Metro, but its fervour also symbolized potential votes in the reconfigured electoral map in the post–*Meek v. Metropolitan Dade County* era.

The Last Wave (2000–5): Miami Lakes, Palmetto Bay, Doral, and Cutler Bay Incorporate; Miami Gardens Arises from Destiny

The final wave of incorporations took place between 2000 and 2005. It was defined by secessionist efforts that stalled after the moratorium. During this wave, a set of communities in the peripheries of Miami-Dade County incorporated, including Miami Gardens, a municipality that arose from the ashes of Destiny. This period represented the final wave of incorporations as community groups returned to the law courts to further discredit Metro's mandate and reclaim political momentum after the moratorium. Secessionism swept to the edges of suburban unincorporated areas, as Metro negotiated solutions to resolve its budgetary challenges.

In 1999, Doral joined a lawsuit with Palmetto Bay, claiming that Metro violated the rights of its citizens because the county commission placed a moratorium on municipal incorporations. The lawsuit was first upheld by a Miami-Dade County court, boosting the case for secessionism, but it was overturned by a court of appeals. In 2000, a new referendum was carried out (Yee, 2000), setting a legal battle in which Doral joined forces with Palmetto Bay in southeast Miami-Dade and Miami Lakes in northwest Dade to argue that Metro should be dismantled because its two-tier system of governance was unconstitutional. The lawsuit played out in the courts until Metro commissioners offered a negotiated solution: municipal incorporation for a mitigation fee. Palmetto Bay, Miami Lakes, and Doral agreed to the proposal and seceded from Miami-Dade County: Miami Lakes in 2000, Palmetto Bay in 2002, and Doral in 2003. Another community of interest, Cutler Bay, joined them in 2005.

Within this timeline, Miami Gardens emerged from the ashes of Destiny in 2003. Seven years after its defeat, African American activists devised a new plan based on the annexation of industrial and residential areas surrounding Hard Rock Stadium. Once again, urban planners carried out feasibility studies for a county commission vote, but their results remained unfavourable. Faced with another round of potential legal battles, county commissioners allowed Miami Gardens to incorporate under a plan requiring a financial assessment of the city's budget after one year. Urban planners explain how the decision played out.

> Destiny was a small area where the tax base was not sufficient to support its services. Incorporation was taken on an economic basis, but it also became a racial issue. If you did an income map and a demographic map, high-income white Anglo areas were saying we want to be our cities. When Miami Gardens was put to a vote, we came to the realization that we couldn't only let all of the high-income areas opt out. (Account drawn from Miami-Dade County urban planner interview)

Miami Gardens remained financially unsustainable in its first year of existence, but a new study showed that Metro's service costs were inflated. The new assessment liberated Miami Gardens from the strict financial oversight. In 2007, two years after Miami Gardens became a municipality, a county task force determined that Metro had a budget surplus. This surplus dissipated with the financial crisis of 2008, ending the rebellion of municipal incorporations. Metro closed a chapter and entered a new phase in its long history of addressing decentralization and managing suburban governance.

Miami-Dade County and the Modalities of Suburban Governance

Hamel and Keil (2015) note three governing forces that define urban decentralization across global contexts: the role of the state, capital accumulation, and authoritarian private governance. The evolution of Miami-Dade County and the rebellion of municipal incorporations offer a historical case to consider the modalities of suburban governance in relation to immigrant empowerment.

Miami's case shows how the role of the state changed over time due to institutional innovations resulting from demographic change. The state was first established in a status quo where speculative development defined governance and decentralization. In this position, the state deployed a regional regulatory apparatus to rein in market-oriented forces of capital accumulation and to plan for the demographic growth driving decentralization. As the state enforced its mandate with Metro's expansion, it encountered new challenges due to the political, social, and economic outcomes of foreign migration. Under these new circumstances, the state's leadership changed to reflect immigrant empowerment, but it also adapted new policy innovations to reclaim its regulatory power over a territory undergoing fragmentation.

Miami's southern geographic location, far from other metropolitan areas in the United States, placed it on the edge of governance innovations during the first half of the twentieth century. The city's condition as a post-war Sunbelt metropolis meant that robust state institutions – particularly at the county level – formed late in its historical trajectory. During the first half of the twentieth century, civic leaders identified the need for regional governance in the management of decentralization, but county government – Metro – did not form until the early 1960s, following several decades of suburban development. Urban planning emerged at this historical juncture to control decentralization against the backdrop of Miami's growing status as a hemispheric destination between the Americas.

The passage of the Home Rule Charter and the introduction of the two-tier system of government represented a disruption in a political context that was set in place during more than forty years of municipal governance after the foundation of the City of Miami and the incorporation of twenty-five municipalities. Earlier, the state's role in decentralization had remained absent and mostly symbolic. Decentralization galvanized around the boom and bust cycles of speculative development in the form of irregular or illegal subdivisions and master-planned communities. Housed in weak municipal administrations, the state apparatus was fragmented according to individual jurisdictions, allowing the expansion of sprawl. It upheld the interests of real estate tycoons and succumbed to the whims of real estate market forces. Decentralization was shaped by the absence of land-use regulations, boosterism, and backdoor local politics.

The establishment of Metro deployed a regulatory apparatus that disturbed this status quo. Metro's mandate coalesced around the need for local services in suburban unincorporated areas, the protection of the natural environment, the regional public interest, and the imperative of comprehensive planning. Prior to this change, municipalities did not converge around county-wide goals. They carried out insular planning agendas according to municipal master plans and directed public infrastructure investments toward affluent areas within their boundaries.

The two-tier system of government aimed to confront these challenges by maintaining the political integrity of municipalities while addressing urban management and local representation needs in suburban unincorporated areas. Metro also aimed to uphold the regional public interest through the establishment of a fiscal system balancing the cost of public services, subsidizing the deficit of poor communities with the surplus of affluent communities. By including the proscription of incorporations, Metro sought to prevent the fragmentation of the Miami-Dade County's territory and the flight of fiscal revenue. These efforts represented not only a vast expansion in the state apparatus through the formation of institutions with a hierarchy and bureaucracy but also the self-colonization of the state over the territory of the county.

As previous sections in this chapter have explored, the provisions of local services and political representation in suburban unincorporated areas remained an unfulfilled promise in Metro's historical development. This failure, combined with the budgetary and fiscal imbalances between donor and recipient communities, the electoral empowerment of Cuban American immigrants during the 1980s, and the *Meek v. Metropolitan Dade County* decision, led to a rebellion of municipal incorporations. The movement confronted county commissioners and urban planners with unprecedented challenges to their state-sponsored mandate. As the demographic make-up of county leadership changed to reflect immigrants in positions of power, the state deployed new regulations and assumed new roles to deal with the repercussions of changing demographics, grassroots activism, and emergent ethnic leadership.

Paradoxically, the fever of secessionism that drove municipal incorporations reinforced Metro's legitimacy and led to the regulatory affirmation of the state. County commissioners, together with urban planners, introduced policies to manage the types of decentralization in the form of fragmentation. At first, they faced the movement in an ad hoc manner. Eventually, policies formalizing the process of incorporation were introduced, including the imposition of a moratorium and the implementation of community councils to provide local representation. Faced with a crisis of legitimacy, the state developed new methods to rein in secessionism and assert its mandate. The county lost fiscal territories, but it reclaimed regulatory power by developing new policies that framed the process of incorporation.

In this transformative context, the practice of urban planning catalogues how the state makes and unmakes political power in suburbia. The account of urban planning practices symbolizes an arena where decentralization is defined by ethnic conflict and suburban governance becomes a tool to reconfigure urban power. Urban planners deployed land-use controls to fight sprawl, advised county commissioners on secessionism, developed feasibility studies to address incorporation, and managed community councils, among other activities. Political power shifted through the medium of urban planning as its policies and practices were negotiated and asserted through the management of suburban spaces. They were claimed and counter-claimed by new and old actors, as county commissioners and planners enforced Metro's directive of central governance. As the example of Destiny and Miami Gardens demonstrates, these reconfigurations were also defined by the dimensions of race and class. The fiscal requirements developed by Metro to address secessionism favoured white affluent residents while they undermined poor African American communities. Groups that were traditionally under-represented by the legacies of segregation and structural racism remained undermined and had to pursue secessionist agendas in other ways. The public interest ideology embedded in comprehensive planning work operated through a colour-blind ideology that conclusively maintained the racial status quo.

Race, ethnicity, and immigration also had deep impacts on capital accumulation as a governing force in Miami's new phase of decentralization. This dimension would also play out differently for immigrant and ethnic groups realigning for political power in the city. Speculative development has represented a key force in Miami's decentralization process since the foundation of the City of Miami. It was traditionally defined by white developers and their master-planned visions in municipalities such as Coral Gables, Hialeah, and Miami Beach. Capital accumulation remained at full strength as decentralization continued to be fuelled by high rates of immigration from the Caribbean and Latin America, and the region's globalizing economy.

However, by the early 1990s, this force began to acquire a new ethnic face. An immigrant-led growth machine and political coalition moulded decentralization and turned suburban governance into a political arena. The Latin Builders Association and Miami's Cuban American construction industry became the new faces of speculative development in suburban unincorporated areas. The Latin Builders Association aligned development interests with Cuban American leaders to influence municipal and county governments. The repercussions of these alliances provoked conflicts over Metro's regulatory power and the secessionist mobilizations of communities of interest. Lawsuits over land-use regulations and counter-mobilizations on behalf of anti-secessionist agendas reveal how Cuban American politicians, construction guilds, corporations, and public-private interests organized to forge a form of clientelism geared around immigrant empowerment and immigrant-based planning agendas.

In this regard, the experience of Miami's African American community stood in sharp contrast to the empowerment of Cuban Americans. While Cuban Americans organized around urban development and secessionism to influence decentralization, the memory of Destiny and the incorporation of Miami Gardens offer an alternative set of tactics taken by African American activists to retool speculative development into a viable strategy for decentralization. The history behind the construction of Joe Robbie Stadium uncovers how race was factored into the top-down imposition of state-sponsored speculative development on an African American suburban community. While public-private partnership cemented the state's role in decentralization on behalf of the public interest, it was to the detriment of African Americans in the suburban locality. The experience was not forgotten. To secede from Metro, years later, African American secessionists identified the taxable land around the stadium as a source of capital accumulation to resolve the fiscal base requirements in their proposal for Miami Gardens. Unlike white affluent residents who framed taxation for local services as an unfair grievance, African Americans embraced state-driven capital accumulation to secure secession. By co-opting the lessons from previous incorporation efforts, they re-envisioned a path toward incorporation. The differences between these experiences demonstrate that capital accumulation and clientelism were different assemblages of power among Miami's empowered immigrant and ethnic communities based on local histories, scales of governance, and access to political power.

The rebellions also demonstrate how political claims and counterclaims unfolding in an urban context transformed immigration in hyper-localism to reshape decentralization. The statements from planners show how, in Miami's milieu, authoritarian private governance acquired a revanchist mantle in the face of immigrant and ethnic empowerment. The rise of the communities of interest in the aftermath of Cuban American electoral gains and the *Meek v. Metropolitan Dade County* decision underlined the mobilization of white affluent residents to reclaim the loss of political power. While these insurgent actors deployed reactionary and progressive discourses to frame their messages – property rights, fear of crime, managing traffic problems, land-use controls, protection of nature, and conservation of the built environment – these discourses also carried anti-immigrant and racist undertones.

Overall, their efforts stood for a suburban social movement composed of homeowner and condominium associations, as well as small neighbourhood groups. Their actions proliferated from Miami-Dade County intercoastal areas to the western suburbs through the mimicry of strategies and tactics that looked to the prospects of municipal incorporation as a model for self-rule. Decentralization was infused with a political effervescence that turned suburban unincorporated areas into a stage for authoritarian private governance. Suburbia erupted into an exuberant field of direct democracy and rogue governing bodies that turned the spaces and processes of decentralization into platforms for electoral activity at the local, municipal, and county levels of government. Referenda after referenda brought new civic leaders to power. County commissioners sought the votes of new constituents in newly formed cities, as new municipalities elected mayors and inducted new city councils. From the public sector, the actors of this political drama included old and new county commissioners who laboured to uphold the public interest through the development of comprehensive planning policies. From the private and non-profit sectors, the actors included members from the business sectors, construction industries, and civil rights groups coming together in complex advocacy alignments for and against secession. In the midst of this activity, the usurpation of power not only took place vertically but also horizontally. The co-option of community councils exemplified by communities of interest shows how a governance innovation deployed by the state was co-opted by small community groups to be redeployed in the name of secessionism.

Conclusion: Immigrant Empowerment and Decentralization

From the early 1990s through the mid-2000s, Miami-Dade County dealt with the incorporation of nine new municipalities. This process carved a vast suburban area into nine new cities, challenging Metro's regional mandate with self-governing territories. The rebellion of municipal incorporations was led by communities of interest representing white affluent residents in suburban unincorporated areas. Their concerns arose against the backdrop of three historical tensions in Metro government: the failure of local representation and service provisions in suburban unincorporated areas, the fiscal imbalance between diverse communities, and the reconfiguration of political power in the city on behalf of Cuban Americans.

Secessionism pitted a new generation of county commissioners and urban planners against an eclectic grassroots social movement in suburbia. As secessionist fever spread from Miami-Dade County's intercoastal areas to its western suburbs, it shaped decentralization with new policy and governance puzzles. Urban planning became a symbolic battleground where the balance between regional versus local, affluent versus poor, public versus community interest, Cuban versus Anglo, White versus Black played out according to changing alliances and policy innovations. The labour and expertise of urban planners were entangled with new conflicts over immigration, ethnic politics, and secessionism.

The experience of Miami-Dade County shows how the modalities of suburban governance develop in a context defined by the political, economic, and social repercussions of immigrant empowerment. Under these circumstances, governance institutions functioning at different geographic scales in the city are not only transformed but also enacted in new ways. The role of the state evolved from a condition where speculative development defined decentralization to the deployment of a state apparatus managing decentralization as a project of self-colonization. During the rebellion, the state's territory was fragmented into subunits of governance – municipalities – turning decentralization into a strategy to forge new cities through emancipation. Faced with secessionism, the state morphed its regulatory apparatus to reclaim power. Capital accumulation was exemplified by a Cuban American growth machine (Nijman, 1997), and authoritarian private governance was embodied in the revanchist politics of secessionist groups led by white affluent communities of interest.

Secessionism was based on notions of independence and self-rule that galvanized community groups to claim political geographies where power could be localized, concentrated, and managed. This process implied legal separation from the county and the making of new territorial boundaries, but it also included the control of fiscal bases, the capacity to decide upon land-use regulations, and the assertion of localist imaginaries adhering to notions of authenticity in a metropolitan context defined by rapid sociopolitical change. Secession, however, was not an accessible path for all communities. The case of Destiny and Miami Gardens demonstrate that the legacies of structural racism and segregation echoed in the colour-blind ideology that exemplified the formulation of a regional public interest during this period.

The rebellion of municipal incorporations was framed by narratives of insurgency, but the right to incorporate largely played out in the theatre of the courtroom. The reconfiguration of electoral power in Miami-Dade County resulted from civil rights litigation. Similarly, throughout the rebellion, incorporation claims played out in law courts in parallel with electoral disputes at the urns and grassroots mobilization on suburban streets. The empowerment of immigrant groups produced not only an effervescent urban democracy but also a long series of ardent court battles that informed suburban governance. The rule of law predominated through this experience as a framework to reshape political power in the city and defined decentralization.

The case of Miami-Dade County shows that suburban governance must be understood through an analysis of the long duration of history whereupon a city's path dependency accounts for the empowerment of immigrants as a major factor in decentralization, the role of the state, capital accumulation, and authoritarian private governance. More recent scholarship on the relationship between urban politics and place demonstrates a mode of historical case study research that considers the spatial dimensions of urban political power (Doering et al., 2021). This process implies accounting for planning policy, recognizing immigrant-based political agendas, and analysing counter-claims that traditional groups make to reassert their political power in the midst of social change.

NOTES

1 This chapter relies on previous research on the history of comprehensive planning in Miami and the impact of Cuban immigration on planning practice and policymaking in Dade County during the twentieth century. The research was conducted between 2008 and 2013, and interviews with planning professionals and policymakers took place between 2012 and 2013.
2 See United States Census, Miami-Dade County, Florida: Population estimates, July 1, 2022. https://www.census.gov/quickfacts/fact/table/miamidadecountyflorida,US#viewtop.
3 "Communities of interest" was a term used by Miami-Dade County policymakers to designate local interest groups seeking incorporation.

REFERENCES

Biddulph, G. (1989, 20 August). Key Biscayne Group pushes incorporation. *Miami Herald*, Final edition, Neighbors KE, 6.
Cauvin, E. (1995, 2 March). County manager proposes satellite government centers. *Miami Herald*, Final edition, Neighbors NE, 3.
Charles, J. (1995, 26 March). Team Metro centers extend county's reach. *Miami Herald*, Final edition, Neighbors NW, 4
Citizens Charter Review Committee. (1986). *Citizens Charter Review Committee on Dade County*. Dade County, Florida.
Dade County Charter Review Committee. (1982). *Dade County Charter Review Commission report*. Dade County, Florida.
Dade County Metropolitan Study Commission. (1971). *Final report and recommendation*. Dade County, Florida.

Dade County Metropolitan Study Commission. (1995). Ordinance relating to incorporation providing procedures for filing and review of petitions for incorporation. Ordinance No. 95-78. Dade County, Florida.

Dade County Metropolitan Study Commission, Citizen's Advisory Committee. (1992). *Metro-Dade County Citizen's Advisory Committee on county-wide incorporation final report*. Dade County Charter, Sec. 5.05. Metropolitan Dade County, Miami, Florida.

Doering, J., Silver, D., & Taylor, Z. (2021). The spatial articulation of urban political cleavages. *Urban Affairs Review, 57*(4), 911–51. https://doi.org/10.1177/1078087420940789

Faiola, A. (1991, 16 June). Key Biscayne: Dade's 1st new city in 30 years. *Miami Herald*, Final edition, Local, 1B.

Filkins, D. (1992, 7 June). Groveites cheer as secession plan okd. *Miami Herald*, Final edition, Local, 1D.

Filkins, D. (1994, 15 August). Concerned residents weighing Metro vote, NE Dade candidates pledge stronger voice. *Miami Herald*, Final edition, Local, 18.

Filkins, D. (1995, 4 June). City fever sweeping the county. *Miami Herald*, Final edition, Local, 1B.

Filkins, D., & Strouse, C. (1992, 8 July). Metro pulls secession issue off ballot. *Miami Herald*, Final edition, Local, 1B.

Finefrock, D. (1996, 8 October). Metro freezes incorporations, annexations. *Miami Herald*, Final edition, Local, 1B.

Hamel, P., and Keil, R. (Eds.). (2015). *Suburban governance: A global view*. University of Toronto Press.

Hartman, T. (1995, 23 April). Metro mulls stricter rules for cityhood. *Miami Herald*, Final edition, Local, 1B.

Hertz, B. (1984). *Governing Dade County: A study of alternative structure*. Dade County, Florida.

Martin, L. (1991, 3 September). Grove activists back board but call secession unlikely. *Miami Herald*, Final edition, Local, 1B.

May, P. (1996, 26 May). Breaking up is hard to do. *Miami Herald*, Final edition, Local, 2B.

Metro-Dade County Boundaries Commission. (1996). *Report of the Metro-Dade County Boundaries Commission on issues of incorporation, annexation and community councils*. Metro-Dade County Boundaries Commission.

Nijman, J. (1997). Globalization to a Latin beat: The Miami growth machine. *Annals of the American Academy of Political and Social Science, 551*(1), 164–77. https://doi.org/10.1177/0002716297551001012

Nijman, J., & Clery, T. (2015). Rethinking suburbia: A case study of metropolitan Miami. *Environment and Planning A: Economy and Space, 47*(1), 69–88. https://doi.org/10.1068/a46281

Petchell, J. (1990, 6 June). Key Biscayne clears 1st hurdle to independence. *Miami Herald*, Final edition, Local, 1B.

Shukovsky, P. (1990). Metro to help Key's study on incorporation. *Miami Herald*, Final edition, Neighbors KE, section 8, 14.

Sofen, E. (1961). *A report in politics in Greater Miami.* Joint Center for Urban Studies of the Massachusetts Institute of Technology and Harvard University.

Tanfani, J. (1991a, 18 July). Grove residents consider council. *Miami Herald*, Final edition, Neighbors CT, 10.

Tanfani, J. (1991b, 28 July). Grove independence sought. *Miami Herald*, Final edition, Local, 1B.

Tanfani, J. (1992a, 9 April). Coconut Grove Council works toward secession from Miami. *Miami Herald*, Final edition, Neighbors NE, 10.

Tanfani, J. (1992b, 15 September). Grove secession issue off ballot, Parks plan on. *Miami Herald*, Final edition, Local, 1B.

Tanfani, J. (1996, 10 March). Drawing election boundaries. *Miami Herald*, Final edition, Local, 1B

Tomb, G. (1985, 3 November). Bridge to carry new era to Key Biscayne. *Miami Herald*, Final edition, Local, 1B.

Touche Ross & Co. (1978). *Report on a review of Two-Tier government in Miami/ Dade County*. Touche Ross & Co.

Ycaza, C. (1989, 19 June). Key Biscayne poll shuns development. *Miami Herald*, Final edition, Neighbors KE, 18.

Yee, I. (2000, 22 October). Municipalities move ahead with incorporation. *Miami Herald*, Final edition, Neighbors WE, 20W.

5 Shaping Suburbanization through Regional Land-Use Planning? The Case of Greater Frankfurt

VALENTIN MEILINGER AND JOCHEN MONSTADT

Introduction

Across the planet, suburbanization pushes diverse urban forms and functions toward the peripheries, where they materialize in post-suburban realities and render city-suburb distinctions increasingly obsolete (Keil, 2017). In the Greater Frankfurt (Main)[1] region, Germany's most suburbanized region, such processes are by far not a new phenomenon. Economically, Sassen (1997, p. 64) lists Frankfurt next to cities such as Paris, Amsterdam, and London as a European economic powerhouse and a central hub in the global economy. Speculations about how Europe's second largest financial centre will "capitalize" on Brexit further nurture growth expectations for the City of Frankfurt.

However, a closer look at this allegedly global *city* reveals a globalized and polycentric *city region* in which cities and suburbs form a continuum – an "in-between city" (Sieverts, 1998). Frankfurt's iconic skyline as a key icon of the region's global economic power, therefore, strikingly misrepresents the actual division of labour and diversified economic specialization of Greater Frankfurt, which draws its global status from economic activities in the region's network: As the centre of the Frankfurt-Rhine-Main Metropolitan Region with currently around 5.8 million inhabitants, Frankfurt, with its 747,000 residents, is surrounded by an archipelago of various other urban centres (Wiesbaden, Mainz, Darmstadt, Offenbach, and Hanau), medium-sized cities with fewer than 100,000 inhabitants (Rüsselsheim, Bad Homburg, Aschaffenburg), and small towns (Regionalverband, 2019). In this suburbanization-fed network, a strong economic specialization comes with a tendency toward weighty intra-regional differences and segregation: extremely high tax revenues and purchasing power of some of Germany's most wealthy municipalities contrast with structural deficits, indebtedness, and economic restructuring of others.

As such, Frankfurt's globally integrated landscape of sociospatial organization seems to fit well into Keil's (2017) depiction of the "suburban planet." Moreover, new suburban forms and politics that alter traditional suburbs under contemporary conditions of economic production and reproduction impinge on Greater Frankfurt (Jansen et al., 2017). Two characteristics of German suburban governance, however, make the Frankfurt case a locally distinct case of suburban governance that requires further exploration. First, the German state pursues a stringent and ambitious spatial planning agenda to promote compact urban growth and to ensure equal living conditions. Second, Greater Frankfurt is unique in that its municipalities have regionalized their land-use planning since 2003 to effectively address suburbanization and confine (sub)urban growth. Thereby, municipal land-use planning was upscaled to the Regional Authority FrankfurtRhineMain[2] (*Regionalverband FrankfurtRheinMain*), pursuing the spatial concentration of retail in central places and the confinement of peripheral growth along designated growth corridors among its key objectives.

This chapter explores this contradictory simultaneity characterizing suburban development and governance in the Greater Frankfurt region: On the one hand, a sophisticated system of spatial planning promotes compact urban growth and spatial cohesion. On the other hand, the economically highly productive region is shaped by ongoing peripheral growth, regional processes of deconcentration, and a striking sociospatial polarization (Hoyler et al., 2006; Monstadt et al., 2012). How do place-based local coalitions mediate the ongoing suburbanization within the spatial, regulatory, and wider politico-economic context of the Frankfurt-Rhine-Main region? And how do collective processes of suburban governance within and beyond the state explain ongoing suburbanization in the face of Germany's strong spatial planning system in general and Frankfurt's regionalized land-use planning in particular?

Our contribution draws on Hamel and Keil's (2015) differentiation between *universal* political-economic and cultural forces that shape global suburbanization, on the one hand, and local specificities of suburbanization, their *diverging* forms, on the other hand. To trace back the mechanisms of suburbanization in Greater Frankfurt between global and local forces, we deploy what Ekers et al. (2012) call the three "modalities of suburban governance" – state, capital, and authoritarian privatism – as analytical lenses.

We start by discussing international literature on suburbanization before we pay attention to German suburbanization dynamics and its regulation by the German spatial planning system. Frankfurt's regional land-use plan will be put centre stage. The empirical part first gives an overview of current patterns of suburbanization in Greater Frankfurt and subsequently traces how state, capitalist, and private interests mediate the production of these spaces. This part is to uncover how Greater Frankfurt's characteristic "local politics of place" produce today's suburban realities within the existing governance arrangements. A close look at the municipality of Bad Vilbel will expose the nature of suburban politics and their spatial forms. We conclude by problematizing the nested relationships between the regionalized and cohesion-oriented spatial planning system in Greater Frankfurt and the local politics of place that drive various forms of suburbanization: municipalities seek to strategically (and thus selectively) link their growth interests with that of businesses and private interest groups to maximize local tax revenues and undermine regional planning goals of confining suburban growth to distinct corridors of growth.

The qualitative empirical case study is based on assessment of secondary empirical literature, grey documents, websites, official city and state documents, statistical data, and newspaper articles. These resources were complemented by a series of twelve semi-structured interviews with municipal planning officials from the cities of Frankfurt, Kronberg, Offenbach, Bad Vilbel, Dreieich, Eschborn, Kelsterbach, Hanau, and the Regional Authority, as well as the responsible lower state spatial planning authority of South Hesse. The selection of municipalities reflects the regional division of labour and covers the entire range of striking differences in municipal economic power and significantly varying forms of suburbanization.

Studying Regional Patterns of Global Suburbanisms

Today, suburbanization as the "combination of non-central population and economic growth with urban spatial extension" (Ekers et al., 2012, p. 407) manifests in manifold ways around the globe. The city reinvents itself in these diverse places that leave the Western "edgeless city" (Lang & Knox, 2009) as only one suburban form among many (see other contributions in this volume). Inspired by comparative approaches to urban research (Robinson, 2014), we are interested in how to categorize the Greater Frankfurt region within this global concert of suburbanization and suburban governance.

The region came to the fore in international debates on "new regionalism" during the 1990s (Keating, 1998). In a globalizing economy, the promotion of regions as terrains of integrated urban and economic policy gained momentum as a means to position cities in a global competition for labour, money, and resources (p. 81). Thereby, entrepreneurial public management approaches and competition across local jurisdictions have found entry into the organization of local government. Amin (2004) problematizes such policies for their territorialist ideas of space. Flows of resources, money, goods, people, and knowledge that cut across various territorial scales produce local spaces. These processes of the production of space, he argues, thereby slip through territorial forms of control and policymaking under the banner of new regionalism.

Current theorizations of suburbanization account for this notion of the production of suburban space as a process that connects the local with the global, partly circumventing or unfolding in between precast territorial scales. There are thus globally *universal* and locally *diverging* forms of how suburbs are constructed, financed, planned, and lived in (Hamel & Keil, 2015). Political-economic dynamics and the practices of the suburban production of space can be grasped analytically by what Ekers et al. (2012) call the three "modalities of suburban governance" – state, capital, and authoritarian privatism.

To begin with, the study of the *state's role* in the political economy of urban growth has undergone a fundamental shift toward what Swyngedouw (2005) refers to as "governance-beyond-the-state." State institutions no longer act as impenetrable governing apparatuses that provide policies for inactive policy recipients; rather, policymaking comes as a negotiation between state authorities, private enterprises, and citizens (Rhodes, 1996, p. 666). Yet, despite the rise of governance, state-interventionism continues to loom large both in fuelling and regulating suburbanization. The local growth machine created enduring suburban realities of functional segregation and low density (Molotch, 1976). At the same time, a new form of state-interventionism occurs alongside (not replacing) these rationales of suburban governance by the state: municipalities increasingly turn to the use value of land and engage in retrofitting strategies by aligning their interests in space strategically with those of businesses and private authoritarian forms of government (Phelps & Wood, 2011).

Second, *capital accumulation* makes another modality of suburban governance. Profit interests affect the geographical and social make-up of development on the urban periphery and shape the allocation of resources, housing density, infrastructure, and zoning (Ekers et al., 2012, p. 413). Strategic action of the development industry, infrastructure companies, industrial and technology firms, and increasingly also the finance and service industries in the suburban landscape are central to understanding the politics of capital in suburbanization processes. By making use of lower land prices in suburban peripheries and lower costs of greenfield compared to brownfield development and by capitalizing on the competitive advantages of suburbs, capital drives suburban spatial forms to maximize return on investments. Moreover, jurisdictional fragmentation and competition within urban regions often result in lower property and corporate taxes, lower regulatory standards, or financial support that can be utilized to draw companies out of city centres (p. 413).

Third, *authoritarian private forms of governance* through non-governmental organizations, public-private partnerships, development corporations, and various stakeholder-based associations impinge on the suburban production of space (Ekers et al., 2012). Despite political decision making in pluralist liberal democracies remaining profoundly entrenched in Western nation-state structures, such organized private interests increasingly wield authority over political decisions. Thereby, stakeholder-based forms of urban governance have proven to be both highly selective and democratically less accountable than ideas of a pluralistic governance might suggest (Swyngedouw, 2005, 2009). While acts of private governance in suburbia only matter *in relation* to state actions, not independently of them, Ekers et al. (2012, p. 408) ascribe authoritarian privatism a "post-political" character. This notion describes how the possibility of challenging a given political order becomes reduced to politics as a managerial form of consensual governing (Swyngedouw, 2009).

Tracing back the interplay of the state, capital, and private authoritarian forms of governance in the production of suburban space allows us to highlight the underlying political-economic structures as well as the practices and mechanisms of suburbanization in Greater Frankfurt. In what follows, we put the emphasis on the German state as both driver and regulator of suburbanization. This focus serves to expose how political action within the state and collective action between the state, capital, and privatism mediate (that is, move around rather than dissolve) inherent contradictions of capitalist urbanization and its regulation.

Suburbanization and German Spatial Planning

In post-war Germany, we observe an array of ideological discourses about state organization that range from entrenched forms of Fordist welfarism to competition-oriented models of state organization that emerged in the 1990s. This shift in statehood was paralleled by profound spatial transformations on the outskirts of major German cities.

German spatial planning policies loom large in tying shifts in statehood and suburban materialities.

Suburbanization in Germany

German debates on suburbanization start out from city-suburb inter-relations that have fundamentally altered since the country's post-war boom. During the 1960s and 1970s, a continuously expanding market economy that was embedded in Fordist-style capitalism set the stage for rapid single-family home suburbanization (Brake, 2001, p. 16). Inher-ited settlement cores became amalgamated, which blurred urban-rural divisions both spatially and administratively (Müller & Rohr-Zänker, 2001, p. 36). Suburban retail development has followed consumers to the peripheries since the 1980s, endowing the suburbs with more "ur-ban" functions (Brake, 2001, p. 16). Later, this dynamic became further consolidated with service businesses settling at the urban fringe in the early 1990s (Keil & Ronneberger, 1994).

This process overlapped with the second significant increase in res-idential suburbanization that had been sparked by Germany's politi-cal unification (Burdack & Hesse, 2007, p. 83). In post-socialist Eastern Germany, the political objective of the "animated city centre" failed; heavy suburbanization was catalyzed due to the growing autonomy of municipalities and the fairly inexperienced planning (see, for example, Franz, 2000; Nuissl & Rink, 2005). In Western Germany, regional urban-ization brought forth "in-between cities" (Sieverts, 1998): extensively growing city-regions that saw their settlement cores become both in-creasingly conglomerated and interconnected.

Despite these major transformations, suburbanization in Germany has never substantially challenged the functional role of the urban core like in North America (Hesse & Siedentop, 2018, p. 99). Rather, recent re-urbanization dynamics mark a "relative centralization" (Brake & Herfert, 2012, p. 412) without, however, radically reframing the inherited functional interrelations in city-regions. These dynamics correspond to what Frank (2018) calls Germany's new "inner-city sub-urbanization," the increasing colonialization of inner cities by middle- and high-income classes that carry suburban lifestyles to the centre. Such centralization tendencies occur in disparate patterns and concen-trate in larger cities, while mid-sized and smaller cities in urbanized regions also continue to grow significantly. The consequences of the COVID-19 pandemic are expected to fuel such urban-regional growth in agglomeration areas (BBSR, 2021, p. 10). The current juxtaposition of re-urbanization and (post) suburbanization in German city-regions brings about an increasing functional and spatial differentiation that city-suburb models fail to adequately explain. Political geographies of state planning struggle to keep up with these shifts in suburban materialities.

Containing Sprawl in City-Regions? Germany's Spatial Planning Framework

The German state has a long-standing history of regulating spatial development on a variety of scales ranging from the national to the local level. This state-interventionism rests on the foundation of a liberal democratic ideology. However, just as much as the post-war welfare state in Germany is depicted as a democratic ideal, Hirsch (1995, p. 82) describes this *"Modell Deutschland"* as a prototype for a state-directed organization of capitalism. Nonetheless, this model is embedded in a welfarist and elaborately organized spatial planning system, which proclaims equivalent living conditions in the subunits.

The German planning system is based on clearly distinct levels of comprehensive spatial planning to integrate and coordinate spatially relevant sectoral policies and plans on each scale (see Figure 5.1). The national level defines the legal framework for both spatial planning at the *Länder* (state) and municipal level, observes national spatial development, and coordinates the general principles and visions of spatial planning with the *Länder* through a coordinating body between the national and *Länder* governments, the Standing Conference of Federal Ministers Responsible for Spatial Planning.

However, in Germany's federal system, the main institutional resources and operational tasks in spatial planning are with the *Länder* and the municipalities. Each devise spatial plans whose preparation is to be coordinated with sectoral policies and further predefined "public interest groups" (*Träger öffentlicher Belange*) such as business associations, utility companies, firefighting, and so on. The *Länder* execute state authority and service provision within their constitutional territories, and most of them organize spatial planning at two levels, the state level and the regional level, through own comprehensive plans. The mandatory "system of central places" guides spatial planning at these levels, ensuring the accessibility of relevant services for all population groups and the efficient spatial division of labour through concentrating spatial development in central places; as such, it has proven to be very effective (Schmidt et al., 2018). Complementarily, the principle of "decentralized concentration" seeks to concentrate spatial development in central places and along major settlement axes. This policy is

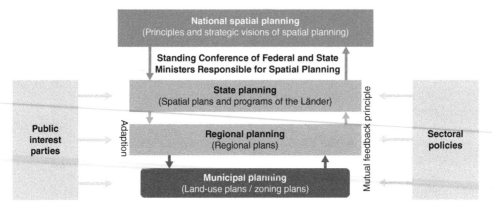

Figure 5.1. The organization of spatial planning in Germany. Source: Adapted from Schmidt-Eichstaedt et al. (2011).

fleshed out in more detail through regional planning by the lower planning authorities of the *Länder*, which thus directly impinges on municipal land-use plans.

While regional planning is mostly state directed (*Länder*), German constitutional law defines municipalities as autonomous bodies, granting them far-reaching autonomy in spatial planning as well as a territorial monopoly over property and business taxes, and a share of income taxes. In line with the "principle of subsidiarity,"[3] municipalities fulfil major public functions within their territories independently and thereby provide a critical counterbalance to the *Länder*. They exercise their constitutional right to planning through a two-tier system of land-use planning. The (preparatory) land-use plans outline all types of land use across the entire municipal territory and prepare the legally binding and detailed zoning plans for settlement areas that regulate the amount and type of building activities. The zoning plan is the only plan that gives landowners the right to development (construction or alteration of land use). The interscalar coordination of integrated spatial planning is guided by the "mutual feedback principle": superior planning authorities amend their goals with regard to spatial-functional imperatives that are articulated on subordinated scales, which, in turn, participate in planning processes at superior levels.

Policy Reforms and New Orientations in Spatial Planning

How effective has this spatial planning system proven to be in containing urban sprawl on the city-regional scale? A major initiative by the

German national government to mobilize spatial planning regulations to contain sprawl was the introduction of the so-called "30-ha target," aimed at reducing greenfield development by one-quarter, compared to a reference period between 1993 and 1996, and thus not exceeding 30 hectares per day. Subsequent reforms of the Federal Building Code have consistently encouraged brownfield development while restricting growth in peripheral areas (Jehling et al., 2018). Moreover, the introduction of the "regional land-use plan" in 1998 came as a means to thwart extensive growth by better coordinating municipal land-use planning. Germany's reform of the Federal Building Code in 2017, however, de facto liberalized regulatory requirements for residential greenfield development to target Germany's current housing crisis.

The repercussions of spatial planning measures geared toward containing suburban growth can be observed most strongly at the interface of the municipal and the regional scales, where city-suburb boundaries have been ruptured in multiple ways since the post-war period. Regions have seen their authority increasing due to concessions in authority from the *Länder* and to joint planning efforts at the municipal level (Blotevogel et al., 2014, p. 103).

Initial cooperative regional planning dates back to the early twentieth century, while more radical institutional changes to respond to suburbanization became effective in the 1960s. Back then, the so-called "metropolitan reform tradition" (Zimmermann & Heinelt, 2012, p. 21) redefined political boundaries within German metropolitan regions to counterbalance suburbanization-fed shifts in city-suburb tax bases that had caused imbalances in the regional organization and financing of public service provision. Knieling and Blatter (2009, p. 229) ascribe a self-referential perspective to these reforms, almost exclusively focusing on intra-metropolitan planning and limited to the public sector.

In the 1980s, this cohesion-oriented planning approach became increasingly dismantled under a new public management paradigm that gave preference to regional competitiveness (Knieling & Blatter, 2009, pp. 229ff.). Later, more flexible forms of regional governance were adopted as a promising means to address the challenges of economic development, ecological sustainability, and social cohesion where existing government structures failed (Fürst, 2001, p. 375). The self-referential perspective gave way to an outwardly oriented striving for stronger collaboration with private stakeholders and a complementary bundling of regional functions and interests to strengthen the global competitiveness of Germany's new "European metropolitan regions" (Zimmermann & Heinelt, 2012). Such paradigms, which proclaim more "flexible political geographies" (p. 21), remain considered as powerful means to foster global competitiveness while balancing local parochialism.

Yet, throughout these developments, the German spatial planning system "suffered from discrepancy between high aspirations and low resources" (Blotevogel et al., 2014, p. 100). This discrepancy applies especially against the backdrop of growing exigencies of regional economic competition. However, the German spatial planning system has not entirely given up its regulating power in the (re)production of space. Legally binding planning regulations and unambiguous scalar responsibilities of Germany's hierarchical spatial planning system still formally constitute a landscape of heavy regulation. Given this fact, it seems fruitful to assess regionalization in German spatial planning and its effects on suburbanization by taking a closer look at the discrepancy between a powerful state and the de facto strong influence of capital accumulation and private forms of governance on suburban governance.

Suburbanization and Regional Land-Use Planning in the Greater Frankfurt Region

The Greater Frankfurt region, as the politically defined territory of the Regional Authority (see Figure 5.2), has an overall population of 2.37 million inhabitants and includes seventy-five member municipalities, with the City of Frankfurt as its biggest urban node. It builds the functional – and globally most integrated – heart of the larger Frankfurt-Rhine-Main Metropolitan Region, which hosts 5.8 million inhabitants stretching over the *Länder* Hesse, Rhineland Palatinate, and Bavaria. Both the Greater Frankfurt region and the metropolitan region have witnessed demographic growth (Greater Frankfurt: +6.2 per cent between 2012 and 2017) and are predicted to grow further over the coming decades (Regionalverband, 2019, p. 4).

Economically, Greater Frankfurt is one of the most productive German regions, drawing its economic strength from inherited economic clusters with strong functional complementarity such as transport and logistics, finance, biotechnology, and media and materials technology. For example, Frankfurt's status as Germany's transportation node for aviation, railways, highways, and shipping; as Germany's financial capital for banking and the stock exchange; and as a principal location for global knowledge, economies, and business support services is highly complementary and owed to its long tradition as a trade fair city.

Spatially, this economic division of labour is organized in a highly interconnected urban network: the Greater Frankfurt region includes a network of urban centres (Frankfurt, Offenbach, and Hanau), medium-sized cities (Rüsselsheim, Bad Homburg, Aschaffenburg), and small towns. It is surrounded by major urban centres that host key

Figure 5.2. Frankfurt-Rhine-Main Metropolitan Region and the Greater Frankfurt region. Source: Adapted from Regionalverband (2010, p. 15).

governmental functions such as the *Länder* capitals of Wiesbaden and Mainz, and Darmstadt as the capital of the regional district of South Hesse. Since the 1970s, transport lines that originally followed radial routes outward from Frankfurt gained increasing importance as tangential arteries to connect specialized businesses and dense housing (see Mettke, 2015, p. 209).

Alongside and in between these regional transport lines, suburbanization has reshaped settlement structures profoundly toward new (sub)urban forms – an "urbanized landscape" or a "landscaped city" (Sieverts, 1998). This blurring of urban and village boundaries has brought forth an economically highly productive landscape, whose interconnectedness in form and function has consistently penetrated into the region's political realm.

Shifting Political Constitutions of the Region

Illuminating the Greater Frankfurt region's political (re)organization and its spatial planning system – the state as a modality of suburban governance – will clarify the entanglements that are at play in this nexus of social forces and material realities. It will also illustrate how suburban governance in Greater Frankfurt unfolds as a relational process where co-dependent stakeholder actions that are either bound to specific spatial scales or cut across them mediate the suburban production of space.

From early visions of regionalism in the mid-1920s onward, Greater Frankfurt has undergone fundamental transformations. Post-war mass motorization and rapid suburbanization turned Frankfurt inside out. Due to territorial asymmetries in governance, the idea of a *Regionalstadt* (regional city), a radical centralization of government, tax collection, and public service provision authority on a regional scale, emerged. In 1975, this debate cumulated in the foundation of the *Umlandverband*, an attenuated form of the *Regionalstadt* that would leave fiscal authority with municipalities. Nonetheless, this change entailed the formation of a directly elected regional council, and priority was given to the equal distribution of regional costs and benefits among local governments. In the 1990s, lobbying for municipal self-interests and organizational inefficiencies of the *Umlandverband* that came under increasing criticism led to its political breakdown (Zimmermann, 2012, p. 230). Meanwhile, private special-purpose organizations such as the Business Initiative Rhine-Main (*Wirtschaftsinitiative Frankfurt Rhein Main e.V.*), which was founded by CEOs of Frankfurt's major banks and the airport-operating Fraport AG, mushroomed, wielding increasing influence on spatial development (Heinelt & Zimmermann, 2011). Supported by the Business Initiative, the Fraport AG successfully turned the airport into Greater Frankfurt's new "Airport City," a gravitating agglomeration of retail, commerce, and research on the periphery, while undermining municipal planning authority (Knippenberger, 2012, p. 148). By 2000, the welfarist *Umlandverband* had given way to the new *Planungsverband Frankfurt*. As its draft law highlights, this new entity entailed a significant shift toward a competition-oriented regionalism:

> The Rhine-Main region has a particularly competitive relationship with other European regions. Hence, the position of the European economic centre Frankfurt am Main and its surrounding municipalities in European and international competition should be enhanced without abandoning the existing, advantageous polycentric structure of the region. (Hessische Staatsregierung, 2000, p. 1; translation by the authors)

The new regional council was composed of municipally elected representatives. While the former *Umlandverband* was assigned a variety of tasks in the provision of public services, the new legislation emphasized the role of voluntary private, public-private, and inter-municipal associations; special-purpose organizations; and partnerships. The tasks delegated to such special-purpose organizations included the provision of waste, water, sanitation, and transportation services; business and locational development; and marketing, the promotion of culture, and the development of a regional greenbelt – all of which are fulfilled within different purpose-specific cooperative arrangements with variable membership and only partly overlapping (task-specific) jurisdictions (Hoyler et al., 2006; Monstadt et al., 2012). Not least, with municipal representatives on the regional council, local utility companies that drive local growth as financially independent but politically influential project developers gained more leeway in mediating suburbanization in the region (Interview 9, 2018).

In 2011, a third groundbreaking reinstitutionalization of the region was enacted by metropolitan legislation to re-encourage "indispensable" regional cooperation (Hessische Staatsregierung, 2010, p. 1). For this purpose, the region's newly founded executive organ, the regional executive committee, prepares issue-based draft resolutions that are then discussed in the regional assembly, where municipal representatives have to negotiate their local interests at the regional level. Most crucially, the Regional Authority in its current form (*Regionalverband FrankfurtRheinMain*) was given authority to oversee regionalized land-use planning within Greater Frankfurt to spatially integrate municipal land-use planning of its seventy-five member cities and municipal districts (see Table 5.1 for an overview of planning scales). This allocation was to reconcile regional spatial planning goals of functionally integrated and spatially confined urban development with municipal autonomy in the interest of a strategic development of the Greater Frankfurt region (Interview 10, 2014). Drawing on the German "system of central places," the plan aspires to channel future local development into compact growth patterns, concentrating retail and other urban functions in central places and confining growth along designated development corridors (Regionalverband, 2010). This most recent regionalization of planning in Greater Frankfurt shows striking similarities with North American "smart growth" paradigms by proposing more compact and less car-reliant urban forms and by confining new developments to the urbanized perimeter of the metropolitan region and satellite communities rather than on greenfield sites (Filion et al., 2016). Characteristically, such smart growth policies take market rationales, growth, and consumption for granted (Krueger & Gibbs, 2008).

Table 5.1. Scales of State Spatial Planning that Shape Suburban Governance in the
Greater Frankfurt Region

Administrative and Territorial Units	Government Bodies	Main Attributions	Inhabitants
State of Hesse	Government of the State of Hesse	State spatial planning (State Development Plan), Law on the Frankfurt-Rhine-Main Metropolitan Region	6.3 million
Region of South Hesse	Regional Planning Authority for South Hesse	Formal regional planning (Regional plan for South Hesse)	3.8 million
Inter-municipal: Greater Frankfurt region	Regional Authority FrankfurtRhineMain	Regionalized land-use planning	2.4 million
Municipalities	Municipal administrations and municipal councils	Zoning plans (as unlike in most parts of Germany, land-use planning is regionalized in Greater Frankfurt)	80 (number of municipalities within Greater Frankfurt region)

Source: Adapted from Macdonald et al. (2021).

Spatial Transformations in Greater Frankfurt's Suburban Patchwork Rug

Suburbanization in Greater Frankfurt unfolds in an environment of constant development pressure, a strong influence of local growth ambitions on spatial development, and recurring regional institutional shifts. Given that, the region has moved away from hierarchical city-suburb patterns long ago. Nowadays, the juxtaposition of expansive suburbanization and peripheral densification of both productive and reproductive functions renders Greater Frankfurt a "prototypical region" (Interview 11, 2014) of contemporary German suburbanization in times of diversified spatial development on the peripheries (see Figure 5.3).

Against the backdrop of ongoing population growth, Germany's housing crisis, and growing speculations about Brexit, Greater Frankfurt's housing market has come under severe pressure: the region's expected housing demand until 2030 is estimated at 200,000 new housing units, equating to an increase of the housing stock by 17 per cent (Regionalverband, 2019, p. 3). Not only is inner-city redevelopment on brownfield sites in Frankfurt restricted due to a limited availability of

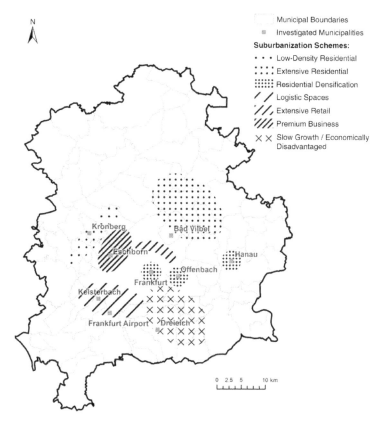

Figure 5.3. Current patterns of regional urbanization in the Greater Frankfurt region. Sources: Based on qualitative interviews conducted by the authors and data from Regionalverband (2019).

land (Interview 9, 2018); even extensive settlement development no longer fully meets the demand for housing, which triggers rising land prices in suburban peripheries, particularly west of Frankfurt (Interview 4, 2014).

These market-induced pressures bear upon Greater Frankfurt's highly diverse landscapes of suburban and post-suburban living, including low-density exclusive residences like in Kronberg; post-war single-family homes on large plots of land that allowed for small-scale agricultural production such as in Bad Vilbel; and peripheral high-rise apartment buildings like in Dreieich, which were once built for social

Figure 5.4. Inner-city redevelopment in Frankfurt's new Europaviertel, 2017.
Source: Sara MacDonald.

housing and are surrounded by residential building restriction areas
(*Siedlungsbeschränkungsgebiete*)[4] due to high aircraft noise emissions
south of Frankfurt (Regionalverband, 2010).

The current transformations of Greater Frankfurt's residential suburbs
are just as diverse. On the one hand, expansive settlement growth in the
northeast is induced by Frankfurt's saturated housing market, which
strongly relies on the market-driven redevelopment of brownfield areas
into high-quality apartments (see Figure 5.4). The "cumulative effects"
(Interview 6, 2014) of these redevelopments push lower income households toward (greenfield developments on) the periphery and not least
threaten Frankfurt's manufacturing businesses due to growing shortages
of building space. While brownfield redevelopment contributes to densifying inner cities, such forms of German re-urbanization frequently
show physical and social characteristics of suburban ways of life, which
is why Frank (2018) discusses them as "inner-city suburbanization."
South of Frankfurt, the saturated housing market led to the mobilization
of substantial reserves in building land from the 1990s for developing

detached or semi-detached single-family housing in Kelsterbach (Interview 7, 2014). Moreover, residential growth occurs far beyond the airport at the southern end of Greater Frankfurt.

On the other hand, new suburban developments have reached the urban fringe. The redevelopment of former harbour areas in Offenbach and the reactivation of military conversions in Hanau bear testimony to this sprawl (Interview 8, 2014). In Hanau, the flexibilization of building and procurement regulations allowed the city to instigate fierce competition among private developers to invest in the city. Similarly, the City of Bad Vilbel strategically issues building permits for row houses and condominium buildings to attract middle- and high-income singles and couples without children, as well as retirees, to avoid high municipal expenditures for education and child care (Interview 3, 2014). Generally, such a suburban densification is in line with both regional planning goals and recent reforms in federal building law that strongly incentivize and deregulate inner-city redevelopment and, paradoxically, for an interim phase, also greenfield development. Ultimately, however, regulations remain a "normative credo" (Interview 1, 2014) until densification becomes factual where market logic implies demand; that is, where developers, investors, politicians, and various interest groups activate their political networks and realize development.

But despite high market pressures, pockets of slower development remain. For one, smaller municipalities south and southeast of Frankfurt face more hurdles to perform developmental strategies due to their smaller reserves of designated building land. In particular, locally designated building land that predated the institutionalization of regional land-use planning in Greater Frankfurt is a critical determinant of suburbanization in the region (see Table 5.1). Furthermore, budgetary constraints to invest in infrastructure that originate in a long-standing tradition of an unequal distribution of costs and benefits in the region put these municipalities at a disadvantage (Interview 4, 2014). Residential development restrictions around the airport lock in such regional imbalances. Second, reservations concerning densification in the northwestern settlement strip along the Taunus Mountains – which locates some of Germany's wealthiest municipalities – stems from local slow-growth aspirations, not from regional political discrimination. Wealthy suburban communities in this area traditionally lobby for restrictive planning in order to protect the swanky idyll of late nineteenth- and early twentieth-century villa suburbanization (Interview 1, 2014).

The suburbanization of businesses equally shows a picture of heterogeneous development patterns. On the one hand, (frequently banking-related) service businesses "going up the country" (Keil &

Figure 5.5. Deutsche Börse building in the Eschborn Süd Business Park, 2014.
Source: Valentin Meilinger.

Ronneberger, 1994) continue to shape Greater Frankfurt's peripheries. The move of the German Stock Exchange from Frankfurt's inner city to the business park Eschborn Süd in 2000 exemplifies the ongoing tax competition between centre and periphery (Jansen et al., 2017, p. 264; see Figure 5.5). Also, the Frankfurt airport's "Gateway Gardens" and the City of Kronberg's southern business park highlight this concentration of specialized business functions in suburban pockets that are located in the northwestern and western outskirts of Frankfurt in close proximity to the airport (Interview 5, 2014). Besides available building land and excellent transport connections, these suburban premium business spaces primarily compete with business taxes that are significantly lower than in Frankfurt; in Eschborn, taxation is nearly half of Frankfurt's rate (Jansen et al., 2017, p. 264). More recently, these cities also engage in retrofitting policies to customize their traditionally mono-functional business parks for altered business demands through land-use diversification by means of zoning amendments, the optimization of multimodal transport connections, or design improvements (Interview 5, 2014).

On the other hand, these premium business spaces find their locally disadvantageous – but for the region functionally indispensable – counterparts south and southwest of Frankfurt. Logistic spaces around the airport are a case in point. Renting large areas of land to airport-related businesses, the Fraport AG profoundly shapes these suburban spaces (City of Kelsterbach, 2015), while the regionally enacted residential settlement restriction south of Frankfurt prohibits land-use diversification. This restriction leaves the affected municipalities with negative externalities of logistics such as high expenditure for road maintenance and low tax rates per square metre. Likewise, unfavourable (public) transport connections and the comparatively late expansion of the regional commuter train system in the east of Frankfurt have caused persistent disadvantages for local business parks there (Interview 2, 2014). Finally, the indebted City of Offenbach bears high social expenditures to high poverty rates among its residents, and to large numbers of refugees, and has become subject to budgetary surveillance by the State of Hesse. Given its budgetary constraints and high social expenditures, the city has limited opportunities to radically apply retrofitting measures and regional competition strategies (Interview 4, 2014). Just as business suburbanization in Greater Frankfurt creates winners and losers, the local attraction of retailers is highly competitive (see Box 5.1).

Box 5.1. "Look at This, There Is a North of Frankfurt, Too!"[5]

Only thirty years ago, a local city planner tells us, people started to acknowledge Frankfurt's north as being "on the map" of the region. Today, the City of Bad Vilbel embodies the vibrant local growth aspirations north of Frankfurt. The actions of only a handful of well-connected businesses, investors, and active individuals in politics and state authorities that keep close personal ties across institutional boundaries have incited skyrocketing development in the city. This growth stirs regional functional geographies and structures of power.

   Aiming to attract a large-scale furniture store to create local business taxes and jobs, the City of Bad Vilbel entered a fierce political fight with the region. The city was determined to permit the furniture store 3,000 square metres of retail space for everyday goods, which clearly violated the region's retail development concept that only allows 800 square metres for these goods to protect inner-city areas. Even though these development plans sparked a years-long judicial settlement with the neighbouring municipality of Bad Homburg, local politicians in Bad Vilbel achieved political support from the State of Hesse for this large-scale retail project. Circumventing the region through bilateral negotiations with the State of Hesse, the city exposed the political instability of the regional retail development concept, which structurally opposes local development interests.

More recently, Bad Vilbel entered the regional competition for premium businesses by promoting a gigantesque office park project of a private investor on its territory. Plans envision creating the "Springpark Valley" office park with 8,000 new jobs and high-rise towers on land that the city has sold to the investor. To increase the economic productivity of the development, the city is experimenting with the German building code's most recently introduced land category, "urban area," which allows for denser construction.

Inner-city development in Bad Vilbel further illustrates characteristic points of friction between local parochialism and regional cohesion goals. Influential individuals with strong personal bonds with Bad Vilbel were very successful in attracting "urban" functions. Over several decades, a long-standing city council member and head of the city's proprietary department acquired large areas of land through the municipality and the local utility company. The development of these areas, partly by the local utility itself, actively boosted Bad Vilbel's inner-city revival, while the sale of formerly agricultural land left the city debt-free.

Generally, the case of Bad Vilbel illustrates one aspect of suburban governance in particular: local specificities in development – despite the rigid formal organization of the region and its planning regime – seem to depend largely on actions taken by well-connected individuals that manoeuvre in between preset boundaries of state, capital, and privatism. Ultimately, the power relations between municipalities and the region that shape suburbanization become visible in such actions – an image that frequently diverges from the institutionalized power structures of suburban governance in the region.

Greater Frankfurt's Political Economy of Suburbanization

Greater Frankfurt's integrated regional land-use planning system clearly targets the confinement of settlement growth and prioritizes inner-city development. While, undeniably, densification occurs in the region, the planning goals remain largely unmatched. Rather, population growth and the increase in settlement space have become significantly decoupled over the last sixty years – settlement development has outpaced population by a factor of 1.7 (Interview 1, 2014). Suburbanization fuels a temporally simultaneous but spatially selective densification and expansion of Greater Frankfurt's inherited urban patterns, favouring certain locations and putting others at a disadvantage. This selectivity leaves the region's suburbs socio-economically splintered and comes with uneven patterns in the regional allocation of costs and benefits of growth.

At odds with regional spatial planning objectives, and yet continually reproduced, regional forms of suburbanization and the underlying processes of the production of space call for further clarification. It is important to emphasize that the sociospatial constellation of the region is not so much a haphazard result of coincidences but the result of deliberate action by competing interests. Suburban governance in Greater Frankfurt can be explained by tracing back the interplay of state, capital, and private forms of governance acting on the region and – specific to the Frankfurt case – by exploring the crucial role of municipalities as mediators between these modalities of suburbanization (see Figure 5.6 for an overview of actors).

"Exponentiated" Fragmentation in the State

The reconstitution of Greater Frankfurt through the 2011 *Metropolgesetz* combines an integration of regional and land-use planning in Greater Frankfurt, which draws on traditional German spatial planning paradigms such as the "system of central places," with economic paradigms of the region as a breeding ground for global economic competitiveness.

Technically, the planning goal to confine settlement development to specific corridors is consistently substantiated by coherent spatial data, through regular meetings of municipal planners, and by a region-wide harmonization of planning procedures (Interview 1, 2014). Formal zoning thus makes a pivotal instrument for a coherent regulation of settlement development. Such regional land-use planning is encouraged by environmental discourses that criticize greenfield development, Germany's recently revised building code that prioritizes brownfield development, and policy initiatives to bundle diverse spatial functions to increase the regional economic productivity.

In practice, however, the power geometries that mediate suburban governance are far more dynamic than they appear on paper, and planning operations are messy and contested. Regional land-use planning

Scale \ Modality	State	Privatism		Capital	
State of Hesse	Government of the State of Hesse (authority over state spatial planning and formal regional planning)	Interstate Strategy Forum Frankfurt-RhineMain		Fraport AG	
Metropolitan	Metropolitan Region FrankfurtRhineMain (collaboration between municipalities, private actors, and state)	FrankfurtRhein-Main International Marketing of the Region	Business Initiative Frankfurt-RhineMain	Logistics and transport sector	Manufacturing and service sectors
Inter-municipal	Regional Authority FrankfurtRhineMain (authority over inter-municipal land-use planning)	Regionalpark GmbH	Rhine-Main Transport Associaton	Retailers	Real estate developers
Local	Municipalities (authority over local zoning plans and vote on inter-municipal land-use planning)	Inter-municipal special purpose associations (e.g., water, wastewater)	Chambers of commerce	Agriculture	Local utilities

Figure 5.6. Overview of actors of suburban governance in the Greater Frankfurt region. Sources: Based on qualitative interviews conducted by the authors.

involves complex political negotiations between municipalities and the region about what development is possible (Interview 1, 2014). This complexity resulted not least from the influence of various local political representatives who sought to maximize their political influence in the region when the latter was institutionalized in 2011. Local interests rooted in the German state's emphasis on municipal autonomy led to an "exponentiated fragmentation" (Interview 6, 2014) of the political region, causing intra-state limits on the regulation of suburbanization.

The inflated regional amount of designated building land is emblematic of this fragmentation within the state. In order to stay competitive in attracting investments, municipalities strive for flexible – and therefore ample – designated areas of building land. Crucially, municipalities succeeded in securing vast reserves of designated building land, which predated the creation of Greater Frankfurt's regional land-use plan, during regional negotiations about the plan. Once enacted, building land in Germany remains legal indefinitely if not repealed in a complex legal process. This law accounts for the ample amount of building land ready for development in the region today. Eventually, the Regional

Authority promotes an amount of building land that allows for "all possible development pathways" (Regionalverband, 2010, p. 43).

Simultaneously, the regulatory upscaling from the local to the regional scale has set free "centrifugal forces" (Interview 6, 2014) in local planning, where planning departments have been downsized. In combination with "a renaissance of informal planning instruments" (Interview 8, 2014) such as urban development concepts and public-private urban development contracts, this upscaling opened up new channels for political and stakeholder-based decision making to impinge on technical spatial planning.

Ultimately, the reorganization of Greater Frankfurt to promote "indispensable" regional cooperation (Hessische Staatsregierung, 2010, p. 1) and to foster economic competitiveness has been paralleled by the delegation of various public tasks to a variety of special-purpose organizations acting formally at arm's length of local and regional governments but promoting task-specific interests. Their influence on suburban governance is substantial but, not least due to their task-specific geographies that diverge from each other, little coordinated and difficult to govern. For instance, Hoyler et al. (2006) already list five different established business development and regional marketing initiatives in the region. In addition to that, the recently founded Interstate Strategy Forum FrankfurtRhineMain (*Länderübergreifendes Strategieforum FrankfurtRheinMain*), a public-private think tank with representatives from various state entities and business organizations, installed distinct task groups on Brexit and the streamlining of building permit processes to fuel the region's economic prosperity (Strategieforum FrankfurtRheinMain, 2018). Equally, the State of Hesse's research and development strategy, which established research hubs in different economic domains (houses of finance, logistics, and mobility, IT, pharma) materializes in Greater Frankfurt's urban periphery: the 2010-founded House of Mobility and Logistics is a key tenant in the "Gateway Gardens" business park at the airport (Hessisches Wirtschaftsministerium, 2016). In addition to these complexities that result from public-private cooperation, the Regional Authority operates within a highly complex institutional architecture of spatial planning with overlapping institutional and spatial jurisdiction. Planning goals need not only to be coordinated with the seventy-five member municipalities but also with the metropolitan region, the region of South Hesse, and the State of Hesse – all of which have specific visions and partially competing interests in regional development.

As a whole, this development conveys a picture of Greater Frankfurt that tends to reflect an "addition of municipalities" (Interview 6, 2014) rather than a coherent region. A comprehensive upscaling of regulatory capacities from the local to the regional level could only be achieved in part or, as an interviewed municipal planner states, it is "formally but not factually existent" (Interview 6, 2014).

Local Politics of Place: The Suburban Production of Space beyond the State

Allocating municipalities a monopoly over property and business taxes, and a share of income taxes, the German tax regime strongly incentivizes municipal governments to promote economic growth. This allocation comes at the expense of regional planning matters and materializes in policies that seek maximized local tax bases (Interview 12, 2014). Rather than imposed by an external abstract market power, these local policy rationales are thus rooted in the very organizational principles of the German state itself.

To attract private investors (*capital*) in order to increase local tax revenues, planning strategies of local politicians and planners adopt market-economy rationales. For instance, large amounts of designated building land are preserved to quickly react to business needs. Also, urban development contracts and the German building code's new land category "urban area," which allows for denser development, create room for municipalities to make land more productive. Profits are sought to be maximized both from greenfield development (denser construction) and from suburban retrofitting (maximizing use values through, for instance, investments in infrastructure or land-use diversification). The example of the Fraport AG shows how private businesses themselves engage in governing suburban spaces to optimize land use for their business models. Turned into a real estate business, the company paves the way for landscapes of logistics around the airport, where state regulations prohibit residential development (Interview 7, 2014). As Belina (2012, p. 87) insightfully puts it with regards to the German Stock Exchange's move from Frankfurt to Eschborn, by avoiding high business taxes in the centre, businesses take recourse to the "region as a cost-cutting measure in service of the shareholder value." Municipal interest in local development and their respective influencing of regional zoning caters to these spatial interests of capital.

Practices of *private governance* further mediate both capital's spatial needs on the peripheries and the interests of the local state within the political-economic architecture of suburbanization in Greater Frankfurt. First, collaborations between individuals in the local state or in local utility companies, private investors, and politicians who frequently uphold strong personal ties constitute the very "market forces" driving the suburban production of space in specific locations. Such personal ties thereby crisscross both territorial scales and boundaries between the state and beyond. Second, Greater Frankfurt's plethora of special-purpose organizations looms large in governing suburbanization. While some organizations like the regional greenbelt initiative and civil society groups against aircraft noise promote a stronger regionalization of land-use planning, business-oriented organizations lobby for mobilizing the region's polycentricity and municipal competition for a highly productive regional division of labour (see Hoyler et al., 2006).

In addition to the multiplied intra-state fragmentation that characterizes Greater Frankfurt's suburban governance regime, capital and private governance contribute to uphold the region's juxtaposition of ambitious land-use planning vis-à-vis continuous suburbanization and strong sociospatial polarization. Political-economic incentive structures that are "opposing" (Interview 6, 2014) regional planning goals thereby de facto place responsibility for regional cooperation in the hands of the politically autonomous municipalities, which impedes genuine regional thinking and planning practices, or even delegitimizes those practices. Negative externalities of local economic development are pinned on those local governments that have a weaker stance in regional negotiations or weaker locational conditions. Cities such as Offenbach bear the burden of regional externalities (such as high social expenditures) while providing cheap labour and affordable housing to keep the region productive. For other municipalities that take recourse to established networks of bilateral municipal and public-private cooperation to attract investment in premium business and living spaces at the peripheries, "regional collaboration allows for cherry-picking" (Interview 3, 2014).

On the whole, it is precisely this interlacing of functionally marginalized municipalities and the strong spatial division of labour that keeps Greater Frankfurt economically booming. Here, we can neither discern a form of suburbanization that is thoroughly market-driven nor one that bypasses state institutions. Rather, what at first sight appears as a contradiction between strong state regulation and suburban materialities that diverge from planning goals is actively mediated through the very interactions of the state with capital and private forms of suburban governance.

Conclusion

Not unlike many city-regions throughout the world (see other contributions in this volume), Greater Frankfurt is shaped by a strong and ongoing dynamic of various "urban" functions being redistributed on the peripheries, a simultaneity of old peripheral settlements becoming retrofitted beside continuous expansive suburbanization, and a juxtaposition of high economic productivity and striking sociospatial polarization.

Dating back more than twenty years, Sieverts's (1998) seminal work on the "in-between city" came as an insightful theorization of early forms of this regional urbanization in Greater Frankfurt. As we have shown, these dynamics persist; suburbanization even seems to gain pace in the wake of Germany's housing crises, the repercussions of Brexit, and global capital searching for investment opportunities in real estate since the financial crisis in 2007. The regional spatial planning system in Greater Frankfurt has not been unaffected since then, but has increasingly adopted market-based "smart growth" policies. Land-use planning became regionalized in 2011, with the region simultaneously gaining importance as a terrain for economic development policy. This duality illustrates contemporary contradictions of German metropolitan development and its regulation: suburbanization continues despite ambitious planning objectives to foster urban forms that are more compact, to confine development along designated growth corridors, and to prioritize brownfield development.

The institutional architecture of the German state itself – integrating a plethora of various (and possibly diverging) interests – and its relationship to capital and private forms of suburban governance explain this contradiction. Greater Frankfurt's current institutional form was not born in a political vacuum. It emerged from a nested landscape of long-standing local economic networks and identities, competing ideologies of governing, and strong (but selective) ties between politicians, businesses, private interest groups, and local elites. First, the state spatial planning regime that was created in this landscape is highly fragmented. An inflated regional amount of available building land that had been locally designated prior to the reconstitution of the region significantly thwarts the development-confining potentials of regional land-use planning. Second, effective regional land-use planning is complicated by the influence of a variety of special-purpose organizations, which shape suburbanization according to their constitutional interests rather than in a thematically or geographically coordinated manner. Finally, local politics of place that seek to maximize tax revenues within municipal territories remain the dominant rationale underlying peripheral settlement development, while undermining regionalized planning and the regional redistribution of the costs and benefits of growth.

The state thereby acts as a terrain of political struggle: on the one hand, an institutionalized system of smart growth and spatial cohesion policies is deeply entrenched and legally secured in the state; on the other hand, entrepreneurial investment policies together with the German municipal tax system trigger locational competition and decentralized growth. Both become enacted in practices of zoning, delineating growth corridors, and negotiating locations for retail, as well as in practices of lobbying the regional assembly with local interests, maintaining personal contacts across institutional boundaries, and channeling private funds into local development projects. Collectively, such locally specific responses to universal forces of global suburbanization perpetuate inherent contradictions of capitalist urbanization in Greater Frankfurt by smoothing them and shuffling them around; sociospatial polarization and high economic productivity thus can further coexist in the region.

However, in order to recalibrate the interplay of Frankfurt's modalities of suburbanization, it seems that a thorough institutional restructuring of planning is not necessary. It is rather the issue of renegotiating the political standing of coherent spatial planning and sustainability goals in relation to municipal growth policies and their legally entrenched incentive system in the German tax system, as well as regional development strategies, that is at stake. Responses to this imbalance could include a regional redistribution of local tax revenues from suburbanization within a functionally adequate geography that corresponds with geographies of regional planning; regionally elected, not locally dispatched, representatives in the regional council; a governance of regional service provision that is better aligned with state spatial planning or a better formal control of special-purpose organizations; a temporally limited effectivity of building land designations; and a legal strengthening of landscape planning to delineate suburbanization. Altogether, our findings thus suggest rethinking welfarist traditions in spatial governance so as to balance economic competitiveness with sustainable suburban land use and sociospatial cohesion more effectively.

NOTES

1 Subsequently, "Greater Frankfurt" or "Greater Frankfurt region."
2 Subsequently, "Regional Authority."
3 According to this principle, policy issues should be dealt with at the most immediate (or local) level that is consistent with their resolution.
4 The *Siedlungsbeschränkungsgebiete* restrict residential development within a delineated area of high aircraft noise emissions in the south of Frankfurt.

5 Quote from municipal planner from Bad Vilbel (Interview 9, 2018). The content of the box is based on this interview and an interview with another planner from Bad Vilbel (Interview 6, 2014).

REFERENCES

Amin, A. (2004). Regions unbound: Towards a new politics of place. *Geografiska Annaler: Series B, Human Geography, 86*(1), 33–44. https://doi.org/10.1111/j.0435-3684.2004.00152.x

BBSR (German Federal Institute for Research on Building, Urban Affairs and Spatial Development). (2021). *Stadtentwicklungsbericht der Bundesregierung 2020*. BBSR.

Belina, B. (2012). Wem gehört die Deutsche Börse? In AK Kritische Geographie Frankfurt (Ed.), *Wem gehört die Stadt? Dokumentation des aktionistischen Kongresses vom März 2012* (pp. 86–93). Forum Humangeographie 9.

Blotevogel, H., Danielzyk, R., & Münter, A. (2014). Spatial planning in Germany: Institutional inertia and new challenges. In M. Reimer, P. Getimis, & H. Blotevogel (Eds.), *Spatial planning systems and practices in Europe: A comparative perspective on continuity and changes* (pp. 83–107). Routledge.

Brake, K. (2001). Neue Akzente der Suburbanisierung: Suburbaner Raum und Kernstadt: Eigene Profile und neuer Verbund. In K. Brake (Ed.), *Suburbanisierung in Deutschland: Aktuelle tendenzen* (pp. 15–26). Leske + Budrich.

Brake, K., & Herfert, G. (2012). Reurbanisierung: Diskurs, Materialität und offene Fragen. In K. Brake & G. Herfert (Eds.), *Reurbanisierung: Materialität und Diskurs in Deutschland* (pp. 408–20). Springer.

Burdack, J., & Hesse, M. 2007. Suburbanisation, suburbia and "Zwischenstadt": Perspectives of research and policy. In D. Scholich (Ed.), *Territorial cohesion* (pp. 81–100). Springer.

City of Kelsterbach. (2015). *Gewerbegebiet Mönchhof*. http://www.moenchhof-info.de.

Ekers, M., Hamel, P., & Keil, R. (2012). Governing suburbia: Modalities and mechanisms of suburban governance. *Regional Studies, 46*(3), 405–22. https://doi.org/10.1080/00343404.2012.658036

Filion, P., Kramer, A., & Sands, G. (2016). Recentralization as an alternative to urban dispersion: Transformative planning in a neoliberal societal context. *International Journal of Urban and Regional Research, 40*(3), 658–78. https://doi.org/10.1111/1468-2427.12374

Frank, S. (2018). Inner-city suburbanization – No contradiction in terms: Middle-class family enclaves are spreading in the cities. *Raumforschung und Raumordnung/Spatial Research and Planning, 76*(2), 123–32. https://doi.org/10.1007/s13147-016-0444-1

Franz, P. (2000). Suburbanization and the clash of urban regimes: Developmental problems of East German cities in a free market environment. *European Urban and Regional Studies*, 7(2), 135–46. https://doi.org/10.1177/096977640000700203

Fürst, D. (2001). Regional governance: A new paradigm in the regional sciences? *Raumforschung und Raumordnung/Spatial Research and Planning*, 59(5–6), 370–80. https://doi.org/10.1007/BF03183038

Hamel, P., & Keil, R. (2015). *Suburban governance: A global view.* University of Toronto Press.

Heinelt, H., & Zimmermann, K. (2011). "How can we explain diversity in metropolitan governance within a country?" Some reflections on recent developments in Germany. *International Journal of Urban and Regional Research*, 35(6), 1175–92. https://doi.org/10.1111/j.1468-2427.2010.00989.x

Hesse, M., & Siedentop, S. (2018). Suburbanisation and suburbanisms: Making sense of continental European developments. *Raumforschung und Raumordnung/Spatial Research and Planning*, 76(2), 97–108. https://doi.org/10.1007/s13147-018-0526-3

Hessische Staatsregierung. (2000). Gesetzenentwurf: Gesetz zur Stärkung der kommunalen Zusammenarbeit und Planung in der Region Rhein-Main. Hessischer Landtag, Drucksache 15/1491, Wiesbaden.

Hessische Staatsregierung. (2010). Gesetzesentwurf: Gesetz über die Metropolergion Frankfurt/Rhein-Main. Hessischer Landtag, Drucksache 18/2733, Wiesbaden.

Hessisches Wirtschaftsministerium (Hessisches Ministerium für Wirtschaft, Energie, Verkehr und Landesentwicklung). (2016). *Innovation durch Interaktion.* Hessens Houses of'. Wiesbaden.

Hirsch, J. (1995). *Der nationale Wettbewerbsstaat: Staat, Demokratie und Politik im globalen Kapitalismus.* Edition ID-Archiv.

Hoyler, M., Freytag, T., & Mager, C. (2006). Advantageous fragmentation? Reimagining metropolitan governance and spatial planning in Rhine-Main. *Built Environment*, 32(2), 124–36. https://doi.org/10.2148/benv.32.2.124

Jansen, H., Wünnemann, M., & Roost, F. (2017). Post-suburban revitalization? Redevelopment of suburban business centres in the Frankfurt/Rhine-Main region. *Journal of Urban Design*, 22(2), 249–72. https://doi.org/10.1080/13574809.2016.1261627

Jehling, M., Hecht, R., & Herold, H. (2018). Assessing urban containment policies within a suburban context: An approach to enable a regional perspective. *Land Use Policy*, 77, 846–58. https://doi.org/10.1016/j.landusepol.2016.10.031

Keating, M. (1998). *The new regionalism in Western Europe: Territorial restructuring and political change.* Elgar.

Keil, R. (2017). *Suburban planet: Making the world urban from the outside in.* Polity.

Keil, R., & Ronneberger, K. (1994). Going up the country: Internationalization and urbanization on Frankfurt's northern fringe. *Environment and Planning D: Society and Space*, 12(2), 137–66. https://doi.org/10.1068/d120137

Knieling, J., & Blatter, J. (2009). Metropolitan Governance: Institutionelle Strategien, Dilemmas und Variationsmöglichkeiten für die Steuerung in Metropolregionen. In J. Knieling (Ed.), *Metropolregionen: Innovation, Wettbewerb, Handlungsfähigkeit* (pp. 223–69). Verlag der ARL.

Knippenberger, U. (2012). *Regionale Governance des Funktionswandels von Flughäfen: Eine Analyse am Beispiel der "Airport City" Frankfurt am Main.* Springer.

Krueger, R., & Gibbs, D. (2008). "Third Wave" sustainability? Smart growth and regional development in the USA. *Regional Studies*, 42(9), 1263–74. https://doi.org/10.1080/00343400801968403

Lang, R., & Knox, P.K. (2009). The new metropolis: Rethinking megalopolis. *Regional Studies*, 43(6), 789–802. https://doi.org/10.1080/00343400701654251

Macdonald, S., Monstadt, J., & Friendly, A. (2021). Rethinking the governance and planning of a new generation of greenbelts. *Regional Studies*, 55(5), 804–17. https://doi.org/10.1080/00343404.2020.1747608

Mettke, C. (2015). *Der öffentliche Personennahverkehr im post-suburbanen Kontex – Toronto und Frankfurt als Fallbeispiele* [Doctoral dissertation, Technical University Darmstadt]. TUprints. https://tuprints.ulb.tu-darmstadt.de /id/eprint/4246

Molotch, H. (1976). The city as a growth machine: Toward a political economy of place. *American Journal of Sociology*, 82(2), 309–32. https://doi .org/10.1086/226311

Monstadt, J., Schmidt, M., & Wilts, H. (2012). Regionale Zusammenarbeit in der Ver- und entsorgung des Rhein-Main-Gebiets. In J. Monstadt, K. Zimmermann, T. Robischon, & B. Schönig (Eds.), *Die diskutierte Region: Probleme und Planungsansätze der Metropolregion Rhein-Main* (pp. 185–210). Campus-Verlag.

Müller, W., & Rohr-Zänker, R. (2001). Amerikanisierung der "Peripherie" in Deutschland? In K. Brake, J.S. Dangschat, & G. Herfert (Eds.), *Suburbanisierung in Deutschland: Aktuelle Tendenzen* (pp. 27–39). Leske + Budrich.

Nuissl, H., & Rink, D. (2005). The "production" of urban sprawl in eastern Germany as a phenomenon of post-socialist transformation. *Cities*, 22(2), 123–34. https://doi.org/10.1016/j.cities.2005.01.002

Phelps, N.A., & Wood, A.M. (2011). The new post-suburban politics? *Urban Studies*, 48(12), 2591–2610. https://doi.org/10.1177/0042098011411944

Regionalverband (Regional Authority FrankfurtRhineMain). (2010). *Regionalplan Südhessen / Regionaler Flächennutzungsplan, Allgemeiner Textteil.* Darmstadt.

Regionalverband (Regional Authority FrankfurtRhineMain). (2019). *Regionales Monitoring 2019: Daten und Fakten – Metropolregion FrankfurtRheinMain.* Frankfurt.

Rhodes, R.A.W. (1996). The new governance: Governing without government. *Political Studies, 44*(4), 652–67. https://doi.org/10.1111/j.1467-9248.1996 .tb01747.x

Robinson, J. (2014). New geographies of theorizing the urban: Putting comparison to work for global urban studies. In S. Parnell & S. Oldfield (Eds.), *Handbook for cities of the global south* (pp. 57–70). Sage.

Sassen, S. (1997). *Die Metropolen des Weltmarkts: Die neue Rolle der Global Cities.* Campus Verlag.

Schmidt, S., Siedentop, S., & Fina, S. (2018). How effective are regions in determining urban spatial patterns? Evidence from Germany. *Journal of Urban Affairs, 40*(5), 639–56. https://doi.org/10.1080/07352166.2017.1360741

Schmidt-Eichstaedt, G., Steinebach, G., and Vallée, D. (2011). Umsetzung der Raumplanung. In Akademie für Raumforschung und Landesplanung (Eds.), *Grundriss der Raumordnung und Raumentwicklung* (pp. 567–635). Hannover.

Sieverts, T. (1998). *Zwischenstadt: Zwischen Ort und Welt, Raum und Zeit, Stadt und Land.* Vieweg.

Strategieforum FrankfurtRheinMain. (2018). *Zielsetzung: Leitlinien und Visionen.* https://strategieforum-frankfurtrheinmain.de/strategieforum -frankurtrheinmain/leitlinien-und-visionen

Swyngedouw, E. (2005). Governance innovation and the citizen: The Janus face of governance-beyond-the-state. *Urban Studies, 42*(11), 1991–2006. https://doi.org/10.1080/00420980500279869

Swyngedouw, E. (2009). The antinomies of the postpolitical city: In search of a democratic politics of environmental production. *International Journal of Urban and Regional Research, 33*(3), 601–20. https://doi.org /10.1111/j.1468-2427.2009.00859.x

Zimmermann, K. (2012). Regionalreformen im Vergleich: München, Rhein-Neckar, Rhein-Main, Stuttgart und Hannover. In J. Monstadt, K. Zimmermann, T. Robischon, & B. Schönig (Eds.), *Die diskutierte Region: Probleme und Planungsansätze der Metropolregion Rhein-Main* (pp. 315–34). Campus-Verlag.

Zimmermann, K., & Heinelt, H. (2012). *Metropolitan Governance in Deutschland: Regierung in Ballungsräumen und neue Formen politischer Steuerung.* Springer VS.

INTERVIEWS

1 Municipal Planning Official. (2014). Urban Planning Department, Kronberg, 23 July 2014.

2 Municipal Planning Official. (2014). Urban Planning Department, Offenbach, 15 July 2014.
3 Municipal Planning Official. (2014). Urban Planning Department, Bad Vilbel, 15 July 2014.
4 Municipal Planning Official. (2014). Urban Planning Department, Dreieich, 3 September 2014.
5 Municipal Planning Official. (2014). Urban Planning Department, Eschborn, 28 July 2014.
6 Municipal Planning Official. (2014). Urban Planning Department, Frankfurt, 29 July 2014.
7 Municipal Planning Official. (2014). Urban Planning Department, Kelsterbach, 29 July 2014.
8 Municipal Planning Official. (2014). Urban Planning Department, Hanau, 23 July 2014.
9 Municipal Planning Official. (2018). Urban Planning Department, Bad Vilbel, 19 June 2018.
10 Regional Planning Official. (2014). Regional Authority FrankfurtRhine-Main, 3 September 2014.
11 Regional Planning Official. (2014). Regional Planning Authority of the State of Hesse, 29 July 2014.
12 Regional Planning Expert. (2014). Hesse Municipal District Assembly, 22 July 2014.

6 How Big Is Grand Paris? Paris, Its Suburbs, and Its Periurbs

MARIE-HÉLÈNE BACQUÉ AND ÉRIC CHARMES

Introduction

In this chapter, we will address two issues. The first is the relationship between the capital city of Paris and its suburbs. Several particular aspects of this relationship will be examined: the persistence of relations of inequality, and even of domination, between Paris and its popular suburbs; the determining role of large housing estates in the representation of the suburbs; and the tensions that accompany the emergence of an intercommunal government uniting Paris and its suburbs.

The second issue concerns the area beyond Grand Paris (Greater Paris) and the place of the periurbs within it. On 1 January 2016, the French government created the Grand Paris Metropolitan Authority (*Métropole du Grand Paris*) – a new institutional entity that brings together the *commune* of Paris, its adjoining departments (*départements*)[1] of the inner ring, and seven *communes* belonging to departments of the outer ring (Figure 6.1). Not all suburbs were integrated into this new entity. Because the institutional choice was to bring together Paris and the departments of the inner ring, periurban territories – which were long considered minor but have been gaining major social and political importance in recent years – have remained outside the perimeter of the Grand Paris Metropolitan Authority (hereafter Grand Paris). Over the last decades, as suburbs have urbanized and turned into in-between cities and post-suburbs (Keil et al., 2017; Phelps & Wood, 2011; Sieverts, 2003), the periurbs developed in a way that takes them back to the original ideal of garden cities, as formulated by Ebenezer Howard. In these territories, the central state has very little presence, apart from largely incantatory summons (at least until recently[2]) to combat urban sprawl. On the institutional level, the periurbs constitute a space of extreme fragmentation, which raises new questions for the governance of Grand Paris and its surroundings.

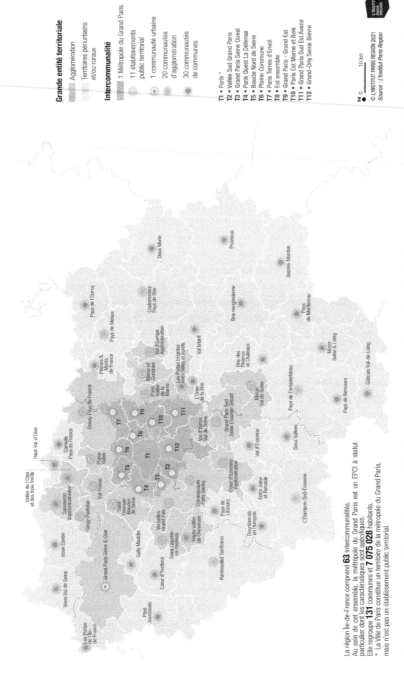

Figure 6.1. Map of Grand Paris and the intercommunal bodies of the Ile-de-France region as of 2021. Grand Paris and its territorial subdivisions (see Box 6.1) appear in dark grey. The intercommunal bodies (see Table 6.2) of the continuous built-up area are in medium grey, and the intercommunal bodies of the periurban area are in light grey (each dot corresponds to one intercommunal body or one subdivision of Grand Paris). Source: Institut Paris Region.

This chapter puts these two issues into perspective in the light of three key ideas. First, the construction and functioning of governance in the suburban territories around Paris city can only be understood with regard to the latter's specific urban and political history. Indeed, population patterns and territorial representations are highly persistent (Sampson, 2012) and largely determine the way in which each of the territories is governed. Hence the large place given here to the history of those territories.

The second key idea is that suburbs around Paris, as elsewhere, are highly diverse, and depending on the context, different types of government and modes of governance are formed within them. Table 6.1 gives an overview of these differences and shows them to be so important that we can wonder about the existence of a mode of governance that would be specific to the Paris metropolitan region. From this perspective, two questions arise: To what extent can this region be considered as a unique case whose specificities might be compared with those of other urban regions? Should we not, on the contrary, construe it as a pool of cases allowing us to study different configurations? It is in this spirit that we wrote the present chapter, which offers not so much an overall picture of the government and governance of the Paris suburbs but snapshots of specific spaces, while also leaving aside territories such as new towns. Although the latter do play an important role, they are already fairly well known in the French and English literature (Berroir et al., 2004; Savitch, 2014).

These choices were guided by a third key idea: France is not only a very centralized country; it is also a highly decentralized country with regard to urban issues. The latter dimension of France's political organization is often ignored to the benefit of the first, especially in the international literature where the image of a hyper-centralized central state in charge of urban development and governance predominates. Yet, since the start of decentralization in 1982, the powers of *communes* and their municipal councils have been decisive (see Table 6.2 for details on these powers). This power shift is why the present chapter gives them special attention to the detriment of an important but better-known actor: the central state.

Paris against Its Suburbs?

A Persisting Physical and Political Boundary

Relations between Paris and its suburbs are marked by a significant urban and political history. The Paris metropolitan area has developed

Table 6.1. Overview of Governance Regimes in the Paris Suburbs and Periurbs

Type of Suburb	Type of Population	Dominant Urban Model	Main Actors (Number of Inhabitants)	Dominant Morphological Changes
Inner- and Middle-Ring Suburbs				
Communes (the further the commune from the core city, the smaller the changes)	Upper classes	Exclusionary zoning; occasional local redevelopment projects	Municipality (10,000–100,000)	Stability with sporadic local changes
	Diverse, with a predominance of middle classes	Redevelopment projects of various sizes	Municipality (10,000–100,000); Grand Paris (from 2016); developers	Densification; brownfield redevelopment; new offices; sporadic changes
	Diverse, with a predominance of lower and lower middle classes	Redevelopment through gentrification (including new-build gentrification)	Municipality (10,000–100,000); Grand Paris; developers	Densification; brownfield redevelopment; new commercial infrastructure; new offices
	Poor, with an important immigrant population	Urban renewal through partial demolition and reconstruction	Municipality (10,000); Grand Paris; central state agency (ANRU); large developers	Transition from modernist to neo-traditional architecture
Major Suburban and Periurban Centres				
New towns (5 around Paris, located at a distance of 40–50 km)	Diverse, with no upper or upper middle classes	Extensive growth from the 1960s; redevelopment from the 1990s	Central state; several municipalities (100,000 or more); large developers	Extensive growth slowing down or ending; renewal in some neighbourhoods
Old urban centres	Diverse, with no upper or upper middle classes	Preserving the influence of old centres over their surroundings	Municipality (10,000 or more); Grand Paris (for those concerned); developers	Renewal in some neighbourhoods; extension of urbanized area through subdivision; business parks; shopping strips

(Continued)

Type of Suburb	Type of Population	Dominant Urban Model	Main Actors (Number of Inhabitants)	Dominant Morphological Changes
Periurbs				
Residential *communes* (first periurban ring)	Middle to upper middle classes, with significant homogeneity at the municipal level	Absence of growth; exclusionary zoning; "clubbisation"	Municipality (typically 1,500)	Stability with occasional redevelopment of old village cores
Towns (about 15% of periurban *communes*)	Diverse middle classes	Extensive growth until the 2010s and/or redevelopment of town centres (the closer to the core city, the lesser the growth and the greater the redevelopment)	Municipality (typically between 3,000 and 10,000); developers	Subdivision; new business parks; new suburban shopping strips; densification of town centres
Rural *communes* in transition	Lower middle classes; rural poor	Extensive growth until the 2010s (relative to size)	Municipality (1,000 or less); small developers and builders	Houses built by individual landowners; small subdivision

Source: Adapted from Charmes & Keil (2015).

around a social tension between the city centre and suburbs, on the one hand, and between east and west, on the other. In the nineteenth century, a few "beautiful suburbs" (*belles banlieues*) were formed around Paris. They appeared mainly in the west, though there were some notable exceptions such as Le Raincy. Yet, the development of bourgeois residential suburbs was much more limited in continental Europe, and especially in France, than it was in the United States and Great Britain. Instead, the suburbs became increasingly dominated by the industrial working class. This occurred mainly because the threat of land invasion was significantly greater in continental Europe than it was in the United States and Great Britain. The idea that the bourgeoisie and the aristocracy might live beyond the city walls was easier to imagine in American and British cities than in Paris (Bacqué et al., 2015). At the time when bourgeois suburbs were beginning to develop around London, Paris had just surrounded itself with new walls: the Thiers fortifications built in the 1840s. These walls were demolished only in the aftermath of the First World War.

In that context, Baron Rambuteau and then, on a totally different scale, Baron Haussmann created a space for the bourgeoisie in the heart of Paris. The large Haussmannian developments of the 1852–70 period were carried out mainly in the west end of the city, toward the villages of Passy and Auteuil where the bourgeoisie used to live. These operations corresponded to an urban model (wide boulevards, tall buildings made of carved stone) and a lifestyle (fashionable dress, use of public facilities and spaces, gardens, opera, and the like) that involved the well-to-do and eventually spread to the rest of society.

This "city of light" project was accompanied by the displacement of polluting activities, cemeteries, and waste dumps to the inner suburban ring, which also became home to the "dangerous classes" (Chevalier, 1958/1984), that is, the emerging working class. In the early 1910s, more than 1.5 million inhabitants of the Paris urban area lived outside the city limits. Housing developments were then composed of rental properties constructed by merchants and private homes built on land with no facilities (Fourcaut, 2000). In the 1920s, the term "red suburbs" was coined to express different realities. First, it described an urban social reality. Suburban *communes*, especially in the northeast (what is now the department of Seine-Saint-Denis, commonly known by its number: 93), saw the arrival of working-class households and became a centre of industrial activity. Second, the term referred to a political reality. A large number of suburban working-class municipalities were dominated by the Communist Party. While the expression "red suburbs" did, in a sense, erase the area's diversity, in particular the very real existence of "chic" suburbs, the picture it offered was fairly accurate overall: a rather bourgeois and conservative city centre (even though it includes many working-class neighbourhoods) surrounded (and even threatened) by working-class suburbs entrenched on the political left. Indeed, in these suburbs, the Communist Party had built a social structure with a specific social, political, and territorial identity that lasted until the end of the 1960s before being progressively dismantled (Bacqué & Fol, 1997; Bacqué & Sintomer, 2001).

In the Paris metropolitan area, as in other large cities, transportation infrastructures play an important role. More specifically, the limits of the city of Paris are marked by a very wide, partly buried highway known as the *Boulevard Périphérique*. Built between 1960 and 1973 on land freed by the demolition of the Thiers fortifications, the *Périphérique* symbolically and physically reinforces the barrier between Paris and its suburbs. This division can also be observed in the public transportation system. While the city of Paris is connected by a dense *métro* network, the transportation system serving suburban commuters is of lesser quality. Even though several *métro* lines have recently been extended into the suburbs, they serve only a few *communes*, all of which are located very close to Paris. Beyond these *communes*, public transport involves buses and the suburban mass transit network known as the *Réseau Express Régional* (RER). This network, laid out under the *Schéma directeur d'aménagement et d'urbanisme* (SDAU) regional plan of 1965, primarily connects Paris and the new towns, which were starting to be built at the time. The lack of suburb-to-suburb connections (a problem that the Grand Paris Express project aims to alleviate, see below) has helped maintain the prominence of the city centre. Although the RER offers rapid access to the capital, it remains symbolically associated with the Paris suburbs, and the most gentrified suburban *communes* today are those that have access to the city centre via the *métro* (Vermeersch, 2011).

Thus, a division has arisen between Paris and its suburbs along several dimensions (Fourcaut et al., 2007). This division is at once political (the city of Paris constitutes a distinct *commune* governed by a municipality – the most powerful in France today – vis-à-vis highly fragmented suburban municipalities), social (the highest income earners are concentrated in the city of Paris), economic (corporate headquarters and subsequent revenues are also concentrated in the city), and morphological (the barrier formed by the *Boulevard Périphérique*).

A Negative Image of the Suburbs

The suburbs are often saddled with a negative image – that of "distressed neighbourhoods," of concrete housing and inhuman urbanism, most often symbolized by large housing estates (*grands ensembles*). Yet, the latter form only part of suburban territories. In fact, they form only part of the popular suburbs. And, if they account for a significant portion of the degraded neighbourhoods, there are also poor old urban centres.

In the beginning, these large housing estates were the very incarnation of modernity, and especially comfort, with well-lit dwellings surrounded by green spaces and equipped with running water, toilets, and bathrooms – all of which were rare in working-class areas in the aftermath of the Second World War. They were populated by young households who saw their standards of living rise during the period of prosperity known as the "Thirty Glorious Years," namely, the three decades that preceded the oil shock of 1973.

The image associated with large housing estates is completely different today. Indeed, they have come to represent social failure. They symbolize the concentration of poor populations in areas that some do not hesitate to refer to as ghettos. Large housing estates are confronted with different kinds of problems. Some of them remain very isolated from the city and are difficult to access by public transportation (though it must be noted that many are now integrated into the urban fabric). These social housing estates are also plagued by physical obsolescence, which can be traced to cheap and often overly rapid construction and, above all, to an obvious lack of maintenance. But the main issue is their impoverishment – though this process is far from homogeneous.

The first large housing estates attracted a diverse population in a context of housing crisis. However, the middle classes were only passers-by, and as early as the 1970s, they began leaving social housing for detached houses. These trajectories were favoured by a central state policy promoting homeownership introduced in the late 1960s under the influence of the free-market approach. In addition, the middle classes sought to distance themselves from the image of the housing estates, which was shifting dramatically at the time, as well as from the social cohabitation implied by life in neighbourhoods whose residents were becoming poorer.

While immigrants of the period, especially North Africans, were kept away from social housing and in particular from large housing estates, in the early 1970s they began to be relocated in the latter as a result of policies for the renovation of unsafe housing and the demolition of slums. Moreover, with the 1976 introduction of the so-called policy of "family reunification," migrations that had involved only single individuals – usually men – became family migrations.

Lastly, the two oil shocks of 1973 and 1977 opened a period of intense and lasting economic crisis. From the late 1970s onward, unemployment increased, affecting in particular the least-qualified groups and immigrants (whose origins diversified, notably with the arrival of sub-Saharan immigrants). The logics of precarity and disaffiliation took hold, leading to the disintegration and weakening of the working class (Beaud & Pialoux, 1999; Castel 1995).

Due to these various phenomena, the social composition of the large housing estates changed rapidly, with a significant expansion of the least-qualified groups, a marked increase in social problems, and a rising proportion of immigrants. Thus, just as they were gaining access to the large housing estates, working-class and immigrant households were also growing more precarious. Their children experienced increasing difficulties in entering the labour market and, more broadly, in achieving social mobility in a post-colonial context where racial discrimination remains strong. In the early 1980s, social tensions became acute, and social revolts broke out in several cities, most often after acts of police violence or blunders. The popular suburbs were then described as "distressed neighbourhoods," as "neighbourhoods of exclusion," and became the focus of a specific policy of social and urban development (*politique de la ville*). But this policy, which was formulated by the central state yet implemented locally, was not equipped to combat inequalities. The social revolts of 2005 and 2023 that set alight the popular suburbs of France are evidence of this failure.

This historical perspective helps to relativize the discourse whereby large housing estates are pathogenic urban forms by showing the weight of social dynamics in their evolution. It also helps to understand how sociospatial segregation structures the Parisian territory and its inner ring of suburbs. This segregation has rather intensified in the last two decades. Inequalities between territories have continued to increase under the double effect of the enrichment of the wealthiest neighbourhoods and the impoverishment of the poorest ones. This trend should not be overstated, however: socially and ethnically mixed neighbourhoods are still dominant, challenging the idea of a dual metropolis (Préteceille, 2012). The working-class neighbourhoods are themselves very diverse from ethno-racial point of view.

From Fragmented Local Powers to the Creation of Grand Paris

While central state policies have played a major role in the development of the Paris metropolitan area, they were not alone in this regard. As shown in Table 6.2, the French politico-administrative system is structured by several local levels of government – municipalities, departments, Ile-de-France region – whose prerogatives were redefined by the laws of decentralization passed in 1982 in the wake of François Mitterrand's accession to power. (The city of Paris also enjoys a specific status, since it is at once a municipality and a department.) Intercommunal bodies were added to these entities, notably since the late 1990s. As shown in Table 6.2, these local entities' prerogatives are significant. Thus, *communes* and intercommunal bodies are responsible for housing and urban planning policies, and it is they who decide, for instance, on the construction of social housing on their territory, even as the central state tries to impose a minimum percentage (set at 20 per cent in 2000 and raised to 25 per cent in 2012).

Table 6.2. Administrative Units of the Ile-de-France Region as of 2017

Administrative and Territorial Units	Government Bodies	Main Attributions	Number of Units
Ile-de-France region	Regional council, headed by an elected president	Regional planning, transportation, economic development, senior high schools (*lycées*; 14–17 years)	1 (12.2 million inhabitants)
Departments	Departmental council, composed of *canton* representatives	Social assistance, junior high schools (*collèges*; 10–14 years)	8 (including Paris)
Grand Paris	Metropolitan council, composed of the representatives of 131 *communes* (from Paris and its suburbs)	Urban planning and housing (by delegation from the *communes*)	1 (7.1 million inhabitants)
Intercommunal bodies (groups of *communes*) outside Grand Paris	Intercommunal council, composed of *commune* representatives (17 on average)	Urban planning and housing (by delegation from the *communes*)	62 (5.1 million inhabitants)
Communes (including the city of Paris)	Municipal council, headed by an elected mayor	Land use, zoning codes, housing policy, business parks, primary schools (3–10 years)	1,268

Sources: Adapted from INSEE; Institute Paris Region.

This administrative complexity is intertwined with political and social issues at the national, regional, and local levels, which make the urban region difficult to govern. Conflicts between local authorities and the central state are also political conflicts. For instance, the Ile-de-France region was governed by a socialist majority from 1998 to 2015, and under the presidency of Nicolas Sarkozy (of the right-wing *Rassemblement pour la République* [RPR] Party), the central state never approved the Ile-de-France Regional Master Plan (*Schéma directeur de la région Île-de-France*, SDRIF) voted by the regional council in 2007. Political tensions are intensified by resource inequalities. Local authorities have access to very uneven fiscal resources because they rely heavily on taxes levied on households, landowners, and businesses.

In this institutional landscape, some divisions are particularly striking. In addition to the division indicated above between Paris and its suburbs, there is a division internal to the suburbs that plays out at the departmental scale. On one side of this division are the Hauts-de-Seine, where bourgeois families and headquarters of the largest corporations are concentrated (notably in the first business district of Paris: La Défense), and on the other side, Seine-Saint-Denis, which has suffered major deindustrialization and is home to some of the poorest populations in France.

It is in this context that the Grand Paris project was formalized, under the impulsion of different actors and according to divergent logics (Gilli & Offner, 2009; Subra, 2012; Veltz, 2012). For the Paris municipality, the aim was to address problems it could not solve on its own, particularly in the field of transport and housing. Despite being home to 2.2 million inhabitants, the city of Paris is not an island. In view of this situation, under the impulsion of Paris's socialist mayor Bertrand Delanoë and with the notable support of Pierre Mansat (a communist elected representative of Paris), a space of cooperation between the city of Paris and its suburbs took shape in the 2000s. This cooperation has taken a flexible form based on mutual agreement.

But, as has often been the case in the history of Paris, the central state got involved and arbitrarily set up Grand Paris: a new intercommunal body that includes the city of Paris, the 123 *communes* of the inner-ring departments (including the Hauts-de-Seine and Seine-Saint-Denis), and a few adjoining *communes*. The central state's involvement has been the subject of criticism, and a number of *communes* have been challenging an approach they view as authoritarian (see Box 6.1). One should regard such involvement as a political manoeuvre in the face of a region and a capital city governed by the left, but also as the desire of the then president of the Republic, Nicolas Sarkozy, to leave his mark on the urban design of the capital region.

The French government was then not only concerned by Paris internal political balances but also by its international status. Grand Paris has a population approaching that of Greater London. This size is not a coincidence. Paris is widely considered as a global city that must secure its rank in the global competition. Yet, its main competitor, London, is governed at the large scale of Greater London, which is home to more than 8 million inhabitants. Moreover, the Grand Paris project is not limited to politico-administrative reform. It includes a strong urban planning component, with the construction of the *Grand Paris Express*, a *métro* double loop that will serve the suburbs, and the creation of peripheral centralities around the newly created *métro* stations. The first *métro* lines should open to the public in 2024.

Box 6.1. The Grand Paris Metropolitan Authority Challenged by Its Popular Suburbs

Grand Paris, as an institutional form and with its urban project organized around a *métro* network, does not enjoy unanimous support among the elected representatives of the popular suburbs. Two personalities have been leading the opposition to the centralized method that has governed the creation of Grand Paris: Patrick Braouezec, former mayor of Saint-Denis (an emblematic city of the former red suburbs) and Front de Gauche (left-wing) president of the Plaine Commune intercommunal body (one of the territories of Seine-Saint-Denis that was severely hit by deindustrialization and economic recomposition); and Patrick Jarry, Communist mayor of Nanterre, a former working-class and industrial city located on the edge of the business district of La Défense. In addition to denouncing a political manoeuvre aimed at regaining control of the last communist bastions of the former red suburbs, the two men have countered this centralized method with "bottom-up governance." The latter approach has been promoted by *Paris Métropole*, a sort of union of local elected representatives created in June 2009 in the wake of the metropolitan conference initiated by the Paris City Hall. *Paris Métropole* relies on a cooperative approach, based on voluntary participation, between more than 100 Ile-de-France governments of different levels (*communes*, intercommunal bodies, departments). This forum for debates, propositions, and lobbying – in which each *commune* has one vote regardless of its size – was renamed *Forum métropolitain du grand Paris* in order to distinguish it from the Grand Paris Metropolitan Authority (*Métropole du Grand Paris*). One of the main criticisms expressed by local elected representatives is that the Grand Paris Metropolitan Authority is undermining existing intercommunal bodies and is thus initiating a movement of recentralization. The latter is accused of breaking territorial dynamics that were built from groups of *communes* with great difficulty. It is true, critics say, that the Grand Paris Metropolitan Authority has been subdivided into twelve territories, with competences in the fields of urban planning, economic development, and housing. But the newly created territorial entities will not have the independence of the former intercommunal bodies because they will not enjoy financial autonomy or have access to state grants as those bodies did. The question of the redistribution of fiscal resources also remains unanswered. Lastly, this process of centralization presents a democratic risk because it creates a distance between citizens and the sites of decision making.

The critique also concerns the substance of the metropolitan project, along with social and urban issues. Thus, Patrick Braouezec asks: "What do we want to do with it? An attractive city making us the best student of the capitalist class, or a city able to offer an alternative to the dominant model by reducing social and territorial inequalities?" (Braouezec, 2011). Braouezec seeks to promote a polycentric development that will rebalance relations between centre and peripheries – in the modalities of urban development as much as in institutional power relations. As he sees it, monocentric development merely contributes to the rise in inequalities – for instance, by creating the risk that processes of gentrification will spread to the suburbs under the effect of a "Grand Paris" address. Thus, a mission officer working with the mayor of Saint-Denis argues:

> The question is less to define peripheries than to render them visible, to give them a voice, to offer them the possibility of setting the metropolitan agenda – and this, not to defend any "status quo," but to invent solidarity, social inclusion, democracy, and the "right to the city" in the metropolitan fact in order to move beyond the "centre/periphery" divide. Moving beyond this divide calls for imagining a new model of governance that combines coordination and decentralization, while respecting the capacity to act of the territories that make up metropolitan areas. (Interview, 10 July 2015)

At the time of writing, it is difficult to predict what will happen to the historical divide between Paris and its periphery, and how far Grand Paris will contribute to reducing it. In any event, changes will be very slow. To begin, experiences of intercommunal cooperation in other French cities have shown that, even after long decades of progressive integration, mayors remain largely in control (Desage & Guéranger, 2011). Indeed, a few years after its creation, Grand Paris is still struggling to assert its authority (Chauvel, 2021; Subra & Serisier, 2012). The political landscape of the Paris metropolitan region has evolved since the birth act of Grand Paris, especially with the Ile-de-France region being conquered by the right in 2015. Yet tensions remain significant between the state and the various local authorities involved.

Moreover, Grand Paris is not going to erase the differences between the hyper-gentrified neighbourhoods of Paris and the impoverished housing estates all at once; the sociospatial specialization of Grand Paris is very likely to persist (Vermeersch et al., 2019). One of the issues at stake in the creation of Grand Paris is thus the affirmation of a solidarity between Paris and its popular suburbs – a solidarity that has so far been sorely lacking. Some suburban municipalities see in Grand Paris an issue of spatial justice, as well as the potential for a redistribution of resources and a rebalancing of power relations between Paris and its suburbs. However, as shown in Box 6.1, redistribution has for the moment been ineffective. Equalization of resources remains a major stumbling block in the negotiations.

Another issue is the establishment of a more democratic government in which suburban residents would have a say in what is happening in the centre. A number of policies, in particular in the field of housing, could be discussed on a scale broader and more consistent with current social and economic dynamics. But this reform would imply working toward democratic forms that involve citizens and civil society organizations at a time when the metropolitan government is moving away from local communities and public-private partnerships are developing, along with often very opaque modes of governance.

However, regardless of what happens to the relations between Paris and its suburbs, Grand Paris leaves two important spaces at its borders: new towns and periurban territories. Yet, the latter have developed in articulation with Paris and its suburbs. In particular, they have constituted a residential alternative to Paris and, as far as the middle classes are concerned, to the suburbs. Today, they are at the centre of debates surrounding issues of spatial justice and metropolitan development.

The Rise of the Periurbs vis-à-vis Grand Paris

Located beyond the suburbs, periurban territories have a rural aspect, with a strong presence of agriculture and natural spaces; at the same time, they are strongly integrated into the orbit of Grand Paris. Unlike suburbs that have urbanized and no longer correspond to the canonical model (Phelps & Wood, 2011), these territories have updated the traditional model of the garden city whereby one lives in a country setting while remaining close to a metropolitan centre. For an estimate of the numerical importance of periurban territories, we will limit ourselves to the definition adopted by the National Institute of Statistics and Economic Studies (INSEE).[3] According to the zoning established by INSEE for the year 2010, the periurban ring of Paris includes approximately 1,400 *communes* and is home to about 1.8 million inhabitants.

The Space of Middle-Class Families

The periurbs are largely dominated by individual housing. Their development is closely linked to the phase of expansion of the middle classes that took place during the second half of the twentieth century (Jaillet, 2004). In accordance with post–Second World War Keynesian stimulus policies, several states invested heavily in road infrastructure, supported the automotive industry by favouring the equipment of households, and promoted home ownership, in particular the acquisition of individual houses (Hayden, 2009). In France, residential housing developed especially in the early 1970s, when public housing policies broke with the large housing estate model. The central state then encouraged the middle classes and the most stable sectors of the working class to acquire property via personalized aid (Steinmetz, 2013). Numerous housing developments were constructed by private developers and builders. These policies contributed to strong economic growth in the context of the so-called Fordist compromise. France therefore experienced the same process as many other countries did.

These policies accompanied and even fuelled a sociological process known in France as *moyennisation* (Mendras, 1988). The term refers to the constitution of a vast constellation of social groups with relatively similar lifestyles and aspirations – a process that relegated the class struggle between dominant classes and proletarians to the background. Indeed, the generalization of access to material comfort favoured the development of a less politicized ethics and tended to align the interests of households with those of the political and economic system. As has been pointed out by many sociologists, including Pierre Bourdieu (2000), access to homeownership with a twenty-year loan tends to moderate revolutionary fervour.

Nevertheless, the relationship between the middle classes and periurbanization can hardly be reduced to individual homeownership. In reality, in France as in many other countries, middle-class children who were coming of age in the late 1960s began to develop aspirations other than material comfort (Bidou, 1984). Meanwhile, the rise in the number of graduates was not followed by a corresponding increase in the number of skilled jobs. A certain frustration developed in professional life, and a section of the middle classes sought the social and political autonomy to which they aspired in local places. This trend led to the development of the post-68 Second Left (the French equivalent of the New Left), which largely contributed to the election of a socialist president, François Mitterrand, in 1981. In parallel with the centres of major cities, the periurbs became a land of conquest for these "new" middle classes or "alternative classes," as their villages offered the promise of genuine social relations, stripped of the flashy rags of consumerism and geared toward the pleasure of being and acting together. Some have described the migratory movements of the time as the "pink wave" of the periurbs – in reference to the pink rose emblematic of the Socialist Party (Jaillet, 2004).

Since the 1990s, the process of *moyennisation* has been reversed (Lojkine, 2005). Globalization has notably broken the connection between the space of investment and production and that of consumption – a connection that was at the heart of the Fordist regime of accumulation. Meanwhile, the middle classes have diffracted, with, on the one hand, lower middle classes that tend to draw closer to the popular classes because of the difficulties they face in coping with ongoing adjustments in the world of work and, on the other, upper middle classes that manage to make the best of the global economy in terms of income and wealth (Bouffartigue et al., 2011). The growing sociospatial fragmentation of the periurbs reflects these divergent trajectories. Thus, while in the 1960s and 1970s periurbanization was associated with the great expansion of the French middle classes and the reduction of social inequalities, today the periurbs seem to reflect the fragmentation of these same middle classes and the rise in social inequalities (Berger, 2004).

As a result, the population of the periurbs has diversified. Executive families are concentrated in the village *communes* that have the best location (for example, Châteaufort, presented in Box 6.2 and Figure 6.2). Meanwhile, the least attractive *communes* are home to the most modest households, whose incomes are typically around 2,500 euros per month. Many of them become solvent only by moving about a hundred kilometres from the centre of Paris. They are then faced with very high transport costs and times, and with scarce local facilities, in particular for the care of children outside school hours. A large portion of the literature on the periurbs has investigated these lower class households (Girard et al., 2013; Lambert, 2015; Rougé, 2007), which formed the terrain on which the Yellow Jackets (or *Gilets jaunes*) movement took shape in late 2018 (Charmes, 2021).

A Myriad of Residential Clubs

Even more so than in the suburbs, local authorities in the periurbs are highly fragmented. *Communes* are usually very small. In almost nine out of ten cases, they have fewer than 2,000 inhabitants. The most typical case is that of a village core surrounded by five or six housing developments of a few dozen houses, complemented by some diffuse development threads along the roads. The village-like fabric

Box 6.2. A "Clubbised" *Commune* of the Paris Periurban Ring: Châteaufort

Châteaufort is a small residential *commune* in the Yvelines, the wealthiest department of Paris's outer ring and the most attractive for executives (see Bacqué et al., 2016). The *commune*'s population is about 1,400 inhabitants. Its village-like atmosphere surrounded by natural or agricultural spaces is typical of periurban *communes*. Châteaufort's demographic growth occurred mainly in the 1980s, with the housing development known as La Perruche. Its population, which from the 1960s to the 1980s had been stable at about 800 inhabitants, grew from 770 to 1,430 between 1982 and 1990. Since then, the population has stagnated or even declined, on the one hand because the families who settled in the 1980s have aged (and their children have left) and on the other because Malthusian land-use regulations have been implemented. Restrictions on urban growth have been reinforced by the *commune*'s belonging to the Haute-Vallée de Chevreuse Regional Nature Park (a park created in 1985 that now covers 63,300 hectares and has 110,000 inhabitants distributed in 53 *communes*).

In Châteaufort, 85 per cent of houses are individual, and 85 per cent of main residences are owner-occupied. This situation, which is common in the French suburbs, fostered a style of government that bears many similarities to that of a private housing estate, according to a logic that can be described as "clubbisation" (Charmes, 2009). Such comparison is all the more justified since the built-up area is limited (it includes approximately 540 homes) and constitutes a unit that clearly stands out from a green background. In this context, the residents of Châteaufort expect their elected representatives to focus municipal policies on preserving village life and maintaining the social standing of the *commune*. Faced with the threats posed by urban expansion, some residents compare their *commune* to the Gaulish village of Asterix, which, as is well known, "still continues to and always will resist the invader." The words of the president of a local association for the defence of the environment are eloquent:

> It's still a village … We've managed to block large constructions, development … No, the protection is solid, I mean the walls of Châteaufort. Because it's a small Gaulish village, they hold firm. The village doesn't move; it can protect itself. We've had no specific constructions. We fought so that Châteaufort would remain in the park [the Haute-Vallée de Chevreuse Regional Natural Park] and not be removed from it. (Interview, July 2011)

Located 27 kilometres from the centre of the capital, Châteaufort is one of the closest periurban *communes* to Paris. Its privileged location in the heart of the Paris urban region combined with a still village-like living environment explains the appeal of this *commune*. Châteaufort has been significantly gentrified. Between 1975 and 2017, the share of blue-collar workers in the employed resident population decreased from 37 per cent to 4 per cent (against 21 per cent for all France), while the share of executives and higher intellectual professions increased from 13 per cent to 48 per cent, against 17 per cent for all France (INSEE data). In 2017, the median taxable income per unit of consumption was €36,000 or €75,600 for a couple with two children under fourteen years of age. This makes Châteaufort one of the wealthiest periurban *communes* of the Ile-de-France region, far removed from the situation prevailing in the poorest *communes* of the distant periurbs.

of residential *communes* is structured by towns of various sizes, with some even constituting real cities. In the vast majority of cases, these towns have a few thousand inhabitants, with eight or ten smaller *communes* gravitating around them. Oftentimes, the link between these *communes* is functionally marked by a high school and by sports facilities, which are located in the town and benefit the inhabitants of surrounding villages.

Like other municipalities, periurban municipalities enjoy significant prerogatives, notably in the area of urban planning (among other things, they can decide on zoning and potential urbanization). The combination of these prerogatives with the expectations of periurban households has turned several periurban *communes* into residential clubs, particularly in the most privileged sectors (Charmes, 2009). In many periurban *communes*, acquiring a detached house is equivalent to purchasing an entrance ticket to a private club. By moving into a detached house, one also becomes a "member" of a *commune* whose residents are united by the shared enjoyment of a particular living environment. Due to the forces of the real estate market, the "clubs" that offer the most sought-after living environment are those for which the "entrance ticket" is most expensive. The clubs that are least in demand, either because they are far removed from the Paris centre or because they suffer nuisances, are the least expensive and are mainly populated by lower middle-class households. Social sorting is especially strong because, inasmuch as the neighbourhoods of wealthy households are in high

Figure 6.2. Aerial view of Châteaufort surrounded by greenery. Sources: IGN 2016; Géoportail.

demand (notably for children's education), privileged families attract privileged families. In this context, residents come together around similar tastes and incomes. They are bound by a shared living environment and are primarily concerned with its management and maintenance, according to an economic logic similar to that governing the functioning of a private residential estate. They are also concerned with monopolizing access to and use of their residential environment, making exclusivism and the determination of the modalities of group membership a key issue. At the *commune* scale, this "clubbisation" translates, among other things, into land-use regulations that aim to control the quality of the population, for instance, by prohibiting the construction of collective housing buildings and even of any new building.

The Political Emergence of the Periurbs

Grand Paris currently has 7.1 million inhabitants, while the metropolitan region has 12.2 million, including 1.8 million in the periurbs. Most importantly, compared with the 1,400 *communes* of the periurban ring, Grand Paris includes, at the time of writing, 131 *communes*. These figures are eloquent. They show that Grand Paris is limited to the dense, agglomerated centre of the metropolitan region. The city of Paris has joined with its nearby suburbs, not with its distant suburbs and new towns, and even less with its periurban rings. If we may venture a prediction, we suspect that, like the *Boulevard Périphérique*, the *Francilienne* (the highway bordering Grand Paris) will gradually become an important symbolic boundary marking the limit between the periurbs and the central cluster – that of the dense agglomeration where wealth and political power are concentrated. This division is anything but trivial.

First, the relationship between the periurbs and Grand Paris, like that between the suburbs and Paris, is one of complementarity. The periurbs do not exist without Paris, and the centre needs its residential hinterland (Davezies & Talandier, 2014). Thus, periurban territories are one of the answers to the issue of housing in the Paris metropolitan region. Although their population amounts to only a quarter of that of Grand Paris, they cover a much larger geographical area. The periurbs are very weakly urbanized, and hence they constitute an important reserve for urban expansion (even if such extensions tend to be restricted by French laws in order to preserve agricultural and natural lands). In short, on the scale of Grand Paris, the nagging and pressing issue of housing can only be partially dealt with. The complementarity between the periburbs and Grand Paris is also obvious for another key issue: mobility. Yet, as is often the case in this domain, transportation is at the forefront of metropolitan governance because the scope of action of the authority that manages public transport around Paris was extended to the entire Ile-de-France region in 1991.

Second, the creation of Grand Paris has reinforced the identity division between the city and the periurbs. It was long thought that periurbanization was a transitory phenomenon and that the periurbs would eventually be integrated into the suburbs. We now know that the periurbs constitute a space with its own perennial characteristics, marked by the hybridization of the city and the countryside (Brenner & Schmid, 2015; Vanier, 2011). As mentioned earlier, in almost nine out of ten cases, the periurban *communes* around Paris have fewer than 2,000 inhabitants, they resemble rural villages, and they wish to retain this characteristic. These *communes* are hybrid, turned toward the countryside as much as toward the heart of Grand Paris. This identity sets them apart from the Paris centre and even more so from the suburbs. For instance, for the residents of Châteaufort, the suburbs – even residential ones – symbolize an environment they wish to keep at a distance. Suburbs are not only associated with impoverished large housing estates; they also embody continuous urban sprawl and hence the negation of what is valuable about their Châteaufort living environment, namely its village character. Thus, periurban residents affirm their rural identity more clearly than do suburban residents, even though they value the countryside more in terms of the living environment it provides than in productive terms (Vanier, 2003).

For the time being, the government of the periurbs consists predominantly of a succession of initiatives taken in hundreds of small *communes*. Overcoming this fragmentation is a slow process. Intercommunal bodies are gradually gaining in importance, but they do not really challenge the influence of municipal authorities because these intercommunal cooperation schemes derive their powers from the very *communes* that have created them. In addition, periurban intercommunal bodies have taken the least integrated form – one intended primarily for rural and less dense territories. Lastly, their limited size leaves them unable to manage the vast spread of periurban territories (many include a few dozen *communes*, but their demographic weight remains limited, with a total population generally between 15,000 and 40,000 inhabitants).

On a broader scale, the institutional and political void might perhaps be filled by the departments of the Paris outer ring (Seine-et-Marne, Essonne, Yvelines, and Val d'Oise), considered as the long-standing, instituted representatives of rural territories. However, departments have little influence because they are regarded at the national level as an obsolete institution, to the extent that the question of their elimination is frequently raised. Another actor not to be neglected is the Ile-de-France region. In particular, it has been in charge of elaborating the Regional Master Plan (SDRIF) since 1995. This document, however, primarily lays down broad guidelines for infrastructure and facilities that leave considerable discretion to municipalities. The main restriction, imposed by national laws, concerns the conversion of non-urban land. Yet, many municipalities are comfortable with this constraint, because it does not frustrate their desire to preserve the living environment by limiting urbanization.

The political emergence of the periurbs primarily took the form of a vote for the Rassemblement National and Marine Le Pen. In the national media, maps and curves regularly show that the Rassemblement National vote reaches its peak in the periurban rings. Based on this observation, some do not hesitate to regard the periurbs as a breeding ground for the far right (Lévy, 2013). This viewpoint is highly reductive, and research has shown that the party's electoral successes are concentrated in specific periurban *communes* (the most remote) and mainly concern some sections of the popular classes (Charmes et al., 2016). In the periurbs, the vote for the Rassemblement National can primarily be related to a system of housing production, which pushes modest families to small outlying *communes* that are generally poorly equipped and very poorly served by public transportation. Moreover, even in the popular classes' periurbs, the Rassemblement National remains a secondary political force (Girard, 2017; Rivière, 2009), as demonstrated by its inability to embody the *Gilets jaunes* movement. This movement was very diverse. On the social networks, some *Gilets jaunes* shared ideas circulated by the Rassemblement National, but many others circulated ideas from other parts of the political spectrum, including the far left (Morales et al., 2021). Convergences between the *Gilets jaunes* and movements from the popular suburbs have also developed, notably around the denunciation of police violence.

Conclusion: Persisting and Emerging Divisions

As shown in several studies (for example, Hamel & Keil, 2015), metropolization is a manifestation of globalization and neoliberalism; it articulates forms of centralization with forms of fragmentation; and its modalities of governance are transforming urban democracy. All these observations apply to the case of Paris, but do so in a specific configuration – it being the result of a political, social, and urban history in which local and national contexts play a significant role.

While metropolization is a relatively recent contemporary global phenomenon, the place of the suburbs in large urbanized territories can only be understood by analysing the historical processes that have led to their formation. We have focused, in particular, on the historical relationship between Paris and its suburbs, which is characterized by a relationship of reciprocal yet unequal dependency – and even of domination as far as the popular suburbs are concerned. In a sense, Grand Paris is probably too big for the popular suburbs to be able to reverse this relationship. Similarly, periurbanization has taken a form determined by the pre-existence of a village framework that is specific to the countryside, which has notably contributed to the formation of well-delimited residential clubs around a series of towns. This process is far from constituting a uniform and continuous urban fabric. The unequal dimension of the fragmented periurban landscape is significant: The upper middle classes monopolize the most attractive villages, while the popular classes are pushed away from the Paris centre and its facilities. The first protect themselves in well-controlled clubs, whereas the second have reduced access to transportation.

At the institutional level, the French system is known for its centralization; however, it has also inherited administrative fragmentation along with 36,000 *communes*. The latter represents an essential dimension of political and administrative life, and of the social and identity anchoring of inhabitants. Thus, the *communes* of the popular suburbs have resisted the centralizing governance of Grand Paris, countering it with bottom-up governance that starts from the local level. Similarly, village *communes* and small periurban towns have implemented forms of local regulation and even of social closure. It is unlikely that the determining role of municipalities will be radically challenged in the near future. From an institutional and urban point of view, the place of the suburbs and periurbs in the Paris metropolitan region is therefore shaped by two contradictory logics. There is, on the one hand, a logic of centralization that has led to the creation of Grand Paris and, on the other, a logic of fragmentation that persists especially in the periurban areas left outside this new institutional entity.

However, one of the main arguments for the creation of Grand Paris is that it will ensure efficiency and coherence, thus countering the fragmentation of local governments. But what project will favour such efficiency, and who will benefit from it? Will the construction of Grand Paris contribute to erasing the historical social divisions and inequalities that characterize the city and its suburbs, or will it favour competition between financialized global cities? Will it promote the right to the city? These questions arise especially with regard to the suburbs. Redressing the inequalities that they suffer would require significant redistribution of resources to ensure, in particular, that public services, accessibility, and environmental quality achieve the same standards as those prevailing in central neighbourhoods and wealthy suburbs – yet without the popular classes being pushed away due to urban redevelopment. Otherwise, there is a strong risk that sociospatial fragmentation will intensify and that inequalities will be further reinforced in the popular periurbs.

These issues raise questions concerning the place of citizens in Grand Paris. While urban practices are already largely metropolitan, at least as far as suburban and periurban residents are concerned, the political relationship between citizens and the Grand Paris Metropolitan Authority is, for the moment, far from secured. Will the centralization brought about by the creation of Grand Paris allow for building such a relationship? Several collectives and social movements (like Métropop'!, a citizens' collective formed in 2010 to challenge conventional representations of the suburbs) are beginning to make themselves heard on this issue. Mobilizations have emerged on the scale of Greater Paris, and even of the region, against the realization of "large useless projects." A project of ecological transition, CARMA,[4] born from a mobilization against the conversion of agricultural land in Greater Paris, is carried by several activist collectives, initiating a debate on the Greater Paris project and governance. Yet questions remain. How will the residents of popular suburbs make their voices heard in Grand Paris? And beyond the suburbs, what institutions will pay attention to the problems posed by the territories located outside the scope of action of the Grand Paris Metropolitan Authority? The Ile-de-France region and the departments of the outer ring certainly have a role to play. But again, what of the democratization of these bodies, and what of the articulation between their decisions and those of Grand Paris?

Acknowledgment

We would like to thank Arianne Dorval for translating this article into English.

NOTES

1 The department is an administrative and political body that corresponds to a territorial division dating from the Napoleonic era (see Table 6.2).
2 From the 2010s onward, the French state passed several laws that significantly restrict extensive growth and land conversion for urban uses.
3 Up until 2020, INSEE used two criteria to define the periurban character of a *commune*: a criterion of functional dependency and a landscape criterion. Functional dependency was defined as follows: at least 40 per cent of the employed resident population worked outside the *commune* in one or more "metropolitan areas" (see the INSEE territorial nomenclature for the definition of *aire urbaine*). According to the landscape criterion, a *commune* was periurban if its main built-up area was separated from the urban cluster on which it depends by an unbuilt strip of land at least 200 metres wide.
4 Coopération pour une Ambition agricole, Rurale at Métropolitaine d'Avenir (CARMA), https://carmapaysdefrance.com/.

REFERENCES

Bacqué, M.-H., Bridge, G., Benson, M., Butler, T., Charmes, E., Fijalkow, Y., Jackson, E., Launay, L., & Vermeersch, S. (2015). *The middles classes and the city: A study of Paris and London*. Palgrave.
Bacqué, M.-H., Charmes, E., Launay, L., & Vermeersch, S. (2016). Des territoires entre ascension et déclin: Trajectoires sociales dans la mosaïque périurbaine. *Revue française de sociologie, 57*(4), 681–710. https://doi.org/10.3917/rfs.574.0681

Bacqué, M.-H., & Fol, S. (1997). *Le devenir des banlieues rouges*. L'Harmattan.

Bacqué, M.-H., & Sintomer, Y. (2001). Affiliations et désaffiliations en banlieue, réflexions à partir des exemples de Saint-Denis et d'Aubervilliers. *Revue française de sociologie, 42*(2), 217–49. https://doi.org/10.2307/3322965

Beaud, S., & Pialoux, M. (1999). *Retour sur la condition ouvrière*. Fayard.

Berger, M. (2004). *Les périurbains de Paris: De la ville dense à la métropole éclatée?* CNRS Éditions.

Berroir, S., Cattan, N., & Saint-Julien, T. (2004). La contribution des villes nouvelles au polycentrisme francilien: L'exemple de la polarisation liée à l'emploi. *Espaces et sociétés, 119*(4), 113–33. https://doi.org/10.3917/esp.119.0113

Bidou, C. (1984). *Les aventuriers du quotidien: Essai sur les nouvelles classes moyennes*. Presses universitaires de France.

Bouffartigue, P., Gadéa, C., & Pochic, S. (2011). *Cadres, classes moyennes: Vers l'éclatement?* Armand Colin.

Bourdieu, P. (2000). *Les structures sociales de l'économie*. Le Seuil.

Braouezec, P. (2011, 11 February). De la gouvernance du Grand Paris. *Métropolitiques*. https://metropolitiques.eu/De-la-gouvernance-du-Grand-Paris.html

Brenner, N., & Schmid, C. (2015). Towards a new epistemology of the urban? *City, 19*(2–3), 151–82. https://doi.org/10.1080/13604813.2015.1014712

Castel, R. (1995). *Les métamorphoses de la question sociale*. Fayard.

Charmes, E. (2009). On the residential "clubbisation" of the French periurban municipalities." *Urban Studies, 46*(1), 189–212. https://doi.org/10.1177/0042098008098642

Charmes, E. (Ed.). (2021). *Métropole et éloignement résidentiel: Vivre dans le périurbain lyonnais*. Autrement.

Charmes, E., & Keil, R. (2015). The politics of post-suburban densification in Canada and France. *International Journal of Urban and Regional Research, 39*(3), 581–602. https://doi.org/10.1111/1468-2427.12194

Charmes, E., Launay, L., & Vermeersch, S. (2016). Le périurbain n'est pas une version dégradée de la ville. In E. Charmes & M.-H. Bacqué (Eds.), *Mixité sociale, et après?* (pp. 81–96). Presses universitaires de France.

Chauvel, J. (2021). La construction territoriale d'un problème public en contexte multiniveaux: Le cas du Grand Paris. *Revue gouvernance/Governance Review, 18*(1), 10–39. https://doi.org/10.7202/1077285ar

Chevalier, L. (1984). *Classes laborieuses et classes dangereuses*. Hachette. (Original work published 1958)

Davezies, L., & Talandier, M. (2014). *L'émergence de systèmes productivo-résidentiels*. La Documentation française.

Desage, F., & Guéranger, D. (2011). *La politique confisquée: Sociologie des réformes et des institutions intercommunales*. Éditions du Croquant.

Fourcaut, A. (2000). *La banlieue en morceaux: La crise des lotissements défectueux en France dans l'entre-deux-guerres*. Créaphis.

Fourcaut, A., Bellanger, E., & Flonneau, M. (2007). *Paris/banlieues: Conflits et solidarités, historiographie, anthologie, chronologie, 1788–2006*. Créaphis.

Gilli, F., & Offner, J.-M. (2009). *Paris, métropole hors les murs*. Presses de Sciences Po.

Girard, V. (2017). *Le vote FN au village: Trajectoires de ménages populaires du périurbain*. Éditions du Croquant.

Girard, V., Lambert, A., & Steinmetz, H. (2013). Propriété et classes populaires. *Politix, 101*(1), 7–20. https://doi.org/10.3917/pox.101.0007

Hamel, P., & Keil, R. (Eds.). (2015). *Suburban governance: A global view*. University of Toronto Press.

Hayden, D. (2009). *Building suburbia: Green fields and urban growth, 1820–2000*. Penguin Random House.

Jaillet, M.-C. (2004). L'espace périurbain: Un univers pour les classes moyennes. *Esprit, 303*(3–4), 40–62. http://www.jstor.org/stable/24249397

Keil, R., Hamel, P., Boudreau, J.-A., & Kipfer, S. (Eds.). (2017). *Governing cities through regions: Canadian and European perspectives*. Wilfrid Laurier University Press.

Lambert, A. (2015). *Tous propriétaires! L'envers du décor pavillonnaire*. Seuil.

Lévy, J. (2013). *Réinventer la France*. Fayard.

Lojkine, J. (2005). *L'adieu à la classe moyenne*. La Dispute.

Mendras, H. (1988). *La seconde révolution française, 1965–1984*. Gallimard.

Morales, P.R., Cointet, J.-P., Benbouzid, B., Cardon, D., Froio, C., Metin, O.F., Ooghe, B., & Plique, G. (2021). Atlas multi-plateforme d'un mouvement social: Le cas des Gilets jaunes. *Statistique et Société, 9*(1–2), 39–77. https://statistique-et-societe.fr/index.php/stat_soc/article/view/822

Phelps, N.A., & Wood, A.M. (2011). The new post-suburban politics? *Urban Studies, 48*(12), 2591–2610. https://doi.org/10.1177/0042098011411944

Préteceille, E. (2012). Segregation, social mix and public policies in Paris. In T. Maloutas & K. Fujita (Eds.), *Residential Segregation around the World: Making Sense of Contextual Diversity* (pp. 153–76). Ashgate.

Rivière, J. (2009). *Le pavillon et l'isoloir* [Unpublished doctoral dissertation]. Université de Caen Basse-Normandie.

Rougé, L. (2007). Inégale mobilité et urbanité par défaut des périurbains modestes toulousains. *Espacestemps.net*. https://www.espacestemps.net/en/auteurs/lionel-rouge-english/

Sampson, R. (2012). *Great American city: Chicago and the enduring neighborhood effect*. University of Chicago Press.

Savitch, H. (2014). *Post-industrial cities: Politics and planning in New York, Paris, and London*. Princeton University Press.

Sieverts, T. (2003). *Cities without cities: An interpretation of the Zwischenstadt*. Routledge.

Steinmetz, H. (2013). Les Chalandonnettes: La production par le haut d'une accession bas de gamme. *Politix*, *101*(1), 21–48. https://doi.org/10.3917/pox.101.0021

Subra, P. (2012). *Le Grand Paris: Géopolitique d'une ville mondiale*. Armand Colin.

Subra, P., & Serisier, W. (2021, 17 June). La Métropole du Grand Paris, enjeu caché des élections municipales de 2020. *Métropolitiques*. https://metropolitiques.eu/La-Metropole-du-Grand-Paris-enjeu-cache-des-elections-municipales-de-2020.html

Vanier, M. (2003). Le périurbain à l'heure du crapaud buffle: Tiers espace de la nature, nature du tiers espace. *Revue de géographie alpine*, *91*(4), 79–89. https://doi.org/10.3406/rga.2003.2264

Vanier, M., (2011, 23 February). La périurbanisation comme projet. *Métropolitiques*. https://metropolitiques.eu/La-periurbanisation-comme-projet.html

Veltz, P. (2012). *Paris, France, monde: Repenser l'économie par les territoires*. L'Aube.

Vermeersch, S. (2011). Bien vivre au-delà du "périph": Les compromis des classes moyennes. *Sociétés contemporaines*, *83*(3), 131–54. https://doi.org/10.3917/soco.083.0131

Vermeersch, S., Launay, L., Charmes, E., & Bacqué, M.-H. (2019). *Quitter Paris? Les classes moyennes entre périphéries et centres*. Créaphis.

7 City with No Boundary: Suburbanization as a Mode of Wealth Accumulation in Istanbul

MURAT ÜÇOĞLU AND K. MURAT GÜNEY

Introduction

Even though there is a lot of discussion on the matter of urban renewal and massive housing construction in Turkey (Asci, 2020; Kuyucu, 2014; Yeşilbağ, 2020), the ongoing city-building practices that we have been witnessing since the early 2000s in Istanbul refer to the massive production of suburban space and the financialization of housing through megaprojects and massive housing projects (Güney, 2019; Üçoğlu, 2019, 2021a). Therefore, suburbanization in the case of Istanbul has had a significant role in the urbanization process of the city in the last two decades. Istanbul stands as the main example to understand the suburban development process in Turkey, and this city has a special place in a global schema regarding the global urbanization process and inter-referencing of different sub/urbanisms due to its geopolitical location (Keil et al., 2019).

In this chapter, we argue that suburban governance has been reorganized in a way to generate a regime of wealth accumulation for certain growth coalitions (we refer to Logan & Molotch, 1987) in Istanbul, and we examine the practices of governance underlying this process of wealth accumulation. Built on the dimension of political economy, our perspective is established through the three modalities of suburban governance formulated by Ekers et al. (2015). The authors, in their work *Governing Suburbia*, emphasize the three major modalities of suburban governance: the role of the state, the role of capital, and the forms of authoritarian governance. These three modalities provide necessary clues needed to comprehend the major dynamics of suburban governance throughout the world. The role of the state is a sophisticated factor in understanding different suburbanisms that one may witness in different geographies. The state might have different positions and causalities in the successes or failures of suburban governance. Ekers et al. refer to Sonia Hirt (2007) in order to examine major regimes of state-level governmentalities that put suburban governance on the table for discussion. Hirt indicates that, historically, there are three general types of state practices that deal with the governing of suburban development. First, there is the developing state practice, which does not have adequate capacity to finance suburban development. That state structure oversees informal suburbanization (to create an industrial reserve army) in the form of squatter houses or slum neighbourhoods. The developing state, after a certain point, tries to govern the already-existing informal suburban morphology. Second, in the already developed capitalist states, the well-known approach to suburban development entails the active role of the state in regulating and financing suburbanization. Developed capitalist states have two major ways of governing suburban development, according to Ekers et al. (2015): (1) regulating the mechanisms of housing through founding necessary housing agencies, a practice quite common in North America as seen in organizations such as the Canada Mortgage and Housing Corporation (CMHC) and the American Federal National Mortgage Association (Fannie Mae); and (2) facilitating access to financial tools so that people are able to own houses through mortgage credits. The purpose of that governing practice is to boost the demand for suburban housing, essentially in certain global city-regions. Finally, to again use Hirt's taxonomy, there is the socialist suburb, which deals with problems of public health and population increase, hence, actively builds high-density suburbs (Ekers et al., 2015, p. 30).

The role of the state, then, appears as the facilitator of wealth accumulation through the suburban production of space. Capital accumulation is one of the basic reasons for suburban development, since it is literally linked to land-rent questions and financialization in the twenty-first century. Approaches to capital accumulation through urban expansion can be depicted within the categories of urban growth machine theory and theories related to the rising financialization of housing. The former refers to urban growth coalitions that aim at boosting the development industry through land-rent speculation, housing market dynamics, and local investments of certain capitalists (see Logan & Molotch, 1987; Molotch, 1976), whereas the latter deals with the spread of financially created money for further wealth accumulation. The financialization of the housing market plays a crucial role in this schema because it inevitably leads to the expansion of the city for further housing projects. The transition of housing from a safe shelter with use value to an investment tool of exchange value reveals itself in the financial markets with different ways of using investment tools such as mortgage-based securities (Aalbers, 2016; Üçoğlu, 2021b). Therefore, in neoliberal times, housing is no longer perceived as a shelter; rather, it is an investment and financial commodity that increases the indebtedness level of a society (Madden & Marcuse, 2016). The third point of suburban modality involves the authoritarian regime of governance (privately led governance). The inevitable urban expansion caused by urban growth coalition incentives and facilitation of financial tools leads to new forms of governing in peripheral areas. In terms of neoliberal social policies, securitization and gated governance have become widespread. Private governance in the form of gated communities has become a dominant way to deal with the securitization of housing and private space. One of the reasons for this practice is the increasing social polarization and the competition between middle classes. Hence, authoritarian urban regimes are inevitably manifested in the suburban housing practices of gated communities.

The case of Istanbul demonstrates the various stages of these modalities, and we will discuss the suburban development process of Istanbul in this chapter. To do so, we will first briefly touch upon the history of Istanbul's suburbanization and its governance structure. Later, we will explain the suburban governance process in Istanbul through the three modalities suggested by Ekers et al. (2015). While doing so, we argue that the suburbanization process in Istanbul during the last fifteen years has served to perpetuate the authoritarian conservative regime imposed by the current governing party in Turkey.

Istanbul's Brief History of Peripheral Expansion

Istanbul is known historically as a major city with the status of a political command centre. Indeed, the city has served as the capital for three empires. But in 1923, after the declaration of the Republic of Turkey, it lost its capital city status. Ankara became the capital city of Turkey, but Istanbul has remained its most populated city. From 1923 to the late 1940s, the planning strategy was to prevent suburbanization in order to create a dense modern city. This practice was supported by modern planning approaches – essentially the plan designed by Henri Prost as a dominant initiative. Henri Prost designed a modern plan that was mostly implemented between 1939 and 1947; his main approach was to prevent peripheral expansion to avoid the potential establishment of squatter houses (*gecekondu*; Tekeli, 2013). Istanbul's population in 1940 was 991,237, and the aim of planning was to increase the population but with a control to prevent informal settlements. The plan was quite successful until the late 1940s. However, in the post-war period, the housing crisis in the city began due to fiscal problems. During this period, the first examples of *gecekondus* began to appear. After their appearance, essentially in the 1950s, the populist policies of the then governing Democrat Party led to the expansion of the city in linear form through the construction of various highways in order to encourage automobile use. Even though the 1960s were known as years of planning conducted by the State Planning Agency, peripheral expansion, especially around the linear highways, prevailed. Gecekondufication became a social reality, and for a very long time, the state played a passive role due to its developmentalist agenda. The 1960s to the late 1970s was a period of import substitution industrialization for Turkey. During that time, the main goal was to bring about an Istanbul-based industrial bourgeoisie. This new economic model entailed an industrial reserve army, essentially situated around the then newly built suburban industrial factories. Therefore, *gecekondus* became widespread, and the state overlooked their spread for the sake of industrial production cluster. However, after the 1980s, following the 1980 military coup, neoliberalization began with an authoritarian regime; that regime wanted to change the structure of local governments since the idea was to spread speculative economies and to facilitate the rise of finance capital (Üçoğlu, 2021b).

Many *gecekondu* neighbourhoods became legal after the amnesties, and many of them were transformed into neighbourhoods of four- to five-storey buildings. Speculators and developers used this opportunity for wealth accumulation, and certain developers later became the major owners of construction companies in Turkey. In the meantime, the Mass Housing Administration (TOKI) was founded in 1984 as an agency to control the housing problem occurring due to the population increase and gentrification. Massive housing projects were launched (Bahçeşehir and Ataşehir) at the peripheries of Istanbul, hence, accelerating suburban development. These projects were funded by Emlak Bankasi (The Real Estate Bank) and TOKI. TOKI's main goal was to provide affordable housing for the middle class by facilitating the financial aspect of becoming a homeowner. In addition, the agency was to develop projects essentially in the periphery of cities. TOKI started to expand suburban development in Istanbul for further projects to boost the construction sector and also to attract more population to the city. Neoliberalization processes accelerated until 2002, when the Justice and Development Party (Turkish acronym, AKP) came to power in Turkey. The AKP government has completely changed the urban dynamics of Istanbul by continuing the neoliberal financialization process under an authoritarian governance and state-led developmentalist economic model. We will deal with the details of that kind of governmentality in the next part of this chapter. However, first we will provide some information on the current demography and local government structure of Istanbul.

Istanbul has witnessed an unprecedented population increase since the 1980s. Since 1980, Istanbul's population has tripled from about 5 million to about 15 million. As of 2022, the population of Istanbul was 15,907,951, which makes the city the largest metropolitan area in Turkey and in Europe. The population increase mainly stems from migration from rural areas, villages, and other cities, because most of the industrial and other types of investments are carried out in Istanbul. Istanbul generates almost one-third of the gross domestic product (GDP) of Turkey, which has a population of 85 million people (2023). Turkey's GDP is $906 billion as of 2022 (World Bank, 2023), and Istanbul produces 31 per cent of the national economic output. Moreover, Istanbul is responsible for 50 per cent of Turkey's imports and exports, and 50 per cent of all tax revenues in Turkey is collected in Istanbul.

State-led developmentalist policies conducted by the governments since the 1980s reached their zenith with AKP governments in the 2010s, and most of the infrastructural investments took place in Istanbul to accelerate local boosterism and land-rent speculation. This developmentalist policy caused a hasty hike in population, which ended up with environmental concerns and a lack of social justice and simple infrastructural services.

Local Governance in Istanbul

In Turkey, there is a specific law called Metropolitan Cities Government for cities with a population of over 750,000. Under this law, these cities are considered to have a metropolitan municipality and are divided into districts with their own local municipalities. For instance, Istanbul now has a metropolitan municipality that deals with all general issues of the city, as well as thirty-nine districts, each with their own local municipalities. District-level local municipalities are designed to respond quickly to the problems people face in terms of street-level infrastructure, beautification, and housing. There is a division of responsibilities between the metropolitan municipality and the local municipalities. The metropolitan municipality is responsible for producing master plans for transportation, housing, infrastructure, and green areas, whereas local municipalities are responsible for neighbourhood-level issues such as cleaning the streets, paving the sidewalks, garbage collection, and providing housing tenure. In the past, distributing housing-tenure licences was the responsibility of the metropolitan municipalities; however, after the neoliberalization process in the 1980s, this duty was given to the local district municipalities. That change of practice also transformed the relations of the housing market, since local district municipalities might be ruled by a different political party from the party in power at the national or municipal level. There also exists a competition between political parties to win the mayor position of local municipalities. Inevitably, this competition serves two matters: (1) better local services to the neighbourhoods because local mayors want to keep their chair in the next election; and (2) a new set of relations in terms of governance, hence a more sophisticated system of crony capitalism and bribery. The latter is also a problem of governance and is linked to legal regulations. We will deal with this dimension of jurisdiction in the next section, but apart from that issue, there also exists another actor created by municipalities. In the 1990s, the metropolitan municipalities started to found companies that act as autonomous private enterprises rather than as public institutions. Istanbul municipality founded an autonomous enterprise called KIPTAŞ for housing issues, and in 1995, Tayyip Erdoğan, then mayor of Istanbul, transformed this enterprise into a construction company. He declared that the aim of KIPTAŞ was to save Istanbul from gecekondufication and to protect people's rights against developers. However, in practice, it did not work that way; rather, it just changed the partnership between KIPTAŞ and developers, and hence, developers would be able to use municipal lands (Uşaklıgil, 2014, p. 47). The reason for founding these enterprises was to find "creative" ways to get the highest amount of revenue from urban growth projects. To wit, Istanbul's local governance consists of metropolitan municipalities, local district municipalities (each of which also has a council with elected members), and private enterprises founded by municipalities (Table 7.1). The rationale behind the establishment of new local district municipalities (Figure 7.1) as the population increases is to control suburbanization through those municipalities. The population continues to increase; hence, the city continues to expand. Each expansion leads to the formation of new local district municipalities.

Suburban Governance in Istanbul

The Role of the State

The role of the state in suburban governance in Turkey is ambiguous since it is not easy to define the responsibilities of authorities while they

Table 7.1. Administrative Units of Istanbul

Administrative and Territorial Units	Government Bodies	Main Attributions	Number of Units
Istanbul Province	Istanbul Governorship – appointed by the central government	Security (police and gendarmerie); securing public order, monitoring public institutions	1 (15.5 million inhabitants)
Istanbul Metropolitan Municipality	Istanbul Metropolitan Municipality Mayorship (elected metropolitan municipality mayor)	Provincial planning, public transportation, parks and green spaces, social assistance, cultural development, water and sewage, recyling, natural gas	1 (15.5 million inhabitants)
Istanbul Metropolitan Municipality	Istanbul Municipal Assembly (311 elected representatives)	Decisions and revisions on urban plans, municipal budget, investments	1 (15.5 million inhabitants) – 312 representatives
Istanbul districts	District municipalities (elected district mayors)	District planning, garbage collection and recyling, cultural events, arts and tourism	39 districts (25 in European side, 14 in Asian side)
Neighbourhood units (muhtarlik)	Neigbourhood representatives (muhtar) – (961 elected representatives)	Monitoring neighbourhood's needs and reporting neighbourhood problems to public authorities	961 neighbourhoods

Sources: Istanbul Metropolitan Municipality (2023); Istanbul Governorship (2023).

are dealing with urban land problems. Since the 1980s, the state started to act as an active player in the suburbanization process rather than remaining a passive actor that disregards suburban development due to lack of financial tools. However, the role of state authorities is not well defined in the legal framework, which brings about an ambiguity in the process of governance. That ambiguity is constantly abused by the central government in order to bypass municipal procedures. In this section, we will discuss in particular those governmental practices that have been applied since 2002. After that time, Istanbul's suburbanization took a new path that has totally changed the socio-economic dynamics of the city.

AKP's neoliberal regime has changed the legal structure for municipalities and facilitated urban transformation projects by introducing

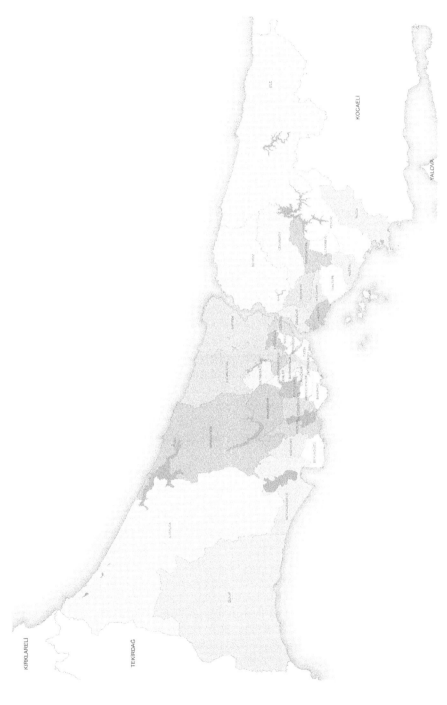

Figure 7.1. Istanbul's districts – each has its own local municipalities. Source: Istanbul Planning Agency (2021).

new ways to intervene in the name of improving the housing stock and making residential buildings stronger, healthier, and more resilient to earthquakes and other risks (Güney, 2022). Thus, the government has been granted the right to expropriate land to protect public safety and health, which in return has rendered the status of land and housing property rights in designated urban transformation zones ambiguous. These practices began after 2004, when TOKI became the major urban growth coalition actor throughout the country. In 2010, more than 175 local municipalities from all around Turkey signed an agreement with TOKI in order to transform neighbourhoods that were considered "risky" (Kuyucu, 2014). The largest projects among those agreements are located in Istanbul. A special governance system exists to acquire land-rent value by transforming both urban and suburban land. TOKI is the major governmental actor that facilitates the formalization of massive suburbanization. Critical scholars describe TOKI's operations as an authoritarian governance of mass housing projects, implemented to create a fragile city with vulnerable communities. Moreover, TOKI's massive housing projects in the peripheries dramatically changed the life-style of Istanbul's inhabitants (Buğra, 1998; Geniş, 2007; Islam, 2010; Kuyucu & Ünsal, 2010; Tanülkü, 2012). The new urban literature on Istanbul focuses on these problems and on the struggles of new residents with the TOKI housing projects. Even though that growing literature broadly explains the dynamics of the new urbanization process in Istanbul and the role of TOKI in that process, there is still very little work on the suburbanization process in Istanbul. Therefore, in this chapter, we particularly examine how suburbanization has become an important hegemonic tool for the AKP government and its cronies.

Suburban development in Turkey has two major social dynamics that are promoted by the local and national authorities as well as by TOKI. On one hand, the new housing projects (usually in the form of high-rise gated communities or luxurious gated communities) are represented as the highest stage of modernism experienced in the city. Such representation aims to make homebuyers believe that they are not simply buying an ideal home but that such a purchase comes with distinction and a privileged status (Keyder, 2005). On the other hand, the new peripheral housing projects reproduce the suburban space by highlighting conservative values such as "Ideal Family House" or "Traditional Turkish House" (Kan Ülkü & Erten, 2013, p. 244). Suburban expansion is promoted as a process of both modernization and exalting familism. Even the smallest apartment in the TOKI projects has at least two bedrooms and is designed for living with family and children. TOKI promotes its social housing projects as the elimination of the *gecekondu* problem and as a process of making the city more modern and beautiful (Asci, 2020). However, in practice, TOKI's urban transformation projects result in the gentrification of the central districts of the city. Such projects relocated vulnerable populations living in the central locations of Istanbul in squatter housing and displaced these populations to peripheral social housing projects, while binding them as new homebuyers with financial debt mechanisms. Although TOKI's social housing units are promoted as an affordable housing option, these apartments still create a financial burden for low-income households, who are displaced from their erstwhile *gecekondu* located in central locations of the city where there are many more job opportunities.

These dynamics of suburban expansion can be described as a new type of neoliberal governance that produces different suburbanisms by an authoritarian urban regime. As David Harvey points out, the neoliberal state works in an unstable and contradicting political platform (2005, p. 64). In theory, neoliberalism claims that free entrepreneurial spirit will expand freedom of choice and that such development would limit the power of the state. Hence, it is assumed that neoliberalism will force the state to be more accountable for its policies and practices. However, in practice, the neoliberal state works in a less transparent manner, which hinders citizens from checking its accountability. As Harvey asserts, in practice the neoliberal state plays an active role, essentially in developing countries, while neoliberalism converges with developmentalism. Neoliberal governance becomes a mechanism to bypass democratic accountability while claiming to bolster economic development for the benefit of all the population. However, such an approach bolsters the cooperation between the government and economic elites. In the Turkish context, such a neoliberal approach results in the governance of urban affairs through crony capitalism (Üçoğlu, 2019). The economic dimension of these ties will be explained in the next section, but first, it is possible to say that the ambiguity in the role of governmental actors serves the well-being of the central government, enabling it to act as the leading figure through TOKI and the Ministry of Urban Affairs. TOKI works as the major actor of the state-driven policy that features an outpouring of overwhelming wealth accumulation greed. This developmentalist process, facilitated by political institutions and TOKI, aims at spreading housing price boosterism in Turkey and particularly in Istanbul. TOKI was initially founded in 1984, but with new legal amendments in the "mass housing law" (law number 2985), the AKP radically restructured TOKI in 2004 to make this government institution the most powerful real estate developer in the country and the most influential actor in the construction of its neoliberal regime (Kuyucu & Ünsal, 2010, p. 1485). Starting from 2004, TOKI became the major actor in construction industry and land-rent speculation in Turkey. TOKI also works as the main agency that facilitates urban gentrification projects. Its function is central to a capital accumulation regime that realizes accumulation by dispossession. In 2007, the AKP passed a significant law that restructured the housing finance sector and institutionalized the mortgage system (p. 1485). This move literally made TOKI the ultimate housing development actor in Turkey and steered the process toward a clearly uneven geographical development. TOKI is now the central government's instrument to intervene in suburban projects and megaprojects, since it has the power to bypass decisions taken by the metropolitan municipality and local municipalities. TOKI's enormous political power also includes the right to expropriate public and private lands to facilitate further housing and infrastructural projects, which in turn increases land-rent speculation. In brief, one can argue that, after 2007, TOKI has become the main actor of urban governance in Turkey. In terms of housing development, TOKI, according to its website, produced more than 420,000 housing units so far; this number was just 43,000 before AKP came to power (Uşaklıgil, 2014). These units include both social housing and luxury housing projects. TOKI claims that the profit obtained from its luxury housing projects is used to facilitate new social housing and infrastructural projects. However, TOKI's budget is not transparent, and one cannot check who benefits from these luxury housing projects. All we know is that the new upper classes and Islamic bourgeoisie engender a demand for luxury housing, which is dependent on the imagination of a safe and peaceful place in the peripheries of the city away from the "crowded and dangerous" city centre. To satisfy such demand, TOKI expropriates land in the peripheries of the city or displaces a former *gecekondu* area in order to re/produce the space for potential land-rent speculation.

The state through TOKI employs an authoritarian approach to suburban land problems, since the developmentalist wealth accumulation process functions by including people in the financial system of mortgage credit or by finding credit for construction companies in order to build large suburban megaprojects. However, this suburban expansion has a legitimate point: homeownership. Turkey's Ministry of Urban Affairs and local municipalities also play a crucial role in facilitating homeownership, since in certain cases local municipalities hold the authority to enable urban transformation projects, and in some cases, the Ministry of Urban Affairs uses public lands for further projects. In order to understand this model, we conducted an interview with an academic expert on urban property relations in Istanbul. We asked the following questions: "What is the role of the state? How does the governance work in this case?" A1 answered as follows:

> In terms of having an authority and organizing a kind of governance, the most important actors are local municipalities because they have the authority in terms of planning, and this authority shapes all property relations. However, since 2010, the Ministry of Environment and Urban Affairs also has this same authority. For the peripheral lands, the property ownership and the authority over the land may vary. The land can be owned by the National Treasury or private actors.

The next question to A1 was, "What is the role of TOKI?" She answered in the following words:

> TOKI is usually involved in the process in accordance with the official contracts signed while transferring the properties from one actor to private actors. For instance, if National Treasury makes a contract with the municipality in order to valorize a land by selling it to private investors, the municipalities either work with their already-existing partner construction companies or they sign those contracts together with TOKI. But in general, TOKI becomes an actor in the projects conducted by the Ministry of Environmental and Urban Affairs or in the large-scale urban transformation projects in the central parts of the city. However, in those urban gentrification projects, TOKI works as a subcontractor instead of being the major actor. In parcel-based land transformations, we do not see TOKI. TOKI usually becomes an actor in certain megaprojects. Indeed, many municipalities do not want TOKI's involvement in land-rent speculation in their areas, because they do not want to share the profit.

A1's answer shows the ambiguity of the situation. The pie for land-rent speculation is large, and all of the actors try to get the best share from that pie. TOKI and local municipalities sometimes agree with urban transformation projects; however, in certain cases they do not cooperate. That is why TOKI usually targets suburban public lands for further projects, since it is easier to allocate and cheaper to transform suburban land. Our interviewee, A1, continued to discuss governmental intervention through TOKI:

> TOKI intervenes during the change of property ownership if there is a specific contract signed by the central government, local municipalities, and private corporations. For instance, if a municipality has a contract with

National Treasury [owner of public lands in Turkey] in order to valorize the land-rent in a particular area, that municipality usually cooperates either with municipal private enterprises or with TOKI for the construction projects, since TOKI has the capacity to mobilize the construction sector. In general, TOKI comes onto the scene in massive housing projects or megaprojects run by the Ministry of Urban Affairs.

This testimony indicates that TOKI has become a central tool to accelerate the authoritarian regime of the AKP by constantly abusing the ambiguity in the legal framework of urban governance.

The Role of Capital

Wealth accumulation may be playing the most important role in Istanbul's suburban development. Indeed, the whole sophisticated system provided by the AKP regime to centralize suburban development in the last fifteen years depends on the practices of wealth accumulation through land-rent speculation. For this very purpose, many infrastructural megaprojects have been constructed or are still under construction in the peripheral areas of Istanbul, and many of these projects are supported by large-scale suburban housing projects. The neoliberalization of the urban process has made the city a tool of the growth machine. Istanbul is now growing day by day, and the massive suburbanization is allocated among those who are adherents of the ruling party. Construction-led economic growth is the major apparatus of the AKP to distribute property-driven wealth among its supporters (Sönmez, 2012). It is basically bypassing all the democratic and social mechanisms of decision-making processes, especially in the level of jurisdiction, through the required networks of both private and public cronyism. As a consequence, that process has literally changed the economic profile of the country. Thus, wealth accumulation is concentrated in the hands of a few cronies, and the rest have been subordinated by a mechanism of indebtedness. That political economic model constitutes the pillar of the AKP's authoritarian regime.

The wealth accumulation process in Turkey is now following a very dangerous path, and economic inequality is rapidly increasing, especially to the advantage of the richest 10 per cent (Güney, 2020). This social and economic inequality has been growing in Turkey since 2003 due to the economic policies imposed by the AKP government, which has fostered a construction and real estate sectors–led economic growth over the last two decades. During that period, major economic investments have been selectively made in construction, infrastructure, and transportation projects. This economic policy has three particular consequences in Istanbul, which has been chosen as the core of this speculative construction economy since the coming to power of the AKP. The first consequence is massive suburbanization in Istanbul due to the expansion of new construction projects. The second is the city's inability to absorb the effects of such big projects, which attract new populations in massive amounts, causing problems regarding insufficient infrastructure. The final consequence is the control and accumulation of wealth in the hands of a few construction companies, financial institutions, and TOKI, which causes subsequent unequal wealth distribution. Indicators show that construction sector–led economic prospects result in the gradual increase in the wealth share of the richest 10 per cent, while the cumulative wealth share of the remaining 90 per cent of Turkey's population is decreasing. When the AKP came to power in 2002, the richest 10 per cent of the society controlled 67.7 per cent of Turkey's total wealth, while the remaining majority owned 32.3 per cent of that wealth. However, as of 2018, the richest 10 per cent owns 81.2 per cent of total wealth in the country, whereas the remaining 90 per cent owns only 18.8 per cent of national wealth (Güney, 2019). Thus, while the already rich classes have increased their wealth share gradually under the AKP rule, the wealth share of other classes, including the poor, has decreased dramatically. Here, one must also note that, according to the same study, in the last two decades about three-quarters of the total wealth in Turkey was in the form of non-financial assets, namely housing and land. This situation is dramatically different compared to the developed economies in Western Europe and North America, where about half of the total wealth is composed of financial assets. Moreover, the trend in Turkey also significantly diverges from other countries in that the proportion of non-financial assets within the total wealth has also been increasing since 2002. The unequally distributed wealth in Turkey was mostly created through the construction and real estate sector–led economic growth fostered by the AKP government over the last two decades. As this dramatic shift in wealth distribution shows, AKP's economic policies, which are based on speculative construction and housing sector growth, have strengthened the economic power of the already rich classes in Turkey. Moreover, such policies have led more and more pro-government capital owners to invest in the construction and housing sector, thereby making them part of that richest 1 per cent by developing a system of crony capitalism (Üçoğlu, 2016, 2019).

We interviewed a housing finance expert in Istanbul (A2) and asked her the following questions: "How can you define the role of construction companies and financial sectors in the wealth accumulation process in Istanbul? Is there an extremely growing risk?" She answered as follows:

> To be honest, housing credits have not really become widespread in Turkey. Only upper middle classes or certain middle-class people have an easy access to housing credit. Because of the economic crisis in Turkey in 2001, the banking system is still conservative right now; they are reluctant to ease the credit lending system. Due to the financial risks and political risks stemming from the authoritarian regime, the demand for financial tools is not high. The low demand for financial tools prevents the derivation of the mortgage system with secondary markets of mortgage bonds and securitizations. In a sense, the financial system branches around mortgage credit are not deepening in Turkey. That is why there is no significant demand from the international markets to the mortgage markets in Turkey. For that very reason, the risk of financial credit is not really growing in Turkey. But let me tell you what risk grows in Turkey. The 1980s and 1990s were the years of high inflation, and because of the Marmara earthquake in 1999, people did not really spend their savings for housing, and there appeared an accumulated demand waiting for the right direction. After the AKP came to power, they just realized this accumulated demand and shifted the country's economic policy into a construction-led growth system with the help of the international conjuncture, since many things became cheapened after the devaluation of the US dollar globally. The central government established this urban growth machine system with the cooperation of state agencies and a few construction companies that are cronies of the AKP regime. The risk burden is not on banks or financial companies. In order to accelerate this system and to sell more houses, the construction companies started to act as a mortgage institution, and they sell houses to the people with a month-to-month payment model for ten to fifteen years without having a bank agreement. Nowadays, the risk burden is carried by crony construction companies, and the failure of these companies would lead to a crisis.

The crony capitalist system in Turkey increases the risk for construction companies and for some homeowners. Even though many construction companies are now in fiscal crisis, the state supports these companies because they are necessary for the well-being of the authoritarian regime.

The Role of Authoritarian Governance

The spread of gated communities is now a dominant reality in the suburbs of Istanbul. The neoliberal risk-management society is reflected

Figure 7.2. Agglomeration of suburban high-rise buildings in the district of Ataşehir. Source: Murat Üçoğlu.

in the housing market of Istanbul because land rent has the highest value in the city, and each young professional and rentier seeks to take advantage of that valuable land-rent speculation. Each new project is promoted in advertisements as the latest stage of modern life, presenting an idealized suburban life in nature with necessary shopping malls and connections to the city centre and financial district. Initially, gated communities emerged in both the inner and outer city adjacent to business and financial districts (Gülümser & Baycan-Levent, 2009). In the inner city, gated communities emerged in the form of residential towers or agglomerations of high-rise buildings; but in the suburbs, they are generally in the form of massive high-rise buildings or luxurious housing (Figure 7.2). At the housing level, projects consist of luxurious gated communities, condominium gated communities, and lower class TOKI-style housing. TOKI and the crony companies that are building these projects are now forming a new type of capitalist elite in the country, and this new crony wealth both increases wealth in the hands of a few corporate capitalists and exacerbates social inequality in the society.

The structure of gated community life facilitates "reducing" the chance to encounter the "other" (Lehrer, 2016). In the same vein, in Istanbul, there are luxurious gated communities of detached houses in which only elites of Turkish society live. These gated communities contain socializing units, including horse-riding pitches, golf pitches, social clubs, and bars, as well as special types of performance venues. They directly exclude people from lower classes as well as those from middle classes. There are also condominium gated communities in which people from the middle classes usually reside. Finally, there are TOKI-style gated communities in the form of so-called social housing on the peripheries of the cities. In one of the project advertisements for a gated community in Istanbul, the investor company explains the term "security" as follows:

> Having security doesn't mean a secluded or guarded life. All the benefits of living in a city that never sleeps, but in a secure environment. 24/7 professional security staff, a closed-circuit camera system, guard-controlled vehicle and pedestrian entries and exits, a visual intercom system in every apartment, and fire and smoke detectors ... All under a professional management that understands how to coordinate these safety measures for your security. (Reclaim Istanbul, 2013)

This advertisement shows the basic point of marketing gated communities in the city. The fundamental discourse relies on the notion of security. Social segregation has become a critical result of this new suburbanization based on gated communities. One of our interviewees (A3) had a very direct answer to our questions: "What is the general profile of people who are buying houses in the new suburban projects? Why are they buying houses in these projects, and what is the everyday life in these new suburban projects?" He answered as follows:

> In general, people who do not own an enterprise but work as a well-paid manager in a good corporate position want to buy houses. They want to have a house in the suburban projects that are relatively close to central business areas. The structure of new suburbs is in the form of mass housing and most generally in the form of huge gated communities. This structure reflects a very isolated life-style, and many of these major gated communities have their own shopping streets and malls full of shops and restaurants. This morphology stems from people's investment in credit to buy those houses. People invest a huge portion of their income in these projects, and they become indebted. That is why, instead of experiencing the city (which would cost them a lot), they are trying to enjoy the gated privatized life provided by these projects. This would cost them less. Of course, this is literally an auto-dependent life-style.

Figure 7.3. Different types of suburban housing: high-rise buildings and low-rise gated communities in the Bahçeşehir area. Source: Murat Üçoğlu.

Hence, financialization and the increase in the number of suburban gated communities are taking place hand in hand with the notion of security. Financialization increases risk, and gated communities provide at least a so-called secure middle-class life-style. Social interaction among different classes and society profiles gradually decrease. Our next question to A3 was as follows: "When people start to live in these suburban projects, they will have to adopt a new life-style that we call the suburban way of life, which is based on auto-dependency and shopping malls. But unlike North American suburbs, Istanbul's suburbs are primarily high-rise [Figure 7.3]. How does this massive high-rise suburban life manifest in the case of Istanbul? How can we depict the suburban everyday life in Istanbul?" In reply, he stated:

In Turkey, detached houses are not that common. There are several reasons for this scarcity, but the tradition is to have high-rise or mid-rise mass housing. The new massive housing projects are full of condo buildings, and only 10 per cent of a single project in certain cases contains detached luxurious houses to attract rich people to that project. Due to the distance from the financial district and central business areas, public transit is not really efficient in these new suburbs. This leads to isolation from urbanity and to an isolated life in a specific suburban area. Many of these gated communities have their own streets, restaurants, cafés, and gyms, or there is a shopping mall nearby. The idea of having this kind of huge gated community with its own shopping street is to give an opportunity to the dwellers to fulfil their everyday needs in these sites, since many of them invested in those housing by taking risk of debt.

The suburban regime leads to an isolated suburban way of life in Istanbul, and this new urban morphology constitutes its own legitimacy over homeownership in the so-called safe and beautiful gated communities. The gated communities are run by gated governance with specific rules and security regulations.

Conclusion

After twenty-five years of AKP rule in the Istanbul Metropolitan Municipality, a new social democratic mayor, Ekrem İmamoğlu, from the main opposition Republican People's Party, was elected in Istanbul with a margin of 20,000 votes during the local elections on 31 March 2019. However, the governing AKP regime did not recognize the election results and called for a new election. The new election took place in June 2019. The second election was won again by the opposition candidate Ekrem İmamoğlu, this time with an even larger – 1 million – vote margin, and the AKP regime could not cancel the results again. To be sure, that victory was a triumph of the opposition against the AKP government. However, following its defeat in the local elections, the AKP government began to take away powers from the municipality and centralize most of the responsibilities of the metropolitan municipalities in order to continue their construction-based hegemony. The AKP government insists on making land-rent speculation and the transformation of suburban land for further megaprojects and housing projects the essence of its urban governance regime.

The type of urban governance seen in the case of Istanbul's suburbanization process can be portrayed as late neoliberalism, which goes hand in hand with nepotism by limiting democratic accountability and fostering the authoritarian regime. It functions in order to stabilize the dominance of the richest classes over the rest of the society by commodifying peripheral lands and speculating to the advantage of political and private actors. This attempt causes two major problems:

an increasing fiscal risk and the widening of wealth inequality. All the stages in that process need closer investigation. Istanbul's case will also show us new approaches to identifying and rethinking the concepts of suburb, surburbanization, and suburban governance. In the case of Istanbul, such investigation also has the dimension of comprehending the structure of suburbanization. The focus of suburban studies in the Global South is no longer on the classical formation of *gecekondu* or shantytowns. New suburbanization has more complex aspects that need to be explained, which is why we would like to use the example of suburbanization in Istanbul to show how it is utilized as a way of new wealth accumulation in Turkey. This insight will also help when analysing current urban politics, not only in Turkey but also in the cities of developing countries. We believe that Istanbul constitutes an important point of inter-referencing for cities of the Global South. Essentially, with developmentalist understanding, the production of space has become very significant, and moreover, facilitating that space production is another step in producing wealth. The ways of facilitating the production of peripheral space constitutes the new urban governance in Istanbul, and the actors of that production pave the way for rich classes as well as those who are close to the government to maximize their wealth. That is why the case of Istanbul shows how peripheral urban space is undergoing a massive reproduction process. Suburbanization in Istanbul means to produce/reproduce the peripheral space for the sake of capitalist wealth accumulation and for the sake of clientalist policies of conservative politics. However, the massive use of peripheral space in this new suburban development process inevitably wipes out the traditional boundaries of the city. Istanbul can now be depicted as a city with no boundary, since it continues to lose its greenbelt and other peripheral lands that used to have the quality of forest, village, or agricultural land. However, apart from that structure, suburban development constitutes the basis of Turkey's authoritarian regime, and that regime gets its legitimacy by providing homeownership to citizens. As a result, the authoritarian regime leads to an indebted society that is reluctant to change the status quo due to a potential financial or political crisis. Suburbanization is the tool that generates this particular dichotomy: being conservative to protect the current regime and yet unable to see the potential risks that could arise with a regime change. The central government's intervention in social life through urbanization is obscuring the crony capitalist system by creating consent through risks. For this reason, the case of Istanbul is quite significant in order to understand how suburban governance could be used as a tool for further authoritarianism.

REFERENCES

Aalbers, M.B. (2016). *The financialization of housing: A political economy approach.* Routledge

Asci, P. (2020). Building the new Turkey: State-space, infrastructure, and citizenship [Unpublished doctoral dissertation]. York University

Buğra, A. (1998). The immoral economy of housing in Turkey. *International Journal of Urban and Regional Research*, 22(2), 303–7. https://doi.org/10.1111/1468-2427.00141

Ekers, M., Hamel, P., & Keil, R. (2015). Governing suburbia: Modalities and mechanisms of suburban governance. In P. Hamel & R. Keil (Eds.), *Suburban governance: A global view* (pp. 19–48). University of Toronto Press.

Geniş, Ş. (2007). Producing elite localities: The rise of gated communities in Istanbul. *Urban Studies*, 44(4), 771–93. https://doi.org/10.1080/00420980601185684

Gülümser, A.A., & Baycan-Levent, T. (2009). Through the sky: Vertical gated development in Istanbul. *The Urban Reinventors Online Journal*, 3, 1–18. http://urbanreinventors.net/3/gulumser/gulumser-urbanreinventors.pdf

Güney, K.M. (2019). Building Northern Istanbul: Mega projects, speculation and new suburbs. In K.M. Güney, R. Keil, & M. Üçoğlu, *Massive suburbanization: (Re)Building the global periphery* (pp. 165–84). University of Toronto Press.

Güney, K.M. (2020). Public health risks of the uneven urban development in Istanbul: Urban inequality, environmental degradation, and earthquake risk. *Urban Anthropology and Studies of Cultural Systems and World Economic Development*, 49(1–2), 1–38.

Güney, K.M. (2022). Earthquake, disaster capitalism and massive urban transformation in Istanbul. *The Geographical Journal*. Advance online publication. https://doi.org/10.1111/geoj.12496

Harvey, D. (2005). *A brief history of neoliberalism.* Oxford University Press.

Hirt, S. (2007). Suburbanizing Sofia: Characteristics of post-socialist peri-urban change. *Urban Geography*, 28(8), 755–80. https://doi.org/10.2747/0272-3638.28.8.755

Islam, T. (2010). Current urban discourse, urban transformation and gentrification in Istanbul. *Architectural Design*, 80(1), 58–63. https://doi.org/10.1002/ad.1011

Istanbul Governorship. (2023). İlçelerimiz. http://www.istanbul.gov.tr/ilcelerimiz

Istanbul Metropolitan Muncipality. (2023). Organizasyonel Şema. https://ibb.istanbul/Home/OrganizasyonSema

Istanbul Planning Agency. (2021). Istanbul Planning Agency: Rethinking Istanbul. https://ipa.istanbul/en/wp-content/uploads/2022/03/ABOUT-IPA.pdf

Kan Ülkü, G., & Erten, E. (2013). Global image hegemony: Istanbul's new gated communities as the new marketing icons. *International Journal of*

Architectural Research, 7(2), 244–57. https://www.archnet.org/publications
/7124

Keil, R., Güney, K.M., Üçoğlu, M. (2019). Introduction: Massive
suburbanization – Political economy, ethnography, governance. In K.M.
Güney, R. Keil, & M. Üçoğlu (Eds.), *Massive suburbanization: (Re)Building
the global periphery* (pp. 3–34). University of Toronto Press.

Keyder, Ç. (2005). Globalization and social exclusion in Istanbul. *International
Journal of Urban and Regional Research*, 29(1), 124–34. https://doi.org/10.1111
/j.1468-2427.2005.00574.x

Kuyucu, T. (2014). Hukuk, mülkiyet ve muğlaklık: Istanbul'un kayıtdışı
yerleşimlerinin yeniden yapılandırılmasında hukuki belirsizliğin
kullanımları ve istismarları. In A. Bartu Candan & C. Özbay (Eds.),
Yeni Istanbul çalışmaları: Sınırlar, mücadeleler, açılımlar (pp. 71–90).
Metis.

Kuyucu, T., & Ünsal, Ö. (2010). "Urban transformation" as state-led property
transfer: An analysis of two cases in Istanbul. *Urban Studies*, 47(7), 1479–99.
https://doi.org/10.1177/0042098009353629

Lehrer, U. (2016). Room for the good society? Public space, amenities, and
the condominium. In H. Rangan, M.K. Ng, L. Porter, & J. Chase (Eds.),
Insurgencies and Revolutions (pp. 141–50). Taylor & Francis.

Logan, J.R., & Molotch, H.L. (1987). *Urban fortunes: The political economy of
place*. University of California Press.

Madden, D., & Marcuse, P. (2016). *In defense of housing*. Verso.

Molotch, H. (1976). The city as a growth machine: Toward a political
economy of place. *American Journal of Sociology*, 82(2), 309–32. https://
doi.org/10.1086/226311

Reclaim Istanbul. (2013, 9 December). Security defined by a gated community
project. *Reclaim Istanbul*. https://reclaimistanbul.wordpress.com/2013/12/09
/security-defined-by-a-gated-community-project/

Sönmez, M. (2012, 13 October). "Transformation" deceit of AKP – The
constructor. *Reflections Turkey*. http://www.reflectionsturkey.com/2012/10
/transformation-deceit-of-akp-the-constructor/

Tanülkü, B. (2012). Gated communities: From "self-sufficient towns" to
"active urban agents." *Geoforum*, 43(3), 518–28. https://doi.org/10.1016/j
.geoforum.2011.11.006

Tekeli, İ. (2013). *İstanbul'un planlamasının ve gelişmesinin öyküsü*. Tarih Vakfı – Yurt
Yayınları.

Üçoğlu, M. (2016, 25 February). Istanbul's suburban dreams fueled by debt.
Bloomberg CityLab. https://www.citylab.com/equity/2016/02/istanbuls
-suburban-dream-is-fueled-by-debt/470550/

Üçoğlu, M. (2019). Massive housing and nature's limits? The urban political
ecology of Istanbul's periphery. In K.M. Güney, R. Keil, & M. Üçoğlu (Eds.),

Massive suburbanization: (Re)Building the global periphery (pp. 185–201). University of Toronto Press.

Üçoğlu, M. (2021a). Financialization and suburbanization: The predatory hegemony of suburban-financial nexus in Istanbul. *Globalizations, 18*(6), 981–94. https://doi.org/10.1080/14747731.2020.1859763

Üçoğlu, M. (2021b). *The financialization of housing as a growth model: New property relations and massive suburbanization in Toronto/Brampton and Istanbul/ Göktürk* [Unpublished doctoral dissertation]. York University.

Uşaklıgil, E. (2014). *Bir şehri yok etmek: İstanbul'da kazanmak ya da kaybetmek.* Can Yayınları.

World Bank. (2023). The World Bank in Türkiye: Overview. World Bank. https://www.worldbank.org/en/country/turkey/overview

Yeşilbağ, M. (2020). The state-orchestrated financialization of housing in Turkey. *Housing Policy Debate, 30*(4), 533–58. https://doi.org/10.1080/10511482 .2019.1670715

INTERVIEWS

A1 – PhD Researcher – Expert in property relations and governance in Istanbul
A2 – Professor – Expert in the housing market in Istanbul
A3 – Manager – Construction market expert

8 What a Difference a Metro Makes! Or Did It? Suburbanization and Local Government Consolidation in Johannesburg

MARGOT RUBIN, ALISON TODES, AND ALAN MABIN

Introduction

The literature on metropolitan or regional government and governance is permeated with the normative view that "metropolitan area governance ... is related with better performance on a range of important outcome variables, such as public transport systems, environmental issues, and urban sprawl" (Ahrend et al., 2014, p. 2).

Consolidation of local government has also been posed as a way to address sprawl and institutional fragmentation (Purcell, 2001). The question remains, what difference does a "metro" or regional government make to urban and suburban development? Does it militate against sprawl, does it favour redistribution, can it accomplish better government performance in general, and how does it respond to residents' concerns and active citizenship? Such issues have been debated in particular city cases in various parts of the world, including the United States and Canada (see Boudreau et al., 2007; Boudreau & Keil, 2001; Keil & Boudreau, 2005; Kipfer & Keil, 2000). This chapter uses the case of consolidation into a single metropolitan government in Johannesburg, South Africa, to explore some of these issues.

Recent literature on suburbs and suburbanization processes has pointed to the complex intertwining and growing importance of non-state actors in the growth, development, and maintenance of non-central urban forms around the world (Ekers et al., 2012; Hamel & Keil, 2015; Mabin et al., 2013; Shatkin, 2014). Ekers et al. (2012, p. 413) argue that

> the restructuring and decentralization of the state has resulted in the emergence of a range of other actors such as non-governmental organizations, community-based organizations, welfare associations, grassroots organizations and the private sector, all of which play a more significant role in governing suburban affairs.

Private sector interests as well as fiercely protective elites are seen to be extremely powerful in the shaping and reshaping of cities, especially where the state has weakened – or has long been weak. Underlying debate have been questions of whether institutional forms of consolidation and fragmentation have contributed to or demoted the ability of these non-state groups to negotiate in the co-production of the cities in which they operate. Pierre Hamel (chapter 1 of this volume) notes that recent changes invite "researchers ... to look more closely at the wide range of actors and practices involved in regulating territorial activities at a metropolitan scale."

This chapter takes a particular "snapshot" of the recent history of Johannesburg. It examines these dynamics in the mid-2010s and explores the modes and mechanisms by which various non-state actors shape their spaces within the City of Johannesburg (CoJ), a local government area remade between 1995 and 2000, and incorporating roughly twenty pre-existing municipal areas. The chapter poses the question of what difference, if any, a centralized or metropolitan local government made to changes in suburban spaces. It addresses the question through exploring the manner in which residents and residents' associations, private developers, and other non-state actors were able to influence the spatial form, land use, and state investments within particular parts of the city space at a particular moment. It looks at three cases, which act as proxies for many of the "suburban"[1] sites within the CoJ: the very large township complex of Soweto, the older elite suburb of Emmarentia, and the northwestern periphery of Johannesburg, which remains a site of new suburban growth. The list is by no means exhaustive, nor does it offer a comprehensive taxonomy of the "suburbs" that exist in Johannesburg, but it does provide some insight into three important types within the city and offers critical inquiry about how power relationships unfolded among constituencies.

The chapter first provides descriptions of Johannesburg's institutional change and policy transition after the first democratic election of 1994. The section offers an overview of the structural shifts and some of the underlying logic of the decisions that were taken for the specific institutional form. It also provides an overview of key policies, especially with regard to spatial planning, which might have been expected to shape patterns of suburban development. Following this contextual section, the chapter offers descriptions of the sites under discussion: the nature of spatial change that took place within them as well as the nature of the suburban constituencies and their abilities to negotiate and ensure that their needs were met. It discusses the strategies that were used within these spaces based on interviews conducted from

2010 to 2015, complemented by relevant documents. We then analyse the commonalities and differences in the ways in which the different constituencies were or were not able to "get their way" and conclude by considering the implications for theories of suburban governance, decentralization, and fragmentation.

Overall, the cases demonstrate that the institutional shape of the metropolitan CoJ has mixed implications for suburban development and the ability of constituencies to negotiate. The chapter argues that it is the specificities of particular suburbs that allow for greater negotiation. But in general, powerful lobbies with shared interests, which can mobilize resources and negotiate through the labyrinthine depths of the metro, coupled with town planning instruments that can be exploited and the know-how to do so, have been key determinants of successfully engaging with a centralized metropolitan government. Both the national and provincial governments also shape much spatial change through, for example, transport infrastructure and other investments, even in a relatively powerful metro government.

A Changing Metro

The present City of Johannesburg (CoJ) is a "metropolitan municipality" in terms of national legislation (Table 8.1). It forms the central part of the "Gauteng city-region," a polycentric but mostly continuously urbanized area of over 15.4 million people with six municipalities within Gauteng province (for detailed information, see https://gcro .ac.za). Together with the CoJ, three of these are "metropolitan municipalities," that is, unitary structures with a single administration, tax base, and elected council.[2] The City of Tshwane (including national administrative capital Pretoria) borders CoJ to the north, and the City of Ekurhuleni lies to the east, both of which have over 3 million people. The notions of "city-region" and "metropolitan" are therefore somewhat complex and cannot be used interchangeably in this terrain.

Johannesburg has South Africa's largest municipal population at around 5.9 million in 2019 (COGTA, 2020a) and is the country's largest economic centre, accounting for an estimated 12 per cent of national employment and 14 per cent of output. The city's population has grown rapidly (3.2 per cent yearly between 1996 and 2019) following economic growth, attracting local and international migrants. The social geography of the city includes large formerly segregated townships that house well over half of the population, as well as a great variety of neighbourhoods of different ages, densities, socio-economic status and mix, and paces of change.

Table 8.1. Key Urban Agents in the City of Johannesburg

Administrative and Territorial Units	Government Bodies	Main Attributions	Number of Units
Gauteng province	Provincial legislature, which elects a premier, who appoints an executive council	Provincial authority in charge of the Gauteng province, responsible for provincial spatial planning and for health, education, and housing; from 1996 to 2010, provincial development and appeal tribunals, headed by appointed professionals and supported by provincial officials, provided a channel for large planning applications and appeals	16.1 (estimate 2022) million inhabitants
Metropolitan municipalities, also called category A municipalities	City councils, which elect a mayor, who appoints a management committee	Vast responsibilities including legislative and executive powers, and responsble for electricity delivery, water for household use, sewage and sanitation, refuse removal, spatial planning, and decisions around land use (inter alia)	Ekurhuleni: 4.05 million Johannesburg: 6.2 million Tshwane: 2.8 million
Johannesburg metropolitan municipality	City has an executive mayor and 260 elected councillors	Responsible for the overall administration, financial control, supply of services, spatial planning, and collection of revenues within its boundaries; the administration of the CoJ	5.2 million inhabitants

		was decentralized initially into 11 regions and finally into 7 regions in 2006 – each region is responsible for the urban management and the operation of local social services	
District councils, also called category B municipalities	Councils that provide some services to local municipalities within their borders; elected mayors who appoint executives	Some types of service provison such as integrated planning, infrastructure development, bulk supply of water and electricity, and public transport	Sedibeng District: 1.4 million West Rand District: 934,000
Local municipalities (not within the metropolitan municipalities), also called category C municipalities	Municipal council, headed by an elected mayor	Each district (or category B) municipality is divided into a number of local (category C) municipalities	Emfuleni Local Lesedi Local Midvaal Local Merafong City Local Mogale City Local Rand West City Local

Non-State Actors

Resident associations	Controlled by executive commitees voted from local residents	Voluntary affiliations of residents in a specific area that come together to represent and protect their interests	
Property development industry	Generally managed by boards of directors	Private companies of various sizes and types involved in the physical development, financing, or management of property	

Sources: Author compiled from StatsSA (2021); United Nations (2018); COGTA (2020b).

The creation of a consolidated metropolitan municipality in Johannesburg after the formal end of apartheid was an outcome of South Africa's larger political decision making, influenced both by the spatial contexts of urban inequality and by international debates around the benefits of consolidation. Prior to 1994 and the first democratic election, the area now included in metropolitan Johannesburg had a number of separate racially defined local authorities, as well as several separate suburban jurisdictions which, like the older and previously smaller Johannesburg City Council, were thought of as "white" areas (although they always contained a significant Black population). These included a set of spatially contiguous autonomous local governments such as Sandton to the north and Roodepoort to the west, which promoted the growth of their areas and constructed new centralities and important residential and commercial zones in the city from the 1970s (Beavon, 2004). Areas housing Black Africans were excised from "white" local authorities in the 1970s, losing access to lucrative property taxes in the rest of the city.

This previous fragmented and racially divided system of local government, on top of steep social hierarchies and divisions, inevitably led to deep fiscal inequalities across the city. It was a key source of protest in areas reserved for Black Africans from the 1980s and underpinned the call for a "one-city" approach, that is, a demand for metropolitan consolidation, allowing a sharing of revenue sources and capacities in city government (Mabin, 1999; Tomlinson, 1999).

Johannesburg's local government was consolidated in two phases. A two-tier structure of a weak metropolitan local government and four municipal substructures with their own rate bases was established in 1995 (Beavon, 2004). However, officials, many of whom were new to their posts, were unclear about the roles and mandate of the two tiers, and there were "vicious party-political contests" over these issues (Beall et al., 2002, p. 77). Financial mismanagement resulted in a fiscal crisis by 1997. In 2001, a single unitary municipality was established as an alternative. The Johannesburg experience was influential in the 1998 White Paper on Local Government, which led to the establishment of several metropolitan municipalities across the country.

The stated intentions behind the centralized local government certainly subscribed to international thinking on the question of consolidated government. Classical consolidation versus fragmentation theory argues that, through centralized government, redistribution to poorer suburbs and areas is possible (Morgan & Mareschal, 1999). The restructuring of the CoJ into a single structure was motivated by an administrative need to have an effective deployment of staff across a metropolitan region … to deal with the equitable geographical distribution of services and opportunities within metro areas. At a financial level … to create a single financial framework and a single budget for metropolitan areas as a whole … there was a need for a single valuation roll and for rates and levies to be set across the metropolitan areas as a whole. (Cameron, 2006, pp. 15–16)

Both Cameron (2005) and Wooldridge (2002) maintain that the desire for a single tier was motivated by concerns that the metropolitan substructures were preventing redistribution and metro-wide development. There was also the fear that African National Congress (ANC) leaders who had been in exile lacked local support bases and so would not be able to drive their agendas in a more decentralized model of governance (Beall et al., 2002). At the time, the civic movements, which had played a key role in the urban struggle against apartheid, thought that a large consolidated authority would be too remote from its citizens. Such thinking was in line with international authors such as Ostrom et al. (1961, p. 837), who argued against "bureaucratic unresponsiveness in gargantua." In Johannesburg, civics were keen to push for a decentralized and locally accountable government, particularly in view of the reconceptualization of local government as developmental and participatory. They were, however, largely sidelined (Everatt, 1999; Seekings, 1996).

The new structure was a consolidated municipality in control of its own legislative and executive functions with a single council and budget. Some eleven administrative subregions were established, with regional directors having enormous power over their internal functions such as hiring staff and the disbursement of their budgets. These subregions were later reduced to seven weaker structures as power was centralized within functional line departments (Beall et al., 2002; Harrison, personal communication, 2012). Control was centralized in the hands of an executive mayor, supported by an executive team with specific portfolios. Municipal-owned entities were also created to deal with a range of services including water and electricity (Pieterse & Gurney, 2012).

It was hoped that a single metropolitan municipality would be able to construct a coherent planning policy across the city, as expected by the national Department of Provincial Affairs and Constitutional Development, which argued that "a citywide metropolitan government is better able to respond to and influence metropolitan-wide spatial, social and economic trends" (cited in Cameron, 2006, p. 14).

Key to the municipality's spatial vision was the desire to densify the city, contain urban sprawl, and improve conditions in areas that had previously been marginalized. These ideas were dominant discourses in post-apartheid spatial planning and have been articulated in all of Johannesburg's post-apartheid spatial plans and in its broader strategic plans, including integrated development plans and longer term city development strategies. While the emphasis on redistribution led to considerable improvement in infrastructure and services in previously marginalized Black African areas, as the case of Soweto shows, plans to restructure the city's spatial form had much less immediate impact.

Despite these policy directions, a laissez-faire approach operated in practice in the 1990s as new municipal structures took time to establish; competition between municipalities continued; and new councillors had to respond to far more experienced developers with strong legal support. In addition, the Provincial Development Tribunal, established in 1997 to enable fast-tracking of low-cost housing projects, was used as an alternative and often quicker route for development approvals,[3] including large up-market proposals such as gated estates and shopping centres (Beavon, 2004). These pressures continued into the 2000s, as the new consolidated metropolitan council established itself and began to put in place policies to support its spatial vision.

The 2001 Spatial Development Framework (SDF) proposed a set of public transport–oriented development corridors and nodes, around which densification would be focused, and the control of urban expansion on the edge. These proposals were supported by regional spatial development frameworks (RSDFs), providing more detailed guidance, and by an urban development boundary. In 2008, a growth management strategy was put in place in response to concerns that the city's infrastructural capacity to support new development was highly constrained and that there was limited funding to extend it. This strategy linked infrastructure investment priorities to the spatial plan. It defined priority areas for infrastructure investment and development around public transport–focused nodes and corridors ("public transport management areas") and in former marginalized areas; "consolidation" areas, where development would be supported if infrastructure was available or if developers were prepared to pay for it; "expansion" areas, where new development was only supported if developers would pay for it; and areas beyond the urban development boundary, where no development would be allowed. Figure 8.1 shows the geographical location of the different designations, demonstrating the low public investment priority of much of the northern part of the city, the high

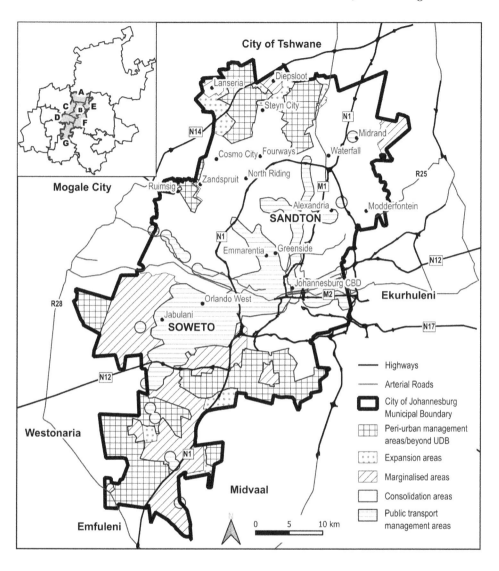

Figure 8.1. Johannesburg 2008 growth management regions. Inset: Gauteng province and Johannesburg administrative regions. Source: Drawn by Michela du Sart based on data from the City of Johannesburg.

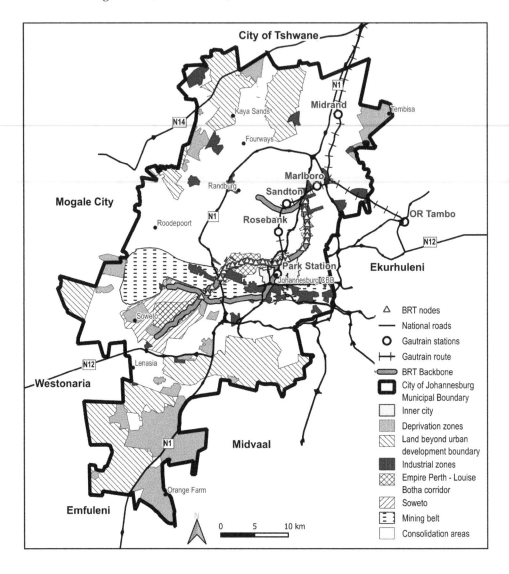

Figure 8.2. Johannesburg 2016 Spatial Development Framework: key elements. Source: Drawn by Michela du Sart based on CoJ (2016).

prioritization of much of Soweto, and the categorization of many of the older suburbs of "white" Johannesburg as consolidation zones.

In 2013, the CoJ embarked on a new transit-oriented development called the Corridors of Freedom, intended to "stitch" the city together utilizing the bus rapid transit system, which had been put in place as the functional spine of the development. The corridors were intended to spatially reconfigure the city through residential densification and the intensification of land use along their length (Harrison et al., 2019). They were part of the city's larger consolidation and densification plans that had been a key focus of the city's planning department since the mid-2000s (Klug et al., 2014). The trend toward consolidation continued with the 2016 *Spatial Development Framework 2040* (Figure 8.2), which identified the city's spatial vision of a compact polycentric, multi-nodal city that "concentrates growth in a compact urban core and around priority transformation areas and key urban and transit oriented development nodes" (CoJ, 2016, p. 18). In line with the SDF, the city has since promulgated a series of policies intended to achieve these ends. They have included an Inclusionary Housing Policy (2019), a Nodal Review (2020), and a new citywide Land-Use Management Scheme (2018), all of which are aimed at ensuring higher densities, spatial integration, and social transformation.

Although policies were slowly put in place from the early 2000s, their impact was limited by the decisions of the provincial development tribunals and the provincial appeal tribunals, where developers could appeal unfavourable municipal decisions (Van Wyk, 2010). Hence, development could occur contrary to the SDF. This situation was challenged legally by the CoJ, which eventually won the power (for all municipalities) as sole decision maker on planning approvals. That victory was almost nine years after the policies had been promulgated, effectively retarding the impact of many of the CoJ's spatial policies.

The following sections investigate how local government consolidation affected the ability of residents and non-state actors to negotiate in the co-production of their spaces and its influence on the outcomes of CoJ's spatial policies.

Soweto: An Old Township Being Rejuvenated?

Soweto, located to the west of the Johannesburg Central Business District (CBD), is nearly as old as the city itself, having been established in 1903 as a site of forced relocations. It later became the city's largest "township" reserved for Black African people. The area accommodates 28.6 per cent of CoJ's population, with a population of 1.3 million people by the time of Census 2011. It is a highly differentiated "suburb" with at least 600,000 people living in poverty (Harrison & Harrison, 2014) and a significant middle-income population, although wealthier Sowetan residents are leaving for the northern suburbs of Johannesburg.

Soweto saw significant spatial transformation from the early 2000s, following substantial investment from the metro's budget. Harrison and Harrison (2014, p. 300) have calculated that

> in 2003/04, 35% of the City's capital budget went to Soweto … As the capital budget grew towards 2008, absolute levels of expenditure were sustained but the proportional expense on Soweto declined to around 17% … However … in 2007/08, Soweto received 78% of the capital budget allocated for so-called "marginalised areas."[4]

The pattern of investment for the intervening years, and in the years since then, supports these claims (see CoJ, 2005, 2006, 2013). Additional attention was given to Soweto through a standing committee[5] intended to drive and manage the regeneration and development of the Soweto areas, established by Mayor Masondo for the 2006 to 2011 mayoral term (CoJ, 2006, p. 14). The following year, a Section 79 committee was established to oversee the development of the area.[6] In both cases, these committees were the only area-based committees in the CoJ. All others were sector or thematically concerned.

CoJ has spent its budget on a range of projects including the tarring of all roads; the bus rapid transit system and its stations, associated cycle lanes, and pedestrian walkways; tourism, focused on the rejuvenation of historically significant areas; and housing and services. Old single-sex hostels have been upgraded to family units, and service backlogs in water, electricity, and sewerage have been addressed (Harrison, personal communication, 2012; Tutu, personal communication, 2013).

Plans were developed to support nodal and transit-oriented development in Soweto (Mohlabane, personal communication, 2013). The main motivation was to ensure that money circulated within Soweto, as historically most households satisfied their needs by shopping in the CBD or in shopping malls outside of the region. Regional strategies and programs, such as the Soweto economic development plans and the "Remaking of Soweto" mayoral project of 2001, sought to develop infrastructure through investment of public funds, which was expected to leverage private money. This strategy has worked to some degree through nodal developments such as in Jabulani, where a theatre, clinic, and regional government offices have been built by the CoJ, and the private sector has invested in the Jabulani Mall (Mohlabane, personal communication, 2013). This development has been followed by a private-public social housing scheme.

However, leveraging has not always worked as planned: the Orlando Ekhaya development, which was designed along Chris Hani Drive to include the development of Bara Mall, a waterfront and hotel area, has met with limited success since the Maponya Mall along the same road has successfully captured many of the anticipated anchor tenants. As has been the case in other parts of Johannesburg (Klug et al., 2014), developers used the provincial development tribunals to gain approval for Maponya Mall, undermining the municipal vision (Mohlabane, personal communication, 2013).

Extensive residential development has also occurred in Soweto. Housing upgrades by private households have become common as the state invests in public infrastructure, and considerable new low-income and affordable housing has been built. There are two anomalies concerning Soweto: Many units were built on the periphery of the area that do not comply with compaction policy; these units require the CoJ to invest in bulk infrastructure. Soweto was not historically included in the Johannesburg town planning schemes, and the legal framework has not been revised. At the time of writing, developers did not have to make a contribution to bulk infrastructure.

Prioritizing Soweto's Development

The large state investment in the area over time raises the question of how Soweto was able to leverage such a significant share of the budget and defend it for such a long time. One line of argument is that Soweto is a highly symbolic space (Laphunya, personal communication, 2013), home to important members of the ANC and historically important events, and had significant backlogs.

Tutu (personal communication, 2013) argues that the development of Soweto and its ability to grasp so much of the budget has roots in the Soweto Civic Association (SCA), which was born out of the 1976 Soweto riots and acted as a federation of separate non-political civic organizations under apartheid. From the late apartheid period, the SCA began to link up with local ANC structures and nominate their candidates, who held SCA mandates to ensure that they would eventually be on the party lists when democratic elections occurred. The first local government elections saw a number of SCA members elected as councillors. In addition, some ex-SCA members were hired into the new municipal substructures as officials since they were familiar with local concerns. By the early 2000s, when the CoJ was consolidated into a single-tier metro and new wards were demarcated, there was a strong contingent of politicians from Soweto sitting in the council in very powerful positions, including the executive mayor, Amos Masondo, and the regional director of the administrative region, who was a former secretary of the SCA (Harrison, personal communication, 2012).

The combination of strong political weight in council coupled with bureaucratic support meant that there was the political will and technocratic know-how to support extensive public investment in the development of Soweto. The council led by Masondo also took the view that public investment would attract private investment, and so a decision was taken by the mayor and his council to retain old town planning regulations that did not require bulk contributions from investors. This decision seems to have encouraged private-sector development in the region.

Public investment in Soweto has tailed off slightly since 2010. Officials in the region attribute this shift to a council that was no longer as heavily weighted toward councillors from Soweto and those with a SCA background. Furthermore, in Masondo's second term, the power of administrative regions was reduced, and much of their autonomy around spatial planning, projects, expenditure, and employment practices was removed (Harrison, personal communication, 2012). As such, the prioritization of Soweto began to diminish, which also coincided with the rise of service delivery protests and more strident calls by other former township and low-income communities for attention and investment (Harrison & Harrison, 2014).

Emmarentia: An Older Suburb Defending Its Character

Emmarentia is one of Johannesburg's older suburbs, established in 1937 from subdivided farmland and mostly developed after the Second World War. It lies northwest of the CBD, with a population of 5,116 in 2011 (ERA, n.d.). Due to the large plots and proximity to schools, open spaces, and the CBD, it has, since its inception, attracted higher income residents (Abrahams, personal communication, 2013). Since the end of apartheid, the demographics of the area have changed as more Black residents have moved in, most of whom are young professionals with growing families, attracted by the location of nearby private and public schools and social amenities.[7] The Emmarentia Residents Association (ERA) describes the area as "the green heart of our city" (ERA, n.d.). The construction of the Masjid-ur-Rahmah mosque has also helped to attract a growing Muslim community to the area (Abrahams, personal communication, 2013).

Development in the suburb has largely taken the shape of house renovations, extensions, and increased security measures in the form of higher walls and electric gates. It has not seen significant densification[8] or the conversion of plots into higher density accommodation (Brugman-Richards, personal communication, 2012), as seen in many other older suburbs. Nor has it undergone the commercialization of the adjoining suburb of Greenside, which has become an entertainment hub with restaurants, bars, and nightclubs along some main roads (CoJ, n.d.).

Managing Suburban Change

Emmarentia has been able to retain its character as a leafy suburb, while others have densified. The reasons seem to lie in a quirk of planning fate and the ability of an active and well-resourced residents' association to exploit the planning instruments at their disposal and actively engage with the precinct planning processes of the CoJ. The Emmarentia-Greenside areas have approved precinct plans that active residents manage and monitor. The residents' association also has a coherent view of the image of the suburb and its subregional context within the city and has been able to fend off unwanted change. The CoJ's spatial policy promotes densification, but the policy is differentiated by region, recognizing that densification must be harmonized with the provision of infrastructure and services. Within Region B, in which Emmarentia is located, the RSDF notes:

> Residential densification … is promoted at nodes, along critical mobility routes, in relation to low income housing initiatives and on consideration of site specifics of a given application. (CoJ, 2010, p. 48)

However, in Emmarentia, densification and land-use change was limited in order to "retain and enhance the residential character and amenity" (CoJ, 2010, p. 140). This position reflects the "strong resistance from residents" to land-use change and the incorporation of "community submissions" into the planning objectives for the area (p. 148). The Precinct Plan for Emmarentia was funded by the CoJ budget but was completed with significant local community participation (Brugman-Richards, personal communication, 2014; CoJ, 2003). The residents' inputs were able to ensure that development conditions included a requirement that all stands be a minimum of 1,000 square metres, restricting subdivisions and densification. The plan also sets out the desirable land uses throughout the suburb and indicates that higher densities are only allowable on the main roads and that commercial activities are largely restricted throughout the area, except for a small commercial node and small professional activities employing up to two people, in line with the RSDF for the region (Abrahams, personal communication, 2013; CoJ, 2003).

The ability of well-organized middle-class residents to limit change in their suburbs is not unusual in Johannesburg (see, for example, Parker & Richardson, 2015; Peens, 2015). However, in Emmarentia, it goes much further. Since the sites were originally part of the same farm, all title deeds contain provisions controlling what changes can occur and requiring that certain land-use changes be approved by the Louw Geldenhuys Trust, established by the farm owners. The Trust may consider anything it "deems necessary" in its assessment. Due to capacity constraints, the ERA acts on behalf of the Trust, granting the necessary approvals (Abrahams, personal communication, 2013.).

Discussions with ERA representatives indicate that there is a coherent vision for the suburb, shared by residents who participate in ERA and articulated as concerns over security and retaining property values (Abrahams, personal communication, 2013). The ERA has significant capacity to carry out its mandate. It has an elected executive committee of fourteen members, including an experienced planner who knows how to navigate the rules and regulations and the CoJ corridors of power. The committee is extremely active and makes sure that the provisions of the various planning instruments are enforced. It was estimated that the members collectively dedicate about 600 to 700 hours of their time each year to carrying out the ERA's activities.

Over the years, the ERA has developed good relationships with the CoJ's planning and building inspectorate, who contact it immediately if building or zoning applications have not been approved by the ERA. All applications for change submitted to the CoJ's building plans section must be endorsed by the Trust before CoJ approval (Abrahams, personal communication, 2013). On occasion, the ERA also drives through the suburb with the building inspector pointing to illegal constructions and land use. The ERA has a close relationship with the local ward councillor, who is actively involved in the area. It is unafraid to use its power and has refused plans that do not comply, forced changes in plans, and ordered the stopping of illegal construction. It has embraced social media and encourages its residents to complain when there are problems, working on the premise that a "squeaky wheel" gets attention.

Despite this very active community and powerful leadership, there have been significant changes since the early 2000s when the suburb's plan was developed. Since the area is an elite space, it has not received much funding, and levels of maintenance have declined. Further, the city's institutional restructuring has posed difficulties, potentially weakening the ERA's effectiveness and its ability to contain unwanted change.

The Northern Arc of Johannesburg

The last site under discussion is the northern arc of the CoJ, generally beyond the outer ring road from the Ruimsig/R28 in the west and across to the east of the city to Modderfontein, north of the R25. Although this area is vast, there are commonalities in its spatial development that allow for a generalized discussion. The following section offers an account of the forces arising from two distinct but powerful impulses: private-sector developers' drive to construct estates and sectional title units for middle-income earners and the elite; and conversely, the construction of very low-income public housing developments as part of the national housing program. Some of this development has been contrary to CoJ intentions of compaction and in places transgresses the urban development boundary. CoJ policies have not been irrelevant, but the effects have been uneven, constructing a patchwork of spatial differences influenced by historical processes, contemporary political directives, and market forces.

A Short History of Change in the North

Historically, much of the northern arc comprised periurban plots used for small market gardening and stables or was undeveloped open farmland. However, since the 1980s, residential and commercial development was actively encouraged by the small municipalities that characterized large parts of the area under apartheid. By 2000, the area included substantial residential developments, informal settlements, and commercial and industrial nodes. Although the CoJ's planning designates much of this area peripheral, where growth should be contained, it is cross-cut by a network of major routes, which has made it highly accessible and thus desirable. From a city-region perspective, much of the area is close to existing and emerging economic nodes, such as Midrand, and is also close to main routes to Tshwane and Ekurhuleni municipalities, with which Johannesburg's growth is increasingly intertwined.

Some of the earlier post-apartheid development took place beyond the urban development boundary: Cosmo City mixed-income housing development, middle-income town-house developments in the north-west (Klug et al., 2014), and large securitized high-income estates in the northeast (Landman & Badenhorst, 2014). Development continued apace into the 2000s. Not all of this development was beyond the ur-ban edge, and at the time, loose planning frameworks allowed property development in large parts of the area, as the CoJ focused its efforts on marginalized areas elsewhere. Thus, during the 1990s and very early 2000s, residential development in the north seems to have been mainly unfettered and uncontrolled by the state, resulting in what the growth management strategy (GMS) later identified as undesirable sprawl.

The GMS designated much of the northern arc as either a "consolida-tion" or an "expansion" area, where "future market-led developments will be determined by the ability of the prospective developments at-scale to be self-sufficient in the upgrading of bulk infrastructure" (CoJ, 2011, cited in Klug et al., 2014, p. 431). Aside from a few nodes at Lanse-ria airport and limited nodes to the north of the N14 around Midrand, development for the area was supposed to prioritize the integration of the township/informal settlement of Diepsloot into the urban system and the construction of a state-subsidized housing initiative to address the significant pockets of informal settlements.

Herbert and Murray's (2015, p. 472) dystopian contention that "the accumulated power of real estate capital has simply dwarfed the regu-latory impulses of municipal planning authorities" has become far less true over the last few years. The northern arc is still much in demand by the developers: Jackson (2015, p. 49) notes that 70 per cent of "all devel-opment applications received by the City emerge from within Region A," which covers large parts of the area. However, Ahmad and Pienaar (2014) argue that the CoJ has become better at managing growth in this area, despite the pressure for development. The CoJ applies more nu-anced approaches to applications, looking specifically to see whether they will contribute to the development agenda or not and refusing those that do not. Jackson (2015) shows that development in Region A largely conforms to the RSDF and has occurred almost exclusively outside of the urban development boundary.

Aside from high-end developments, informal settlements in the north have grown, following formal property development in the area (Huchzermeyer et al., 2014). Several public housing projects have also been established in the northern arc. In a recent case, a new pro-vincial-led housing project near Zandspruit beyond the urban devel-opment boundary was finally approved after a significant dispute between provincial and local government. There are also two massive private estates planned and well underway, Steyn City and Waterfall

City. They offer elite, securitized work/live/play spaces for their residents (Herbert & Murray, 2015). Steyn City was beyond the urban development boundary but was approved in 2006 through the Provincial Development Tribunal. It is thus entirely legitimate in some senses but does defeat many of the objectives discussed in CoJ documents. Further, in 2021, a new master plan for a major "new city" in Lanseria in the northwest was approved, building on earlier proposed development.

Explaining the Patterns of Growth

A number of reasons account for the uneven pattern of development in the north. Many of the large developments being built are the legacy of permissions that were granted years ago through the Provincial Development Tribunal or under older, weaker policies. These projects take years to develop and are built in phases, so if previous permission was granted, it cannot be retracted. Since the legal decision that the municipality has sole responsibility for planning within the municipality, the CoJ's policies have had greater power. Nevertheless, some of these large developments have been proposed by individuals or groups with powerful political connections or claims (see, for example, Herbert & Murray, 2015; Klug et al., 2014), which influences the approval process.

The CoJ has followed a "passive" rather than an active set of interventions, that is, not providing bulk infrastructure or encouraging development in certain areas but not completely preventing it. It has not tried to drive a hard transformation agenda in the north or to shape how the area grows in a proactive way. Thus, in this context, the CoJ responds to developer applications and needs strong reasons to turn them down. There are few senior officials who are able to negotiate and engage with the private sector over plans and projects. The private developers also employ professionals to push their planning applications through the relevant processes in order to make sure that projects are not delayed.

There is some contestation over the effectiveness and buy-in of CoJ policy. Representatives from the private sector argue that they are not really concerned about the CoJ's policies (Representative from private equity group, personal communication, 2012). Bethlehem (personal communication, 2013) claims that the CoJ's spatial policies have very little effect on development, which is instead driven by where the private developers calculate they are able to make profit. If developers have to put in their own bulk services and a project is still profitable, then they will go ahead irrespective of the CoJ's policies. The CoJ argues that it has buy-in into its spatial policies through participatory and consultative processes (CoJ housing official, personal communication, 2014).

The growth of public housing projects in the area is in some ways in line with the promises made by the GMS, which prioritized housing for low-income residents. However, some of the other developments seem to have been a response to the lack of affordable land elsewhere in the province and the need for housing located close to existing settlements (Charlton, 2014). Since 2014, a politically driven national and provincial proposal for "megaprojects" – major housing projects of more than 10,000 to 15,000 units including a range of income groups, facilities, and economic opportunities – threatens to shift the focus of provincial housing expenditure further to peripheral locations where large land parcels are more likely to be available and affordable. The impact of this idea remains to be seen, but it does demonstrate that the metro's spatial planning continues to be challenged by other spheres of government. Likewise, the recent approval of the Lanseria new city master plan, driven by provincial and national government, has forced a shift in the metro's spatial planning, accelerating what might otherwise have been a very long-term possibility.

Suburbs and Spatial Change: Some Common Threads

Some common threads link how and why certain kinds of spatial change take place in the areas discussed. The first is that, in each suburb, there are powerful constituencies able to determine the changes that are in their best interests. In Soweto, the original group drawn from the Soweto Civic Association (SCA) was able to gain political and technocratic traction; in Emmarentia, residents and their representative association, the Emmarentia Residents Association (ERA), have risen to the fore; while in the north, private developers have been key in shaping space. Provincial government departments have also driven their own agendas. In addition, informal settlements and housing projects have emerged beyond the urban development boundary, legitimized through political support.

There are clear commonalities in how different groups have managed to control development within their suburbs: each have a clear vision of what they are trying to achieve that motivates their actions. The ERA has the clear mandate of protecting the area's residential and suburban character and property values; the SCA saw that the previous "imbalances needed to balanced" and understood that to mean significant public investment and improving the quality of life and public amenities for Soweto's residents. Private property developers in the north have a different kind of vision, an "entrepreneurial urbanism." They have seen a chance for significant returns on investments, which has driven their actions. Similarly, the provincial government is driving its agenda of providing state-subsidized housing units and promoting the development of a "smart new city," in line with recent national government support for the idea.

However, the visions would have come to naught if these groups did not have the capacity and resources to negotiate for what they want. All of the constituencies have worked out ways of navigating the labyrinthine corridors of power that constitute municipal planning systems. The SCA infiltrated the City of Johannesburg and became part of the system itself, whereas the ERA wooed city officials and constructed long-term working relationships with key people. The private sector devoted resources to hiring experts and professionals who usher their applications through the various processes. There are also rumours of political connections being used to push through applications and approvals. Political support has apparently also been key in the case of public housing and new city development, whereby a powerful provincial department has been able to push through its agenda despite the CoJ's spatial plans.

These urban agents have also had the expertise and ability to leverage the town planning instruments at their disposal. In some cases, the private sector, having gained approval of their plans under previous spatial policies, stood on their rights and refused to let more recent spatial policies influence their agendas. In others, the private sector has been prepared to pay for the bulk infrastructure and services, which was completely legitimate under the GMS but did not contribute to curtailing sprawl. The issue of legacy is important in Emmarentia, where the professionals in the ERA have used the historical planning tools at their disposal to maintain the identity of their suburb. In the case of Soweto, the fact that the suburb was not part of the city's planning scheme and the lack of need for bulk contributions have been leveraged to gain private-sector investment layered on the public-sector budget. The provincial housing department has used the fact that it is the sphere of government constitutionally obligated to provide public housing to bulldoze the local authority. All of these are peculiarities of historical legacies that have been leveraged by well-resourced and well-informed constituencies in order to achieve their visions.

Implications for Theory: Fragmentation Versus Centralization

The desire for a more centralized local authority to ensure better standardized planning and a coherent vision across the city does not consider the ability of interest groups to disrupt visions, no matter how unified or coherent they may be. Thus visions of densification, prioritization, and restrictions of development have clearly had some effect in Johannesburg, particularly on the northern edge, and have been able to redirect, even in a limited way, where developers choose to invest. However, the plans are never completely successful and are disrupted by the ability of some groups to circumvent the rules and ensure that their goals are met irrespective of the desires of those in power. Further, the plans are disrupted by the sometimes contradictory agendas of other spheres of government and by shifting politics over time.

What do these findings mean for larger questions of suburbanization, suburban governance, and the centralization of the Johannesburg metro? The answer seems to be mixed.

The arguments concerning fragmentation and centralization do not sufficiently consider the intra-institutional politics and the ability of certain coalitions within the state to direct investment. Unbiased redistribution is not a fait accompli just because a local authority has centralized, and much is related to how different coalitions are able to leverage their interests. In the case of Soweto, the Sowetan councillors and officials had much say in how and where the city's budget was spent. This tactic would not have been nearly as successful if the CoJ still operated under a more fragmented structure. A further reason for the success of this coalition was the structure of regional governance within the city: the original functions and autonomy given to regional directors meant that specific local interests could come to the fore. Thus, arguments around suburban development and spatial change seem to be less about a central versus fragmented structure and more about substructures and their political alignments as well as the nature of intra-institutional political alliances, which shape and direct government expenditure.

Our findings fly in the face of claims that fragmentation creates contexts of local competition, whereas consolidated municipalities ensure coordination (Post, 2002). Such thinking underlay the decision to centralize in Johannesburg (Cameron, 2006). Rather, it would seem there is often significant internal competition between the different coalitions of councillors and officials for limited resources, despite a centralized structure. There is also competition between spheres of government concerning whose agenda or mandate should prevail.

There is no question that the unified CoJ has succeeded in putting together comprehensive spatial policies for the entire municipality and has over the years attempted to balance the needs for development against growth. It has also very effectively redistributed resources toward poorer and formerly marginalized areas, although sites of exclusion and elite areas persist. Spatially, the policies have seen some success, and sprawl in the north has been reduced but certainly not eradicated. The cases clearly demonstrate that, despite these planning regimes, the different constituencies have been able to negotiate for their own specific visions and use the tools at their disposal to ensure that their visions influence how suburban landscapes are produced and what they look like. In short, at least in the Johannesburg case, metropolitan consolidation can make some differences to suburban trajectories, but those differences have significant limits. To understand contemporary suburban governance in the context of metropolitan situations requires, as Hamel (chapter 1, this volume) argues, much closer scrutiny of multiple actors and their interactions. It might be speculated that older coalitions and forces may in future find it more difficult to have their way, now that the city is equipped with stronger and more explicit instruments aimed at spatial densification. However, the acceptance in 2021 of the development of the Lanseria "new city" may well undermine these intentions. Diverse directions of spatial change continue, both because of and yet despite creation of a single metropolitan government.

NOTES

1 "Suburb" has both general and special meanings in South Africa: its most common use is to describe districts or quarters of the larger cities, not only referring to low-density and peripheral housing environments but, unusually, also applying to high-rise areas. By contrast, technically "townships" is the term under law for all urban subdivisions, but it is generally applied to the apartheid-produced areas reserved for Black people. Historically, suburbs were "white" enclaves, while townships were the unique residence of "Black" inhabitants. The use of racial terms in this chapter reflects a pervasive reality in South Africa and is not intended to condone it. The term "Black African" refers to indigenous African people following census definitions; "coloured" refers to people of mixed race; and "Black" to all groupings other than whites.
2 South Africa has eight metropolitan municipalities, all in cities with populations over 700,000. The electoral system in metropolitan municipalities combines local ward councillors with proportional representation at the metropolitan level on a 50/50 basis.
3 These tribunals were established under the 1995 Development Facilitation Act and were used in a similar way across the country.

4 Budgeting for the "marginalised areas programme" included all former Black African townships except Alexandra, where budgets were allocated through a separate program.
5 Standing committees are permanent committees established to deal with council matters.
6 Section 79 committees monitor the delivery and outputs of the executive.
7 In 2011, 41 per cent of residents were white, 27 per cent Indian/Asian, 26 per cent Black African, and 6 per cent coloured.
8 The population has increased only marginally, from 4,452 in 2001 to 5,116 in 2011.

REFERENCES

Ahmad, P., & Pienaar, H. (2014). Tracking changes in the urban built environment: An emerging perspective from the City of Johannesburg. In P. Harrison, G. Gotz, A. Todes, & C. Wray (Eds.), *Changing space, changing city: Johannesburg after apartheid* (pp. 101–16). Wits University Press.

Ahrend, R., Gamper, C., & Schumann, A. (2014). *The OECD Metropolitan Governance Survey: A quantitative description of governance structures in large urban agglomerations*. OECD Regional Development Working Papers. https://ideas.repec.org/p/oec/govaab/2014-4-en.html

Beall, J., Crankshaw, O., & Parnell, S. (2002). *Uniting a divided city: Governance and social exclusion in Johannesburg*. Earthscan.

Beavon, K. (2004). *Johannesburg: The making and shaping of the city*. University of South Africa Press.

Boudreau, J.-A., Hamel, P., Jouve, B., & Keil, R. (2007). New state spaces in Canada: Metropolitanization in Montreal and Toronto compared. *Urban Geography, 28*(1), 30–53. https://doi.org/10.2747/0272-3638.28.1.30

Boudreau, J.-A., & Keil, R. (2001). Seceding from responsibility? Secession movements in Los Angeles. *Urban Studies, 38*(10), 1701–31. https://doi.org/10.1080/00420980120084822

Cameron, R. (2005). Metropolitan restructuring (and more restructuring) in South Africa. *Public Administration and Development, 25*(4), 329–39. https://doi.org/10.1002/pad.383

Cameron, R. (2006, 23–25 April). Preliminary draft: Metropolitan government reform in South Africa: The limits of formal reorganisation [Paper presentation]. International Workshop: Governance and Spatial Discontinuities: Reterritorialisation or a New Polarisation of Metropolitan Spaces?, Montreal, Canada.

Charlton, S. (2014). Public housing in Johannesburg. In P. Harrison, G. Gotz, A. Todes, & C. Wray (Eds.), *Changing space, changing city: Johannesburg after apartheid* (pp. 176–93). Wits University Press.

City of Johannesburg. (n.d.). The best restaurant neighbourhoods. Retrieved 6 June 2023 from https://www.joburg.org.za/play_/Pages/Play%20in%20 Joburg/Places%20of%20interest/-The-best-restaurant-neighbourhoods.aspx

City of Johannesburg. (2003). *Emmarentia/Greenside/Parkview development framework / Precinct plan*. Developed by CoJ Development Planning and Facilitation in conjunction with Mafulela Architectural Studio. Johannesburg, June 2003.

City of Johannesburg. (2005). *Annual report 2005/2006 financial year*. https://www.joburg.org.za/documents_/Documents/2004567/The%20 200506%20Annual%20Report/annual_report20056.pdf

City of Johannesburg. (2006). *Annual report 2006/2007 financial year.* City of Johannesburg. https://www.joburg.org.za/documents_/Documents /Annual%20Reports/20062007%20Reports/annual_report20067.pdf

City of Johannesburg. (2010). *Regional spatial development framework: 2010/11 Administrative Region B.* City of Johannesburg Metropolitan Municipality.

City of Johannesburg. (2011). *Growth management strategy: Growth trends and development indicators 2010/2011.* City of Johannesburg Metropolitan Municipality.

City of Johannesburg. (2013). *2012/16 Integrated development plan: 2013/14 review.* https://www.joburg.org.za/documents_/Documents/Intergrated%20 Development%20Plan/2013-16%20IDP%2017may2013%20final.pdf

City of Johannesburg. (2016). *Spatial development framework 2040: City of Johannesburg Metropolitan Municipality.* https://unhabitat.org/sites /default/files/download-manager-files/SDF%20JOHANNESBURG.pdf

COGTA (Cooperative Governance and Traditional Affairs). (2020a). *City of Johannesburg Metropolitan Gauteng: Profile and analysis: District development model.* Department of Cooperative Governance and Traditional Affairs. https://www.cogta.gov.za/ddm/wp-content/uploads/2020/11/City -of-Johannesburg-October-2020.pdf

COGTA (Cooperative Governance and Traditional Affairs). (2020b). *Sedibeng profile and analysis: District development model.* Department of Cooperative Governance and Traditional Affairs. https://www.cogta.gov.za/ddm /wp-content/uploads/2020/07/District_Profile_SEDIBENG-1.pdf

Ekers, M., Hamel, P., & Keil, R. (2012). Governing suburbia: Modalities and mechanisms of suburban governance. *Regional Studies, 46*(3), 405–22. https://doi.org/10.1080/00343404.2012.658036

Emmarentia Residents Association (ERA). (n.d.). Emmarentia Residents Association. Retrieved 20 June 2023 from https://era.org.za/

Everatt, D. (1999). *Yet another transition? Urbanization, class formation and the end of national liberation struggle in South Africa.* Woodrow Wilson International Center for Scholars. https://www.wilsoncenter.org/sites/default/files /media/documents/publication/ACF1B6.pdf

Hamel, P., & Keil, R. (Eds.). (2015). *Suburban governance: A global view.* University of Toronto Press.

Harrison P., & Harrison, K. (2014). Soweto: A study in socio-spatial differentiation. In P. Harrison, G. Gotz, A. Todes, & C. Wray (Eds.), *Changing space, changing city: Johannesburg after apartheid* (pp. 293–318). Wits University Press.

Harrison, P., Rubin, M., Appelbaum, A., & Dittgen, R. (2019). Corridors of freedom: Analyzing Johannesburg's ambitious inclusionary transit-oriented development. *Journal of Planning Education and Research, 39*(4), 456–68. https://doi.org/10.1177/0739456X19870312

Herbert, C., & Murray, M. (2015). Building from scratch: New cities, privatized urbanism and the spatial restructuring of Johannesburg after apartheid. *International Journal of Urban and Regional Research, 39*(3), 471–94. https://doi.org/10.1111/1468-2427.12180

Huchzermeyer, M., Karam, A., & Maina, M. (2014). Informal settlements. In P. Harrison, G. Gotz, A. Todes, & C. Wray (Eds.), *Changing space, changing city: Johannesburg after apartheid* (pp. 154–74). Wits University Press.

Jackson, A.D. (2015). How is planning managing urban growth in Region 'A' of the City of Johannesburg [Honours research report]. University of the Witwatersrand. https://core.ac.uk/download/pdf/188772548.pdf

Keil, R., & Boudreau, J.-A. (2005). Is there regionalism after municipal amalgamation in Toronto? *City, 9*(1), 9–22. https://doi.org/10.1080/13604810500050302

Kipfer, S., & Keil, R. (2000). Still planning to be different? Toronto at the turn of the millennium. *disP – The Planning Review, 36*(140), 28–36. https://doi.org/10.1080/02513625.2000.10556731

Klug, N., Rubin, M., & Todes, A. (2014). The north-western edge. In P. Harrison, G. Gotz, A. Todes, & C. Wray (Eds.), *Changing space, changing city: Johannesburg after apartheid* (pp. 418–36). Wits University Press.

Landman, K., & Badenhorst, W. (2014). Gated communities and spatial transformation in Greater Johannesburg. In P. Harrison, G. Gotz, A. Todes, & C. Wray (Eds.), *Changing space, changing city: Johannesburg after apartheid* (pp. 215–31). Wits University Press.

Mabin, A. (1999). From hard top to soft serve: Demarcation of metropolitan government in Johannesburg for the 1995 elections. In R. Cameron (Ed.), *A tale of three cities: The democratisation of South African local government* (pp. 159–200). Van Schaik.

Mabin, A., Butcher, S., & Bloch, R. (2013). Peripheries, suburbanisms and change in sub-Saharan African cities. *Social Dynamics, 39*(2), 167–90. https://doi.org/10.1080/02533952.2013.796124

Morgan, D., & Mareschal, P. (1999). Central-city/suburban inequality and metropolitan political fragmentation. *Urban Affairs Review, 34*(4), 578–95. https://doi.org/10.1177/107808749903400403

Ostrom, V., Tiebout, C., & Warren, R. (1961). The organization of government in metropolitan areas: A theoretical inquiry. *American Political Science Review*, *55*(4), 831–42. https://doi.org/10.1017/S0003055400125973

Parker, A., & Richardson, K. (2015). Houghton Estate. In A. Todes, P. Harrison, & D. Weakley (Eds.), *Resilient densification: Four studies from Johannesburg* (pp. 106–26). Gauteng City Region Observatory.

Peens, B. (2015). *The influence of public participation on the Corridors of Freedom policy-making process and project: The case of Empire-Perth Development Corridor* [Master's research report]. University of Witwatersrand, Johannesburg. https://wiredspace.wits.ac.za/items/1b1ddea4-2ace-405b-b9e2-a6b3a7eac0d5

Pieterse, E., & Gurney, K. (2012). Johannesburg: Investing in cultural economies or publics? In H.K. Anheier & Y. Raj Isar (Eds.), *Cultures and globalization: Cities, cultural policy and governance* (pp. 194–203). Sage.

Post, S. (2002, 29 August–1 September). *Local government cooperation: The relationship between metropolitan area government geography and service provision* [Paper presentation]. Annual Meeting of the American Political Science Association, Boston.

Purcell, M. (2001). Metropolitan political reorganization as a politics of urban growth: The case of San Fernando Valley secession. *Political Geography*, *20*(5), 613–33. https://doi.org/10.1016/S0962-6298(01)00014-2

Seekings, J. (1996). The decline of South Africa's civic organizations, 1990–1996. *Critical Sociology*, *22*(3), 135–57. https://doi.org/10.1177/089692059602200307

Shatkin, G. (Ed.). (2014). *Contesting the Indian city: Global visions and the politics of the local*. Wiley.

StatsSA (Statistics South Africa). (2021). *Mid-year population estimates, 2021*. Statistics South Africa. http://www.statssa.gov.za/publications/P0302/P03022021.pdf

Tomlinson, R. (1999). Ten years in the making: A history of the evolution of metropolitan government in Johannesburg. *Urban Forum*, *10*(1), 1–39. https://doi.org/10.1007/BF03036625

United Nations. (2018). World urbanization prospects 2018. https://population.un.org/wup/

Van Wyk, J. (2010). Parallel planning mechanisms as a "recipe for disaster." *PER: Potchefstroomse Elektroniese Regsblad*, *13*(1), 214–34. https://doi.org/10.4314/pelj.v13i1.55361

Wooldridge, D. (2002). Introducing metropolitan local government in South Africa. In S. Parnell, E. Pieterse, M. Swilling, & D. Wooldridge (Eds.), *Democratising local government: The South African experiment* (pp. 127–40). UCT Press.

PERSONAL COMMUNICATIONS

Abrahams, G., Executive Committee member, Emmarentia Residents Association, January 2013.

Bethlehem, L., director of REI Development Management, Standard Bank's
    Corporate Investment Banking Division, April 2013.
Brugman-Richards, P., Democratic Alliance, former ward councillor, July 2012.
City of Johannesburg housing official, April 2014.
Harrison P., former CoJ executive director of Planning and Development,
    currently University of the Witwatersrand, July 2012.
Laphunya, P., director of Region D, City of Johannesburg, December 2013.
Mohlabane, L., deputy director, area-based management, City of
    Johannesburg, December 2013.
Representative from private equity group, October 2012.
Tutu, V., Jabulani municipal regional manager, City of Johannesburg,
    December 2013.

9 State Strategies, Market Instruments: Governing Suburban Shanghai under State Entrepreneurialism

FULONG WU

Introduction

This chapter examines the governance of suburban development in Shanghai. In order to interrogate the dynamics in a more nuanced way, I use an example of major suburban development in Lingang, located 75 kilometres from central Shanghai. Lingang is an indisputably suburban area outside the main built-up area of Shanghai, under the jurisdiction of Pudong new district. It is a gigantic new town, in terms of space, occupying 315 square kilometres. In a sense, the suburban area has become a new city in itself. While Lingang new town has its specificities because of its scale and significance, it reveals some key features of governing suburbia under state entrepreneurialism in China. However, administratively, Lingang is not a level of government, fitting into the government hierarchy (Table 9.1). Under the district government of Pudong, Lingang is a collection of street offices and towns as well as the functional areas (industrial development and logistic zones). This collection is managed economically by a quasi-government agency – Lingang management committee – but the street offices and towns, administratively under the Pudong district government, manage social affairs. The municipal and district government have planning power. In Lingang, the power is delegated from the municipal government to the Lingang management committee, which can receive direct endorsement from the municipal government.

Governed by state entrepreneurialism, which uses state strategic intervention and the instruments of market development (Wu, 2018), Shanghai has seen a shift from urban sprawl driven by residential development adjacent to the core city to the development of new towns in its city-region (Wu, 2021). The development of Lingang is an example that illustrates this changing suburban governance. The

Table 9.1. Administrative Units of Shanghai as of 2019

Administrative and Territorial Units	Government Bodies	Main Attributions	Number of Units
Shanghai municipality	Shanghai municipal government	Overall government responsibility directly under the central government	1 (24.28 million inhabitants)
District	District government	Comprehensive political, economic, and social governance	16 (including Pudong)
Town and street office	Town government and street office	Town is a rural administrative unit (not fully urbanized) Street office is an urban administrative unit They used to have combined economic and social management responsbilities but are now mainly social governance	106 towns; 107 street offices
Residents' committee and villagers' committee	Not an official government body but de facto they are the bottom-level governing units	Residents' committees are urban and villagers' committees rural "mass organizations" Social management and assistance	4,507 residents' committees and 1,570 villagers' committees

Source: Compiled from *Shanghai Statistics Yearbook* (SSB, 2020).

development was initiated by the Shanghai municipal government, driven by major state-owned development corporations, and governed by a special government agency that is specialized in economic development.

Lingang's suburban governance faces two major challenges: First, the introduction of a municipal development agency and market instruments such as development corporations have led to fragmentation and coordination problems. Institutional innovations have been made in response to this challenge, including, for example, reassigning the agency (the management committee) from the Shanghai municipal government to the Pudong district government. Second, the industrial-oriented development park alongside the new town has led to physical separation of land uses and functional disconnection between employment and residence. To respond to this challenge, two previously separate governing bodies have been merged into a single management committee.

As illustrated by this development, suburban development in the metropolitan periphery has been strategically initiated by the municipal government to transform Shanghai into a city-region, which has profoundly changed urban-rural dualism under socialism (Wu, 2022b). A third category – the suburb – has been created between the city and countryside. This category is a Chinese version of the space in-between cities (Sieverts, 2003). In the post-suburbia literature, this emergent space and its governance are explained through post-Fordism, neoliberalism, retrofitting, densification, and more recently globalization (Charmes & Keil, 2015; Fishman, 1987; Peck, 2011; Phelps & Wu, 2011; Teaford, 1997). Keil (2018) has noted:

> The dichotomies of city-suburb that underlie much of mainstream urbanist discourse and practice are insufficient. Suburbs are no simple and linear extensions of city cores but the product of a combination of dynamics … The post-suburban in-between city has developed its own logic and dialectics of space, contradictory and productive of new centre-periphery relationships beyond the old city-suburban binary. (p. 75)

The case of Shanghai shows the need to interrogate politics in the specific local context or, in Keil's expression, "new centre-periphery relationships," so as to understand changing urban governance in the metropolitan periphery.

State Entrepreneurialism: Understanding Chinese Urban Governance

The introduction of market mechanisms in its economic development is a salient feature of post-reform China, similar to the global ascent of neoliberalism (Harvey, 2005). Specifically investigating Chinese urbanization and urban development, Logan (2008) documented many aspects of "urban transition," and Yeh et al. (2015) interrogate the interplay of the state and the market. Currently, in the literature of China's urban governance, there are extensive applications of "entrepreneurialism," the growth machine thesis, and land-based finance (Chien, 2013; He et al., 2018; He & Wu, 2009; Hsing, 2010; Lin, 2014; Shen & Wu, 2017; Wu, 2003). The analytical tension between the roles of the state and market, however, remains. While these roles are not necessarily mutually exclusive, since Ekers et al. (2012) show that three modalities – state, capital, and private governance – are all possible, it is not entirely clear how they operate in the governance of Chinese suburban areas.

While the thesis of neoliberalism has been applied to China (Peck & Zhang, 2013), there is a need to situate China's market transition within its historical changes and continuation. Wu (2010) suggests that the introduction of market players into urban development may not follow a neoliberal ideology but rather, practically, uses the market approach to find space for growth. Evolving around this growth imperative, Chinese planning, in a broader sense beyond city design, strives to find its position in economic governance and impose its significant imprint on the built environment (Wu, 2015). Not relying on Chinese uniqueness, Wu (2017) suggests that the core mechanism underlying neoliberalization is still relevant to China. The concept of spatial fix developed by Harvey (1978) is about using an instrument of the built environment to solve the internal tension of capital accumulation of capitalism. It is possible to understand Chinese urban governance through a "more unified framework of analysis, namely the dynamics of accumulation and the regulatory form to support the structural coherence" (Wu, 2017, p. 154). To critique the neoliberal city, Wu (2017) provides the explanation of the "business model" and its political economic foundation of China as the "world workshop."

As for the concept of "state entrepreneurialism," Wu (2018) defines it in this way: "Through institutional reform, the state apparatus, in particular the local state, demonstrates a greater interest in introducing, developing and deploying market instruments and engages in market-like entrepreneurial activities" (p. 1384). These activities, as will be shown in this chapter, evolve around state strategies. Hence, state entrepreneurialism demonstrates greater planning centrality. Centrality does not necessarily mean that development is well planned or implemented according to plans. Rather, planning centrality indicates the end of entrepreneurialism, while market instruments are used as the means. While actual development processes may involve corruption, vested interests, and complex politics, development is often justified by a rationale that enhances the state's governance capacities rather than reducing or abandoning state control.

Suburban Strategies

Chinese cities have seen rapid spatial expansion along with economic growth and urbanization. Pudong new district, set up and developed in the 1990s, is an example of such spatial extension (Shen et al., 2020). It is aimed to accomplish the vision of developing Shanghai as the "dragonhead" of the Yangtze River region and the gateway to China. In the 1990s, the decentralization of economic decision making in the lower tiers of government led to inter-city competition and urban sprawl (Zhang, 2000). Since the tightening of land regulation (Xu & Yeh, 2009), a more orderly suburban development has been envisioned. The Shanghai master plan in 1999 developed a polycentric spatial structure, which later evolved into a multilayered settlement system. Suburban new towns were adopted as a development strategy, which has led to a much more "ordered" suburban development and "designed suburbs." Chinese suburbs have been characterized by their heavy concentration of manufacturing industries (Wu & Phelps, 2011). Indeed, the development of suburbs is a "state strategy" that is purposely adopted, as the suburb is regarded as a new space for capital accumulation (Shen & Wu, 2017, 2020). Even for more-developed Shanghai, which has experienced significant economic restructuring from manufacturing industries to the tertiary services sector, the suburbs still accommodate industrial development and are major sites for Chinese strategies as a nation of industrial manufacturing.

In the newest round of the urban master plan (2017–35), Shanghai aspires to be an "excellent global city." This global city not only foresees Shanghai as a "global finance and economic command centre" but also forges high value-added manufacturing and innovation capacities. The four suburban new towns – Lingang, Songjiang, Qingpu, and Jiading – are trusted with economic specialization. Lingang specializes in heavy equipment manufacturing.

Lingang is especially important because it is near the Shanghai deep-water port at Yangshan. In fact, the new town was originally named "harbour new city" (*hai gang xingcheng*). The port has been regarded as a strategic development to build Shanghai into a global shipping centre. Foreseeing such a status and a "new international division of labour" to relocate heavy equipment manufacturing, Shanghai assigned Lingang to capture export processing industries, maritime services, and advanced manufacturing industries:

> The deep-water port must have a support that is connected to the land, a port alone in the sea, actually, would not be able to form a development ... [F]or this reason, Shanghai is researching how to create an "interconnected development." This is to use a port to bring prosperity to a whole city; therefore, at that place, a new city needs to be constructed as a proper support to the port; at the same time, it can bring in an "interconnected effect," which would also stimulate Shanghai's growth and achieve synergy. (Interview, former senior planner, Lingang, August 2016)

The development of Lingang is thus not an incidental relocation of population. Behind it is the state strategy (advanced manufacturing plus port development). Its development started from the establishment of a heavy

Figure 9.1. Lingang industrial park. Source: Fulong Wu.

equipment manufacturing industrial park (Figure 9.1). Further, to support the industrial park, a new town was planned. The new town is a residential and commercial centre plus some service industries. The master design of a German-based architectural firm, Gerkan, Marg and Partners, won the design competition. The new town features a large lake in the centre (known as "water-drop lake"; Figure 9.2), surrounded by circular zones of commerce and residential uses. The master plan of Lingang has transformed the area from an administrative or jurisdictional structure to a "functional" structure, comprising the new town proper, several local towns, manufacturing parks, logistics zones, and the port (Figure 9.3).

The Networked State: The Management Committee

The governance of Lingang is not only "entrepreneurial" but also involves complex coordination between different scales and stakeholders (Shen et al., 2020; Wu, 2018). Although Lingang is a municipally led project, Shanghai had to motivate the support of the district government. The development is located in an underdeveloped district

Figure 9.2. Lingang new town by the lake. Source: Fulong Wu.

of Shanghai, the Nanhui district, which was annexed to Pudong new district in 2009. This process of "suburbanization" is not due to economic decentralization as seen in the early stage of reform. The central city remains powerful and has organized the development through development agencies, which is in contrast to the widely known model of the local business-centred growth machine (Logan & Molotch, 1987) or neoliberal suburbanism (Peck, 2011). The management committee (*guan wei hui*) in China is quite special, acting more like an agency on behalf of the upper government in the local territory, which has streamlined functions (focusing on attracting investment and organizing economic activities) and acts across different scales. Its operation has been explained in a case study of Beijing Economic and Technological Zone in Yizhuang (Wu & Phelps, 2011): the management structure as the model of "combined government and business." The composition of the committee reflects a corporate style:

> In Yizhuang, this entrepreneurial governance is, if anything, more pronounced in that a specific government agency has been inserted into the local

Figure 9.3. The port near Lingang industrial park. Source: Fulong Wu.

sphere and invested with significant national economic development objectives. Thus developers indicated the advantages of a streamlined and speed-
ier process for their projects in Yizhuang compared with elsewhere. (p. 424)

In short, the management committee is a government agency that is
responsible for the management of development zones. It is a quite
unique institution, introduced after economic reform as a task force for
coordinating economic development across administrative hierarchies
and departments. As a streamlined government authority, the institution leaves traditional social management to existing local governments such as district and town governments (Wang & Wu, 2019). The
management committee initiates city planning and coordinates developments in designated areas. These areas, such as various high-tech
parks – economic and technological development zones (ETDZs) – are
literally "zones of exception" where new market mechanisms are introduced and implemented. The management committee in this case
represents the municipal government as its agency to control the development, while the town or district government of the area gives up

development management. The management committee can be set up at various levels of government. For example, the district government can set up a management committee to govern the development zone at the district level, as development zones bear different administrative ranks. In short, management committees are government agencies set up specifically for governing local spaces. They are task-oriented, usually toward economic development. Because Lingang new town is a strategic project of the Shanghai municipal government, its management committee was set up directly under the municipal government.

As the management committee connects various parts of the state across scales, it can be regarded as a form of the "networked" state. Lingang also experienced governance innovation. Originally, there were two separate management committees: one for the industrial park and the other for the new town centre. To better coordinate the development of the Lingang area, these two committees were merged into a new Lingang management committee. Another major change was the reassignment of the Lingang management committee from the municipal government to the district government. Thus, the Lingang management committee is now *shishu quguan* (municipally owned but district managed). There is a tax implication as a result. The industrial output of enterprises registered in the district is normally counted under the district government, and the industrial and commercial tax is shared by the central and local government (in this case, the district). In Lingang, as a municipal agency area, local development is controlled by the municipal government since the territory is under the control of a municipal government agency. However, the reassignment of management to the district means that the local district has the right to retain local tax. In addition, Lingang has a special policy that allows it to retain local taxes (rather than for the district or municipal government). This special treatment is known as "double special policies," that is, Lingang can retain its own monies and can make its own decisions. As a result, Lingang has greater autonomy and financial resources for economic development. It is perhaps because of this policy that Lingang aims to generate future economic growth and taxes rather than short-term profits from selling state land.

The guidance of the municipal development agency is necessary in these rather underdeveloped suburban areas. In essence, before Lingang, Nanhui was a rural county, which was converted to district status in 2001 and annexed to Pudong in 2009. The local government lacked the capacity to guide or implement the strategic development of Shanghai. The Lingang management committee is thus a powerful municipal government agency inserted into Nanhui to coordinate development in the area. Indeed, many officials in the Lingang management committee were sent from various functional bureaus of the municipal government to this locality:

> Before the Pudong new district taking over Lingang, Lingang itself was under the municipal administration. It had complete authority to act independently [from the district government]. At that time, we represented the city bureau [of planning] when participating in the management of Lingang. I was able to communicate with the city bureau, with its leaders and staff. Because I was a deputy director in the city bureau, the leaders sent me here. I also acted as the deputy principal planner of Lingang new town. Actually, there was no principal planner. There was only me managing the place, only five to six of us completed the master plan of the region, implemented the plan, and made examination and approval. There was no need for the leaders to worry about the project. Anyway, we did not deviate from the approved, statutory planning procedure. (Interview, former senior planner of Lingang, August 2016)

Such a streamlined agency focusing on economic activities appears to be quite effective:

> About five or six years ago, we only had a few people, so it was a very able and efficient team working there … Before we were in good harmony with the developer [Lingang Group], they worked on planning and were actually working like a family with us; we were managing the planning. We would meet and discuss if there were any issues, and if we reached an agreed decision about planning, it would be executed according to the plan. If you thought the plan had any problem, we would start to think how to solve it and how to adjust the plan immediately, and the problem could usually be solved within a few days. (Interview, former senior planner of Lingang, August 2016)

Market Instruments: Development Corporations

Despite the powerful state agency in suburbs, actual developments are usually carried out by various development corporations. The development corporations are the primary market player, responsible for converting rural land into developable land and for infrastructure investment. Since Lingang started with the heavy equipment manufacturing park, the main development corporation is Shanghai Lingang Economic Development Group (hereafter Lingang Group), which was established in 2003. It is funded by the Shanghai municipal government and hence belongs to the state-asset management committee of Shanghai. It is responsible for land, infrastructure, and industrial development and for attracting external investment. The development model is mainly based on using land as collateral for bank loans. In other words, debt-driven development is the major feature (Robinson et al., 2020).

In 2004, Shanghai Industrial Investment Group used the asset of Caohejin High-Tech Park as registry capital in Lingang, at a price of 450 million Yuan. Since its establishment in 1984, Caohejin High-Tech Park has become a profitable and well-managed high-tech park in Shanghai. In other words, although the Shanghai government used the asset of an established park in the central city to support Lingang in the suburbs, this arrangement was achieved through increasing the capacity for capital mobilization of the latter in addition to cash capital investment by other municipal corporations. It proved very important for Lingang. Another way of reading this transaction is that Lingang Group together with Lingang Investment Corporation invested in Caohejin.

However, because of heavy investment and the slow return of income, Lingang Group had a debt ratio of 83.20 per cent in 2014. To reduce its debt ratio and maintain further capital mobilization capacity, the municipal government of Shanghai "reassigned" profitable assets inside Shanghai city proper to Lingang Group. The shares of Lingang Investment Corporation were transferred to Lingang Group. As a result, Caohejin became a subsidiary enterprise under Lingang Group, which controls 95 per cent of its shares. As a consequence, the debt ratio of Lingang Group was reduced to 75.19 per cent in 2015, 70.02 per cent in 2016, and 69.10 per cent in 2017. Through asset reassignment, the state-asset committee of Shanghai increased its share of Lingang to 51.7 per cent, while other corporations under the state-asset committee of Shanghai invested the majority of the remaining investment. One of the original investors, Nanhui Urban-Rural Construction, Development and Investment Corporation, an urban development and investment corporation (UDIC) belonging to the former Nanhui district and now to Pudong new district, has a 2.15 per cent share in Lingang Group. The Nanhui UDIC is also a state-owned company but belongs to the district government.

In other words, the municipal government injected initial capital for a major development corporation to develop a suburban industrial park and new town by leveraging bank loans and used its assets in central areas of the city to redefine the balance sheet of a suburban development corporation. The Lingang Group also managed to raise capital from the stock market. It bought an existing listed company in the Shanghai Stock Market and transformed it into its subsidiary in 2015. Shanghai Lingang Holdings reached a value of 13.11 billion Yuan in the Shanghai Stock Market, and the net value of the shareholders was 6.51 billion Yuan in 2017. In 2018, the company raised 1.0 billion Yuan green bonds in the capital market to finance its Lingang Science City project. In 2017, the total net value of Lingang Group reached 19.27 billion Yuan. As a state-owned enterprise under the municipal government, Lingang Group is the major developer of this suburban industrial area. Although Lingang Group is an industrial development corporation, it also plays the role of a UDIC in infrastructure investment.

As can be seen from the history of the development corporation, Lingang Group exists to realize the "strategic goal" of Shanghai and has not made profits in the short term. While its average net profit in the period from 2014 to 2016 was 200 million Yuan, in the same period it received 142 million Yuan, 262 million Yuan, and 237 million Yuan in financial subsidies from the Shanghai government. From this account, it is clear that Lingang Group did not make a financial contribution to Shanghai but has continued to expand its investment. It managed to use financial subsidies from the Shanghai government, investment from the state-asset committee, and capital from the capital market to develop the suburb of Lingang in Shanghai. As stated in the special tax policy formulated in 2012 that "all profits generated from Lingang are retained in and used by Lingang," Lingang Group is allowed to use the special fund set up under this tax policy to rebate its investment in infrastructure. In other words, it carried out the development for the municipal government.

In addition to the major development corporation of Lingang, a district-level development corporation is responsible for developing the residential area. Shanghai Gangcheng Development Group ("Harbour-city" group) was established in 2002, originally under Nanhui and now under the Pudong state-asset management committee. It is responsible for the development of the main new town centre (the new town surrounding the water-drop lake, now named Nanhui new town).

The area of Lingang is usually presented in functional terms rather than by jurisdiction boundaries because, administratively, it does not form a level of government or an administrative unit. This ordinary area at the metropolitan periphery was in essence a rural area. In this area, there are rural towns and a new town converted from an original rural town. Most of the land for Nanhui new town came from land reclaimed from the sea. However, this area has now become suburbanized. Multiple governments and their development corporations have participated in this process. There are joint developments between Shanghai municipal government (and its industrial groups), district governments, and town governments (and their development corporations). Outside the original administrative area of Nanhui district, there are a joint investment with Minhang district through Minlian Lingang United Development Corporation and a joint investment with Fengxian district through Lingang Fengxian Economic Development Corporation. These can be seen as cross-border developments but under the economic governance of the Lingang management committee. For example, the rural town of Haiwan, adjacent to Lingang, administratively belongs to Fengxian district. But it has become Lingang Fengxian Park, which was developed as a joint development between Lingang Group, Guangming Group (a municipal industrial group), and the Fengxian district government. Economically, it also became part of the Lingang area and is now under the Lingang management committee in terms of economic governance. In addition to four major development corporations in Lingang, in 2013, to speed up the development of Lingang, the Shanghai municipal government required four major development corporations in Pudong district to develop their Lingang branches (Shen et al., 2020).

The (Civil) Society and Social Innovation

In contrast to a highly mobilized civil society in Western economies, Chinese cities show a lack of formal mechanisms for community participation in decision making. In former rural and now suburbanized areas, the governance structure is particularly weak because former rural township governments are under-resourced. Gated communities are the ubiquitous landscape of new Chinese suburbs. To attract home-buyers and, practically, to manage these estates, developers appointed property management companies, which sounds similar to rising "authoritarian private governance" (Ekers et al., 2012). But the services provided by property management companies are limited to property management such as cleaning and security within the estates. While homeowners' associations have been set up, they have not become a social force in suburban development. Their role is limited to the delegation of property management to property management companies and perhaps to reporting some social needs to the local government agency (the residents' committee under the subdistrict government office). The influence of homeowners' associations over suburban development is fairly limited (Wu, 2022a, 2022b). They are "retrofitted" features to strengthen neighbourhood governance. They do not constitute an alternative form of "private governance" that residents can choose. A resident of an upper market gated community explains:

> [For the theft case], we did report to the police. But eventually they didn't catch the thief. The previous security guard team was not so good. But we could not go to [live in] open communities. For open communities, how many policemen would you need? The cost would be too high. The government would say your community is not secured enough – there are too many "leakages"! For these individual houses, the government would have to send ten policemen. But when these policemen come, they would tell themselves, "Ok, today you two should be on duty, the other eight go to sleep." You see, this would be quite low efficiency. That is why it would be ineffective! However, the homeowners' association also has difficulties, because all board members are volunteers. But they don't even have to use legal means. They just come to force you – do you really want to live here any longer? (Interview, an upper market suburban gated community resident, November 2018; translated by the author)

The government requires the developers to install gated features, which effectively offload certain duties and costs to residents themselves. This measure, however, is not an active choice by residents as a selection of governance attributes. The explanation of authoritarian private governance may sound attractive. But it is not a result of residents seeking private governance in the suburbs. In other words, the selection of suburban living, for most residents, is not a choice for greater self-management (Wu, 2022a). Legally based management such as contract, conveyance, and restriction (CCR), widely seen in American gated communities (Low, 2003), is rare in Chinese suburbs, and even if there is such a condition, it is difficult to enforce through legal processes. Homeowners' associations are not legal entities. They do not act through market means to replace the government to create a corporate form of governance (McKenzie, 1994). Rather, they are an enhanced form of "collective control," as illustrated by the interview.

In terms of governance form, the suburban residential area does not represent a distinctive category from other areas, as participatory governance is generally weak. These suburban gated residential areas are the product of market development, but that does not mean they are self-governed by market mechanisms. The developers designed the qualities, styles, and services according to their prediction of the market preferences of different consumers. Once the residential areas are built, the residents of different estates do not merge and form political "communities" to exert influence over the government, owing to the absence of participatory politics. These areas are instruments of the state to extend its governance capacities.

Despite the absence of participatory politics, suburban Shanghai has experienced some social innovation to enhance the management of social affairs and the provision of social services. In 2015, a pilot policy of "the joint operation of town and management committee" (*guan zhen lian dong*) was launched. As mentioned earlier, in industrial suburbs, development has been implemented by state-owned development corporations supervised by management committees. The management committee mainly coordinates economic development and leaves the social management functions to the local town government. On the other hand, to maintain its own revenue, the town government is also engaged in economic development, setting up its own industrial park. The lack of social coordination and management has remained a long-term problem in suburbs developed from industrial projects. This situation is often described as "separation between industries and cities" (*chan cheng fengli*), in terms of not just physical distance but also the absence of urban functions in industrial areas. Development in suburban areas has been split into economic and social functions. While the economic function is managed by a committee outside the administrative system across scales, the social function remains the duty of local government, that is, the town or subdistrict offices under the district governments. The separation of industrial and residential functions is fundamentally due to this division between economic and social governance.

Since 2015, the function of economic governance (attracting investment and managing enterprises) of four towns in Lingang has been reassigned to the Lingang management committee. Accordingly, their tax is counted under the management committee. However, their tax revenue is kept and returned to them. In addition, the value added from attracting new enterprises is returned to the respective town. In other words, town governments now rely on fiscal redistribution rather than direct income from economic activities. Their performance is accordingly evaluated in terms of social management rather than gross domestic product (GDP) growth. According to the party secretary of Nicheng town, it means that, from that moment, "I only need to consider spending money rather than earning money." This change not only enhances the involvement of local society in state-led mega-urban projects but also strengthens environmental maintenance and social functions for suburban residents working in industrial parks.

Conclusion

Ekers et al. (2012) suggest three modalities of governing suburbia: state-led, market-led or capital accumulation, and self-built or authoritarian private governance. By now there are ample examples of each modality or combinations of them (Hamel & Keil, 2015; Keil, 2018). In previous work (Wu & Shen, 2015), we discussed the relevance of each modality to China and suggested that Chinese suburban areas were highly heterogeneous. Just as in other places, these three modalities may contribute to the mechanism of suburban governance to varying degrees. In this chapter, I further develop an explicit view about the relationship between these modalities. Referring to "state entrepreneurialism" (Wu, 2018), I argue that governing suburbia in China conforms to state strategies, while market instruments are deployed. I emphasize that, while suburban development has seen real estate development and profit-making market endeavours, the development is far more strategic than earlier urban sprawl, evolving around efforts to upgrade urban economies. It does not mean that society is passive. As Logan (2018) noted about the agencies of people, "rather than seeing residents as the passive victims of larger political and market forces, an alternative vision understands them as actively adapting, strategizing and manipulating the conditions of their lives, certainly not in the control of their futures but both knowledgeable and active" (p. 1376). In suburban Shanghai, various social and management innovations try to incorporate local communities into the state strategic development.

Governing suburban Shanghai now involves a networked state across scales and horizontal coordination between stakeholders. The hierarchy of local governments consists of the Shanghai municipal government, district governments, town governments, and street offices (also known as subdistrict government; see Table 9.1). The street office, strictly speaking, is not a level of government but rather an agency of district government. Further, under the street office are the residents' committees, which in theory are "self-organized social organizations" but in reality become the bottom level of government, which manages residential neighbourhoods (Wu, 2002). Parallel to this government structure are the management committee and development corporations. The Lingang management committee, representing the municipal government, is responsible for the supervision and coordination of economic development in the area. The management committee is not a level of government but undertakes some economic management functions for the municipal government and now the district government, after its reassignment. Thus, in the territory of Lingang, multiple governments and development corporations play their roles under the coordination of the management committee (Shen et al., 2020). The salient feature of governing suburbia, as shown in suburban Shanghai, is the way underlying state strategies are implemented through the market instruments of development corporations. Chinese suburban development presents a salient business model (Robinson et al., 2020). Just like the overall approach to China's urban development, the financial method is deployed together with state development agencies to capture perceived opportunities (here, heavy equipment manufacturing in Lingang) and cope with development and economic challenges (Wu, 2023). We have seen both governance and social innovations transform a peripheral rural area into a suburbanized metropolitan region.

Acknowledgment

The first draft of this chapter was prepared in 2015 and presented in the workshop "Suburban Governance in an Era of Globalizing Urbanization" in Montreal, organized by Pierre Hamel. It has been updated subsequently after other later publications became available ahead of this chapter. In addition to grant support from the Major Collaborative Research Initiative "Global Suburban Governance, Land and Infrastructure in the 21st Century" from the Social Sciences and Humanities Research Council of Canada, the research has received funding from Jenny Robinson's UK ESRC project "Governing the Future City" (ES/N006070/1) and "The Financialisation of Urban Development and Associated Financial Risks in China" (ES/P003435/1) and research assistance from Zheng Wang and Jie Shen.

REFERENCES

Charmes, E., & Keil, R. (2015). The politics of post-suburban densification in Canada and France. *International Journal of Urban and Regional Research*, *39*(3), 581–602. https://doi.org/10.1111/1468-2427.12194

Chien, S.S. (2013). New local state power through administrative restructuring: A case study of post-Mao China county-level urban entrepreneurialism in Kunshan. *Geoforum*, *46*, 103–12. https://doi.org/10.1016/j.geoforum.2012.12.015

Ekers, M., Hamel, P., & Keil, R. (2012). Governing suburbia: Modalities and mechanisms of suburban governance. *Regional Studies*, *46*(3), 405–22. https://doi.org/10.1080/00343404.2012.658036

Fishman, R. (1987). *Bourgeois utopias: The rise and fall of suburbia*. Basic Books.

Hamel, P., & Keil, R. (Eds.). (2015). *Suburban governance: A global view.* University of Toronto Press.

Harvey, D. (1978). The urban process under capitalism. *International Journal of Urban and Regional Research, 2*(1–3), 101–31. https://doi .org/10.1111/j.1468-2427.1978.tb00738.x

Harvey, D. (2005). *A brief history of neoliberalism.* Oxford University Press.

He, S., Li, L., Zhang, Y., & Wang, J. (2018). A small entrepreneurial city in action: Policy mobility, urban entrepreneurialism, and politics of scale in Jiyuan, China. *International Journal of Urban and Regional Research, 42*(4), 684–702. https://doi.org/10.1111/1468-2427.12631

He, S., & Wu, F. (2009). China's emerging neoliberal urbanism: Perspectives from urban redevelopment. *Antipode, 41*(2), 282–304. https://doi.org/10.1111 /j.1467-8330.2009.00673.x

Hsing, Y.-t. (2010). *The great urban transformation: Politics of land and property in China.* Oxford University Press.

Keil, R. (2018). *Suburban planet: Making the world urban from the outside in.* Polity Press.

Lin, G.C.S. (2014). China's landed urbanization: Neoliberalizing politics, land commodification, and municipal finance in the growth of metropolises. *Environment and Planning A: Economy and Space, 46*(8), 1814–35. https://doi .org/10.1068/a130016p

Logan, J.R. (Ed.). (2008). *Urban China in transition.* Blackwell.

Logan, J.R. (2018). People and plans in urbanising China: Challenging the top-down orthodoxy. *Urban Studies, 55*(7), 1375–82. https://doi.org/10.1177 /0042098018763552

Logan, J.R., & Molotch, H.L. (1987). *Urban fortunes: The political economy of place.* University of California Press.

Low, S. (2003). *Behind the gates: Life, security, and the pursuit of happiness in fortress America.* Routledge.

McKenzie, E. (1994). *Privatopia: Homeowner associations and the rise of residential private government.* Yale University Press.

Peck, J. (2011). Neoliberal suburbanism: Frontier space. *Urban Geography, 32*(6), 884–919. https://doi.org/10.2747/0272-3638.32.6.884

Peck, J., & Zhang, J. (2013). A variety of capitalism ... with Chinese characteristics? *Journal of Economic Geography, 13*(3), 357–96. https://doi.org/10.1093/jeg /lbs058

Phelps, N., & Wu, F. (Eds.). (2011). *International perspectives on suburbanization: A post-suburban world?* Palgrave Macmillan.

Robinson, J., Harrison, P., Shen, J., & Wu, F. (2020). Financing urban development, three business models: Johannesburg, Shanghai and London. *Progress in Planning, 154,* 100513. https://doi.org/10.1016/j.progress.2020.100513

Shanghai Statistics Bureau (SSB). (2020). *Shanghai Statistics Yearbook*. SSB.

Shen, J., Luo, X., & Wu, F. (2020). Assembling mega-urban projects through state-guided governance innovation: The development of Lingang in Shanghai. *Regional Studies*, *54*(12), 1644–54. https://doi.org/10.1080/003434 04.2020.1762853

Shen, J., & Wu, F. (2017). The suburb as a space of capital accumulation: The development of new towns in Shanghai, China. *Antipode*, *49*(3), 761–80. https://doi.org/10.1111/anti.12302

Shen, J., & Wu, F. (2020). Paving the way to growth: Transit-oriented development as a financing instrument for Shanghai's post-suburbanization. *Urban Geography*, *41*(7), 1010–32. https://doi.org/10.1080/02723638.2019 .1630209

Sieverts, T. (2003). *Cities without cities: An interpretation of the Zwischenstadt*. Routledge.

Teaford, J. (1997). *Post-suburbia: Government and politics in the edge cities*. Johns Hopkins University Press.

Wang, Z., & Wu, F. (2019). In-situ marginalisation: Social impact of Chinese mega-projects. *Antipode*, *51*(5), 1640–63. https://doi.org/10.1111/anti.12560

Wu, F. (2002). China's changing urban governance in the transition towards a more market-oriented economy. *Urban Studies*, *39*(7), 1071–93. https://doi .org/10.1080/00420980220135491

Wu, F. (2003). The (post-) socialist entrepreneurial city as a state project: Shanghai's reglobalisation in question. *Urban Studies*, *40*(9), 1673–98. https://doi.org/10.1080/0042098032000106555

Wu, F. (2010). How neoliberal is China's reform? The origins of change during transition. *Eurasian Geography and Economics*, *51*(5), 619–31. https://doi .org/10.2747/1539-7216.51.5.619

Wu, F. (2015). *Planning for growth: Urban and regional planning in China*. Routledge.

Wu, F. (2017). State entrepreneurialism in urban China. In G. Pinson & C.M. Journel (Eds.), *Debating the neoliberal city* (pp. 153–73). Routledge.

Wu, F. (2018). Planning centrality, market instruments: Governing Chinese urban transformation under state entrepreneurialism. *Urban Studies*, *55*(7), 1383–99. https://doi.org/10.1177/0042098017721828

Wu, F. (2021). A governance perspective on new towns in China. In R. Peiser & A. Forsyth (Eds.), *Towards 21st century new towns: Past, present, prospects* (pp. 152–66). University of Pennsylvania Press.

Wu, F. (2022a). *Creating Chinese urbanism: Urban revolution and governance changes*. UCL Press.

Wu, F. (2022b). Intertwined modalities of suburban governance in China. In R. Keil & F. Wu (Eds.), *After suburbia: Urbanization in the 21st century* (pp.179–200). University of Toronto Press.

Wu, F. (2023). The long shadow of the state: Financing the Chinese city. *Urban Geography*, 44(1), 37–58. https://doi.org/10.1080/02723638.2021.1959779

Wu, F., & Phelps, N.A. (2011). (Post)suburban development and state entrepreneurialism in Beijing's outer suburbs. *Environment and Planning A: Economy and Space*, 43(2), 410–30. https://doi.org/10.1068/a43125

Wu, F., & Shen, J. (2015). Suburban development and governance in China. In P. Hamel & R. Keil (Eds.), *Suburban governance: A global view* (pp. 303–24). University of Toronto Press.

Xu, J., & Yeh, A.G.-O. (2009). Decoding urban land governance: State reconstruction in contemporary Chinese cities. *Urban Studies*, 46(3), 559–81. https://doi.org/10.1177/0042098008100995

Yeh, A.G.O., Yang, F.F., & Wang, J. (2015). Economic transition and urban transformation of China: The interplay of the state and the market. *Urban Studies*, 52(15), 2822–48. https://doi.org/10.1177/0042098015597110

Zhang, T. (2000). Land market forces and government's role in sprawl: The case of China. *Cities*, 17(2), 123–35. https://doi.org/10.1016/S0264-2751(00)00007-X

10 Conclusion: Suburban Governance Facing Uncertainty

PIERRE HAMEL

The diversity of the suburban landscape, which ranges from sprawling "boomburbs" to gated residential communities and from edge cities to planned "new town" projects on the urban periphery, has made the suburbs a dynamic component of urbanization (Teaford, 2006). Since at least the 1960s, suburban areas have played a direct role in the expansion of metropolitan regions (Fishman, 1987; Hayden, 2003; Scott, 2019). This development means that suburbs can no longer be exclusively discussed in terms of their subordinate relationship to central cities. Rather, they have a central role to play in facing the uncertainties of the urban future.

Within the metropolitan regions discussed in this book, suburban communities have followed diverse trajectories that vary not only according to past experiences and/or national constraints but also according to the availability of resources, prevailing market conditions, and various modes of political regulation imposed at different levels by the state. Meanwhile, it can be difficult to assess the capacity of local actors to cope with these determining factors because agency and structural considerations are so interconnected. From this perspective, suburbs are essential to understanding urban space as an element of the highly ambivalent "current modern social conditions" (Martuccelli, 2017a). This summary all points to at least two important observations.

First, it is important to remember that contemporary "modern social conditions" – what sociologists used to consider a "sociological template" (Martuccelli, 2017a, p. 36) – have proven hard to apply analytically in a way that fosters a better understanding of how individuals experience life in society. In any case, studying how social life is experienced requires more attention to the fact that individuals face an ongoing tension between the need to engage in commoning and the emptiness of their solitude in relation to society (p. 41). In today's world, the experience of modern social conditions remains shaped by the breakdown of totality and certainty, as well as by the integration of objectivity and subjectivity that accompanied the emergence of the project of modernity. Western intellectuals have traditionally expressed this loss of certainty through the ideology of progress, which served to give meaning to the Western world. The end of Western hegemony now adds yet another dimension to this process and opens the way for other regions to play a new and different role.

A lot can be said about the decline of Western hegemony and the role played by countries previously deemed or treated as subaltern. In many regions, the ongoing hybridization of cultural traditions can be tied to specific trajectories that point to the emergence of so-called geo-modernity. The latter is defined as a perspective that emphasizes various geographic factors over political ones (Martuccelli, 2017b). Accordingly, relations between the global and the local are characterized by the growing interactions between the two, which means that, even if, to a certain extent, modernity continues to be experienced within a national framework (Dubet, 2017), the meaning of that experience is not universally shared, largely because values, traditions, and cultural life provide individuals and households with a distinct sense of belonging. As reflected in the diverse circumstances described by the contributors to this book, there are significant differences between countries. And this variety brings me to the second key observation on how suburbs help define "current modern social conditions."

Despite its controversial nature and the importance of historical developments and cultural traditions for understanding the emergence of geo-modernity, the theory of individualization remains vital. This theory emphasizes the importance of citizen rights, the growing prominence of subjective singularity, and the unavoidability of life course choices as key features of the modern experience (Bauman, 2001; Beck & Beck-Gernsheim, 2002; de Singly, 2017; Touraine, 2018). However, it is important to remember that individual recognition remains connected to strong identities and social frameworks. At issue here is how social solidarity can be redeployed or what conditions can support a redefinition of solidarity given the current democratic context and the growth of both inequality and pluralism (Dubet, 2016). This predicament cannot be resolved without considering the wide range of paths toward individualization or individuation that exist across different national contexts, how these paths converge, and how they circumvent or redefine institutional constraints: "the individuation process in the modern occidental society is related to a set of social representations and especially institutional interpellations, a fact well expressed by the importance given to the relationship between the welfare state and individuation modalities … the amount of support that they have available to answer to institutional prescriptions … or the effects of the institutional subjection mechanisms, as discussed by Foucault" (Araujo & Martuccelli, 2017, pp. 26–7). So how can individuals and households reject an "institutional prescription" when institutions "are the ones that offer representations and support" (p. 27)?[1]

This dilemma is reflected in several sociopolitical controversies, including those related to suburban planning. I will now expand on this idea in relation to suburban governance on the basis of two theoretical principles or pillars: (1) the production of space, and (2) democracy and challenges to democratization.

Treated as an open process of interaction between actors and institutions, suburban governance is tied to the fact that cities and especially metropolitan regions can no longer be defined as "bounded territorial entities" (Lukas, 2019, p. 9). The scalar relations that engulf local components of regions are made possible by innovations introduced through the functioning of sociotechnical systems that have become integrated into the very fabric of the city (Amin & Thrift, 2017). More importantly, this process involves the restructuring of political culture. The emergence of governance would not have been possible had it not been for elements in civil society demanding more accountability from those in power and more input into decision-making processes. These demands were what triggered changes in the meaning of government (Le Galès, 2021; Stoker, 1998).

The new political culture within which governance has taken shape did not necessarily transform the power dynamics associated with the functioning of the state (Bevir & Rhodes, 2010). However, it did introduce new rules based on networking, cooperation, and partnership. Theoretically speaking, governance can be understood as a better way of conceptualizing the development of the state. Gilles Pinson (2015) therefore argues that this theory can be labelled "pragmatic" and "neo-pluralist." In terms of its capacity to regulate a given territory, the state has lost the monopoly of power. It has become entangled in a web of interdependency with units that were previously under its control. And yet, the theory of governance does not portray a weakened state. On the contrary, the state has been able to redefine its relationship with society and its territory without giving up its rational function (p. 505). As a result, from a governance framework perspective, the state is often even more present than before.

From this point of view, the theory of governance has taken up where the sociology of organizations in the French tradition left off by providing a general understanding of public policy through the analysis of collective action and associated forms of coordination. But unlike the sociology of organizations, the theory of governance has addressed, albeit in a rather piecemeal fashion so far, a historical dimension that had previously been largely ignored. As a result, it has been able to raise fundamental questions regarding the definition of both collective action and authority, as well as regarding the legitimacy of the political (Pinson, 2015).

Below, I will address suburban governance processes from the perspective of this emerging theory of governance with the aim of better understanding how it sheds new light on the ways that suburbanization processes are shaping metropolitan regions. But first, I need to return to the two theoretical principles identified above, namely production of space and democracy.

Production of Space

Suburbanization is central to current debates in urban theory (Hanlon & Vicino, 2019; Keil, 2018; Phelps & Wu, 2011). For researchers who argue that, from a historical perspective, suburbanization has been regulated through diverse processes – state policy, capitalist accumulation, and private (often authoritarian) forms of politics (Ekers et al., 2012) – problems affecting a metropolitan region's periphery can no longer be understood and solved exclusively with reference to the centre. Rather, the direct contribution of suburban communities must be considered. It is therefore no longer enough to simply address the concerns raised in recent years by the New Regionalists, who see suburban expansion primarily as a threat to the renewal or reconfiguration of central cities (Brenner, 2019; Savitch & Vogel, 2000; Swanstrom, 2001). Understanding the production of urban territories requires giving more attention to the conceptualization of space within its inherent processes.

Even if there are "many different modes of producing urban spaces" (Schmid et al., 2018, p. 25), each marked by "difference" and "heterogeneity," spatiality serves as a valid point of departure when understood broadly and through the Marxist notion of "concrete abstractions" (Lefebvre, 1974, p. 462). In particular, certain aspects of Doreen Massey's (1996, 2005, 2013) efforts to clarify the conceptual significance of space deserve attention.

Space may seem a rather obvious reference point for urban studies. However, the way it is understood needs to be clarified in order to open up new avenues of understanding. In the history of philosophy, unlike time, space has most often been treated as a so-called residual category. It has therefore simply been "defined as a kind of flat surface out there" (Massey, 2013). Breaking with such a static representation of space not only makes it possible to rethink the relationship between space and time but also to appreciate the full importance of space in structuring society and politics. Above all, space must be understood as the product of complex relationships. By stressing how space is a dynamic category, Massey offers an opportunity to rethink the narrative of Western modernity by abandoning the subordination of space to time.

Defining space as the "product of relations" (Massey, 2005, p. 91) helps reveal its multiplicity and how it can be understood as "a precondition for the temporal" (p. 89) through a range of interactions "from the immensity of the global to the intimately tiny" (p. 9). In this way, it becomes easier to conceive of space as a sphere where multiple trajectories coexist side by side: space cannot exist without multiplicity, which opens the door to "heterogeneity," among other things.

In addition to addressing the relationship between time and space, Massey introduces two other binary oppositions. First, she looks at the interaction between place (defined in reference to its empirical, concrete, and sensory characteristics) and space (understood as an abstract reality). Second, she explores the interplay between the local and the global, both of which simultaneously shape urban communities – the global being just as concrete as the local in how places are defined. These assumptions make it possible to better "understand space as an open ongoing production" (2005, p. 55). Space is always "under construction" (p. 9). Four elements of this process deserve special attention.

First, in light of the case studies presented in this book, a focus on local variations is not enough to shed light on current suburban issues because globalization cannot be understood solely as an external and/or abstract force. Rather, globalization plays a direct role in the relationships and experiences that shape local settings or communities, all while imposing a logic of its own.

Second, a focus on the spatial connections associated with the production of space and with the relationships rooted in living spaces reveals the need to rethink the reading of place. On the one hand, it is not sufficient to simply emphasize the extent to which "spatial connections" are "involved in the construction and understanding and impact of any place or economy or culture and everyday life and actions" (Massey, 2005, p. 90). On the other hand, space no longer seems to pose an obstacle to mobility; it is as if distance had vanished. These two considerations underscore the fact that space is "more than distance": "It is the sphere of openended configurations within multiplicities. Given that, the really serious question which is raised by speed-up, by the 'communication revolution' and by cyberspace, is not whether space will be annihilated but what kinds of multiplicities (patternings and uniqueness) and relations will be co-constructed with these new kinds of spatial configurations" (p. 91).

Third, a focus on globalization always risks minimizing "the appreciation of difference" (Massey, 2005, p. 99) or overemphasizing how territorial components inhibit dynamic relationships: "envisioning space as always-already territorialised, just as much as envisioning it as purely a sphere of flows, misunderstands the ever-changing ways in which flows and territories are conditions of each other" (p. 99).

Finally, places provide a context for understanding how Massey's definition of the spatial is both dynamic and open to social and political interactions. Going back to Lefebvre's (1974) categories, places – defined in reference to realities that are urban, suburban, or somewhere between the two – are perceived, understood, and inhabited as evanescent phenomena. Cities never remain the same. They are constantly being reshaped, constantly transforming themselves: "Thus something which might be called there and then is implicated in the here and now. 'Here' is an intertwining of histories in which the spatiality of those stories (their then as well as their here) is inescapably entangled. The interconnections themselves are part of the construction of identity" (Massey, 2005, p. 13).

The transitoriness of suburban areas is difficult to grasp, since relationships within polycentric metropolises add new layers of interaction and establish a new horizon for the urban experience. As Richard Harris (2013) has pointed out, "the transitional aspect of suburban land is obvious, with its intermediate levels of population density. To understand how it is transitory, however, we must make an effort: to see the city block as one-time urban fringe; to see the rash of homes on a rural sideroad as future urbanity. Suburban land does not just lie between the country and the city, but in the long view each parcel and tract itself undergoes that transition, begging us to view it historically" (p. 33).

The eight case studies presented in this book highlight not only the numerous challenges facing suburbs, from poverty and social exclusion to environmental concerns and/or planning issues related to technology and infrastructure, but also other material and living components – human and non-human – of city life. While exploring the connections between places and their surroundings – at both a local and a global scale – each chapter also addresses the role of periurban zones in the expansion and restructuring of metropolitan regions.

Competitive global capitalism is often used to explain the current turbulent times. And yet, such turbulence dates back to the very origins of modernity, when the feeling of the end of totality was first experienced (Martuccelli, 2017a). Regionalization has always meant that metropolitan regions face a constant process of expansion and adjustment (Bailey et al., 2020; Harrison et al., 2019; Paasi & Metzger, 2017). Leaving behind the traditional urban-suburban dichotomy (Tzaninis & Boterman, 2018), the social and economic development of metropolitan regions is now governed by cross-national networking (Davidson et al., 2019). Granted, the regions examined in the previous chapters are not necessarily engaged in direct communication with one another. Nevertheless, they share very similar preoccupations with environmental issues, social inequality, social justice, and cooperation among various categories of actors at multiple scales of governing (see, for instance, the chapters on Toronto, Montreal, Paris, Frankfurt, and Miami).

However, important changes have occurred in the role that local governments, including suburban authorities, play in shaping the future of local spaces and their amenities. The two Canadian regions examined in this book provide particularly relevant examples. Canadian municipalities are historically and legally defined as creatures of the provinces; the constitutional status of the latter corresponds to that of states in other federal systems (Savoie, 2019). Nevertheless, municipalities and metropolitan regions have seen their power increase in recent decades as their economic and social role has grown with globalization. As a result, a gap has developed between their official status and their effective capacity for action.

Understanding the reshaping of suburban governance requires returning to the notion of the "local state" (Cockburn, 1977). In line with the analysis developed by Warren Magnusson (1985, 2015), I see forms of local self-governance interacting with diverse components of the state, including state agencies present at the local level. This interaction presents social actors with both constraints and opportunities. The role of the local state can never be reduced to the activities and/or decisions of the municipality. Other levels of government are also involved at different stages of local decision-making processes.

Nevertheless, as Magnusson (1985) also points out, it is important to remember that the state is both "fundamental" and "misleading." On the one hand, it is fundamental in the sense that, as a major political force, it reflects the configuration of power relations between actors at any given moment. On the other hand, it is misleading in the "sense that the state is in many ways an ideological illusion from which all of us suffer" (p. 17). For Magnusson, it is most important to redefine the political – and, more specifically, political space – both locally and globally. In this respect, the political cannot be understood exclusively within the framework of the state. To break with such state-centred thinking, the political needs to be experienced in urban settings on an horizontal basis, whereby legitimacy and social recognition are connected to "democratic mutualism" – a form of cooperation among equals defined as "the necessary condition for genuinely inclusive engagement with others" (p. 268).

The local state does not intervene or participate in suburban governance in the same way everywhere (Robinson, 2016). In some contexts, higher levels of government are more assertive. Although this phenomenon can be explained in terms of historical or structural factors, it is important not to entirely dismiss the role of conjunctural factors. Although evident to varying degrees in all the case studies, the role of upper levels of government is most obvious in the Shanghai city-region and in Istanbul. In both these cases, albeit for different reasons, the reforms introduced by central state authorities and ruling political elites regarding the control and/or regulation of territories once again point to the importance of the historical national context. The existing authoritarian regimes have been able to mobilize resources and regulatory measures through a mix of coercion and hegemony.

In post-reform China, the introduction of "market mechanisms" endorsed by the state can be associated with the rise of global neoliberalism. But this process can also be understood as an initiative by local authorities faced with the new "interplay of the state and the market," which is central to the new orientation of state policy. For that matter, the central role of planning at various scales has been reaffirmed and adapted to a "business model" imposed by "state entrepreneurialism." This model is well explained through the analysis of the suburban area of Lingang in the chapter on Shanghai.

As Fulong Wu points out, Lingang's development has depended on several initiatives launched by the Shanghai authority, starting with the master plan for the region. The latter is based on a "polycentric spatial structure" that provides for the creation of new towns. The Lingang Group, a major development corporation, has received financial support from various corporations. Its interactions with both corporations and units of local government have been organized in a hierarchical manner.

In their chapter on Istanbul, Murat Üçoğlu and K. Murat Güney point out how suburban expansion is closely tied to a process of gentrification supported by TOKI, the state agency responsible for mass housing administration. A series of reforms have made this agency "the ultimate housing development actor in Turkey" and a key decision maker in matters related to suburban development. Characterized by "massive high-rise buildings or luxurious housings" in gated communities, as well as by "lower class TOKI-style housing," this approach to development took shape in a context of "crony capitalism." Indeed, the AKP (Justice and Development Party) government has relied on local boosterism and land-rent speculation to support wealth accumulation by a privileged class. Faced with this turn of events and the fact that Istanbul's population has tripled since the 1980s, a large portion of the population has become increasingly concerned about social segregation, a lack of infrastructure and services, and environmental degradation. In this case, the process of suburbanization can be best understood in terms of an authoritarian and conservative suburban regime, given that urban expansion on the periphery represents one of the main components – if not the main component – of not only economic development but also "rising financialization" practices.

As is the case with metropolitan governance (Storper, 2014), there is no well-established or proven model for suburban governance. Alongside the growing number of local interdependencies within metropolitan regions – associated with multiscale governance involving various institutions and actors – the contributions to this book point to a series of strategic adjustments for coping with public issues and social choices. Under suburban governance, collective action relies on interactions between actors, as well as between actors and institutions. Activities need to be coordinated through networks and at multiple scales in order to respond to social needs and to adjust to uncertainty, including what stems from global challenges (Keil, 1998; Keil et al., 2017).

Given the diversity of local spaces, the presence of conflicting interests, and the pluralism inherent in contemporary modernity (Leca, 1996), coordination at a metropolitan scale poses a challenge that can be better assessed by revisiting the notion of "the institutional entrenchment of binding relations" (Hamel et al., 1999, p. 165). However, even if they have played a fundamental role by prescribing regulation models, institutions cannot account for all social interactions. As Araujo and Martuccelli (2017) point out, beyond and often through fighting against institutions "individuals are forged confronting social life's vicissitudes by means of their capacities and skills, which include the mobilization of interpersonal relationships, and through a singular set of strategies and competencies" (p. 35). In other words, interpersonal relationships can provide social actors with the confidence and resources they need to abandon institutional prescriptions that are unable to protect them, allowing them to recognize that they are "obliged to take charge of themselves, on their own" (p. 36). This insight should not be forgotten when considering how the chapters of this book portray the emergence of suburban governance as a way of coping with the global suburbanization of the current era, given that individuals and households cannot always or exclusively rely on the state to carry out public responsibilities. Once again, this idea is in line with Massey's (2005) understanding of the tension between place and space, in addition to that between the local and the global. From this point of view, political identities and political engagement are mediated through a space defined as "the sphere of openended configurations within multiplicities" (p. 91).

Despite the convergent topics mentioned above, suburban governance has been experienced in a range of different ways. National contexts, national societies, and national cultures have all played a role in shaping processes where the state no longer has the exclusive prerogative of defining and promoting the general interest, as it did within the Weberian tradition. If the notion of governance means that the state is "de-differentiated" and "trivialized" – having invited civil society actors to play an active role in the formulation and implementation of public policy (Pinson, 2015, pp. 506–7) – its influence still cannot be dismissed. This point is particularly relevant to the case of Frankfurt-Rhine-Main, where there is a strong tradition of comprehensive and spatial planning involving both the national and state level. The regionalization of land-use planning in Germany since 2011 has challenged the "institutional architecture of the German state itself," given how the dominant ideology is now based on the logic of the market economy. Nonetheless, the state has not vanished as either an actor or an institution.

The metropolitan regions of Paris and Miami are affected by economic competitiveness as much as Frankfurt-Rhine-Main. As in the latter context, public and collective action in these two other regions has led to the development of solutions similarly based on economic competitiveness, even if the corresponding local and regional strategies are not the same.

The two European metropolitan regions discussed in the book serve as a reminder that spatial planning systems belong to specific national traditions, whose influence persists even though functional specializations are increasingly defined on a global scale. Even while recognizing that globalization is not an abstract and universal law capable of generating "an integrated planetary capitalism" (Ong, 2011, p. 6), it remains important to remember that local and national authorities still need to cope with the consequences of international economic integration. In the case of the Frankfurt-Rhine-Main region, the collective decision to adapt to a context of "global competitiveness" seems to have been almost inevitable. This issue is directly addressed by Valentin Meilinger and Jochen Monstadt in the conclusion to their chapter: "Greater Frankfurt's current institutional form was not born in a political vacuum. It emerged from a nested landscape of long-standing local economic networks and identities, competing ideologies of governing, and strong (but selective) ties between politicians, businesses, private interest groups, and local elites." The redistribution of the "costs and benefits of growth" is constrained by the "inherent contradictions of capitalist urbanization," as regional initiatives are undermined by efforts at the municipal level (the "local politics of place") to capitalize on "settlement development" and maximize tax revenue.

In Paris, historically persistent social divisions and inequalities have been accentuated by the competitive financialization of global cities. However, in this case, an analysis of metropolitan governance also shows that the administrative complexity associated with managing urban functions on a regional basis has not been addressed by the promoters of "Grand Paris," even though its creation was initially intended to better coordinate relations between the central city and its periphery. As a result, the issue of inequality, especially social inequality, in the suburbs has not been effectively dealt with. Marie-Hélène Bacqué and Éric Charmes clearly recognize this problem in their conclusion: "Redressing the inequalities that [suburbanites] suffer would require significant redistribution of resources to ensure, in particular, that public services, accessibility, and environmental quality achieve the same standards as those prevailing in central neighbourhoods and wealthy suburbs – yet without the popular classes being pushed away due to urban development."

For reasons that are not only historical and geographical, but also economic and political, Miami's situation can hardly be compared to that of the French metropolis. Nevertheless, although social and physical divisions within suburban areas are expressed differently through the built environment on the two sides of the Atlantic,[2] the underlying class conflicts and social diversity end up defining relations between people and places in similar ways. In the same vein, the "dual city" model adopted by some researchers in the 1990s (despite its reductionism) shows how social issues have increasingly become urban issues (Le Galès, 2002). This convergence reflects the leading role of class conflict in the structuring and occupation of territories, serving as a reminder that social conflicts often go hand in hand with polarized behaviour (Morales et al., 2019). In other words, looking beyond the so-called American mosaic, social, ethnic/racial, and class divisions can lead to polarized if not crude conflicts when they are transposed onto the built environment. This conflict is what some ethnic communities – especially the Hispanic population of Cuban origin – in Miami-Dade County faced between the early 1990s and the mid-2000s, when a series of new cities were created within what had previously been "suburban unincorporated areas."

Although Miami is considered a major city and metropolitan region, its history only goes back to "the early 20th century" (Nijman & Clery, 2020, p. 66). Indeed, significant urban growth, in the form of "infill development along the coast and gradual westward expansion," did not occur until after the Second World War, "in part owing to the advent of air conditioning" (p. 68).

In addition to Miami-Dade County, Greater Miami includes Broward County and Palm Beach County. In fact, the consolidated Metropolitan Statistical Area of Miami is home to more than 6 million people, making it the seventh most populated region in the country. By studying suburban governance in Miami-Dade County, Fernando Burga focuses on the area with not only the highest percentage of foreign-born citizens but also the highest proportion of Hispanics in the entire metropolitan region: "Miami-Dade County ... is a majority-minority region, where immigrant, racial, and ethnic minorities represent the majority of residents."

In Miami-Dade County, suburban governance is rooted in an older suburban growth model based on speculation that favours "sprawl and segregation." It was not until the late 1950s that the "establishment of a county government became a prescient issue." A central governing body – the Metro tier – was introduced following the adoption of the Dade County Home Rule Charter in 1957. The Metro tier's responsibilities included planning and providing services related to transportation, health care, public housing, and the environment. The "lower tier" of governance, which corresponded to suburban unincorporated areas, had a mandate to represent local residents and provide community-based services. This division meant that the Metro tier was responsible for managing certain local services in unincorporated areas. This model's weakness lay in the possibility of having its legitimacy questioned by new social and political movements demanding secession. Indeed, the incorporation of new municipalities remains an extremely sensitive issue in regional planning.

The Miami chapter's analysis of secessionism provides a good illustration of the difficulties associated with regional planning in a context where social and territorial divisions are debated in the political arena. Demands for secession are seen very differently by affluent white communities, compared to Hispanic and/or Black communities: "The rebellion of municipal incorporations was led by communities of interest representing white affluent residents in suburban unincorporated areas. Their concerns arose against the backdrop of three historical tensions in Metro government: the failure of local representation and service provisions in suburban unincorporated areas, the fiscal imbalance between diverse communities, and the reconfiguration of political power in the city on behalf of Cuban Americans."

The narrative of suburban governance in Miami-Dade County highlights the uncertainty associated with governance at the regional or metropolitan level. Despite the appeal of "good governance" (Rothstein, 2012; Weiss, 2013) and the possibility of collective action, building the degree of consensus required for public action involves overcoming tensions and conflicts that can never be permanently resolved. This situation is a challenge for local municipalities, since local spaces serve as both an arena and a resource for social actors (Damay, 2018). In this way, local culture is an indispensable source of support for social and political action, alongside and sometimes in opposition to highly constraining national traditions.

In the case of Johannesburg, diverse categories of non-state actors have mobilized in one way or another to "influence the spatial form, land use, and state investments within particular parts of the city space." Although they have often achieved success, it does not mean that municipal decision making and/or regulatory authorities have become any more open or inclusive.

At the outset, a collective choice was previously made to consolidate "roughly twenty pre-existing municipal areas" into a single metropolitan government, the City of Johannesburg. The latter covers most of the Gauteng city-region, a conurbation with more than 15 million inhabitants. Focusing on three suburban areas – "the very large township complex of Soweto, the older elite suburb of Emmarentia, and the northwestern periphery of Johannesburg" – Margot Rubin, Alison Todes, and Alan Mabin compare the strategies used by interest groups to promote their projects and priorities, while coping with the new regulatory authority (the consolidated metropolitan municipality) and planning system.

The creation of a consolidated metropolitan municipality in Johannesburg was made "after the formal end of apartheid." It was the result of a political decision taken by the national government. The aim was to overcome the fiscal inequalities that had existed during the apartheid era. However, the choice of consolidation over fragmentation in support of redistribution was not endorsed by everyone. Leaders of civic movements, who played a key role in the struggle against apartheid, feared that a centralized authority "would be too remote from its citizens."

Nonetheless, the idea of a new consolidated metropolitan municipality won the day. It was seen as the best option for addressing the damage done by the previous "fragmented and racially divided system of local government," which had created "deep fiscal inequalities across the city." But whereas this reform brought with it spatial planning practices that helped improve infrastructure and services in "previously marginalized Black African areas," competition between municipalities persisted. As efficient as it might be, comprehensive spatial planning does not take place in a vacuum: "unbiased redistribution is not a fait accompli just because a local authority has centralized, and much is related to how different coalitions are able to leverage their interests."

When it comes to planning, implementation almost always falls short of initial expectations. Planning practices have inherent limits that are far from just rhetorical. So should it really be surprising when the concrete implementation of a plan fails to fully meet its strategic objectives or other goals (Flyvbjerg, 1998)? Planners are not demigods. More importantly, the analysis of suburban development in the Johannesburg metropolitan region underscores how plans are discursive proposals influenced by the planner's capacity for "acting with things" (Beauregard, 2015). In this regard, applying actor-network theory means accepting the general need to understand situations in relation to their materiality – not only in the case of stated plans but also that of arguments, expertise, buildings, and so on. This approach recognizes the pre-eminence of objects, things, or matter over mind and ideas.

From this perspective, planning practices are also accountable to powerful "constituencies" capable of "navigating the labyrinthine corridors of power." Among social actors, the ability to influence "development within their suburbs" can be attributed to several factors, including an understanding of institutional complexities and a mastery of "town planning instruments." Whatever the case, a capacity for mobilizing residents remains essential. It is therefore not surprising that local strategies were developed based on matters of concern to residents: "the SCA [Soweto Civic Association] infiltrated the City of Johannesburg and became part of the system itself, whereas the ERA [Emmarentia Residents Association] wooed city officials and constructed long-term working relationships with key people." Centralized metropolitan government allows for the implementation of various modalities of suburban governance (as in the Istanbul region), but services and amenities can remain fragmented, while the agencies responsible for them fail to respond equally to the needs of all constituencies (Storper, 2014, p. 123).

The various chapters of this book show how issues of suburban governance are often regional or metropolitan in nature, even though they are often also defined at the local level (as in the case of Johannesburg). Relations between public authority and private power, including both synergies and conflicts, are the result of diverse and multiscalar negotiations involving communities of interest and institutions. There are simply no previously imagined or projected models of "real existing regionalism" (Addie & Keil, 2015). As a result, it largely consists of social, political, and urban compromises. These forms of cooperation need to be better understood, given that space remains "an open ongoing production" (Massey, 2005, p. 55).

Here, I should mention that the theory of governance remains incomplete. Reasons for this shortcoming include the lack of anthropological foundations and the difficulty of understanding the relationship between collective action and authority (Pinson, 2015). More importantly, there is a need to properly understand the growing tension between the political principle of democracy and its sociological underpinnings in a context of plural, diversified, and segmented interests. In other words, these factors are poorly addressed by traditional forms of political governance (Mouffe, 2018). If the general interest can no longer be expressed solely through the management of public services and the formulation of public policy by a centralized state (Dubet, 2009), how can it be pursued in urban everyday politics, such as through suburban governance?

Democracy and Processes of Democratization

As the so-called suburban periphery acquires increasing economic and demographic weight in the development of metropolitan regions, new practices are emerging. But this transformation is not necessarily acknowledged by the dominant actors, who see such practices as limiting or challenging their authority. Indeed, metropolitan regions and their specific identities tend to be a work in progress (Booth & Jouve, 2005; Heinelt et al., 2011; Jones et al., 2015; Keil et al., 2017; Lefèvre et al., 2013), and it can be difficult to recognize the need for political coordination at such a scale (Scott, 2019). Nonetheless, the innovative practices and dynamic actors described in the various chapters of this book reflect the fact that metropolitan integration can no longer be thought of exclusively in terms of expansion of the central city (Tzaninis & Boterman, 2018). This shift in perspective is particularly clear in the case of

Toronto, as discussed by Pierre Filion, Roger Keil, and Michael Collens in their chapter. Based on their analysis of the interview data, they point out how the diversity of suburban populations has helped suburban municipalities increase their presence on the metropolitan scene over the years: "there is growing sophistication in how Toronto's suburbs meet the specific challenges of a maturing suburban environment that is increasingly diverse in population and economic make-up, in built form and infrastructure." To a lesser extent, this analysis is also true for the case of Montreal's suburbs.

Urban and regional studies have been pointing out this change for at least two decades (Keil et al., 2017), describing how local development is constantly being restructured in the context of a globalized land nexus where local and global networks are intertwined (Sassen, 2004). As a result, economic, social, and environmental priorities are constantly being reassessed, providing new perspectives on the crisis of the political (Crouch, 2004; Eatwell & Goodwin, 2018; Mounk, 2018).

The question of democracy and its concrete forms looms beneath the crisis of the political. The capacity of democratic institutions to mediate ongoing conflicts based on interests and values is declining, while national populism is on the rise (Eatwell & Goodwin, 2018). In what one French researcher has labelled the "century of populism" (Rosanvallon, 2020), politics is being defined by upheaval, disengagement, and uncertainty. In response to widespread protests and discontent within civil society, several ways of democratizing decision-making processes have been explored. Numerous principles inherent to democracy as a political form have been called into question: How legitimate is majority rule under representative democracy? What is the general will, and how can it be defined? What makes authority legitimate? How much confidence should be placed in decision makers? If, as argued by Massey (2005), "interrelatedness" between local residents always "implies a spatiality" (p. 189), to what extent is this fact fundamental to how the political realm operates? These are just some of the questions that have been raised to different extents by new forms of collective action (Hamel, 2018) or new ways of expressing the general will that have emerged in the context of participatory and/or deliberative approaches to governance.

One of the hypotheses tested in this book is that projects based in everyday politics and initiated by households and social groups living in suburban areas can serve to refine our understanding of governance in action provided that the distinctive social, cultural, and geographical circumstances of metropolitan areas are addressed. Given the diverse spatial components of metropolitan regions, the urban-suburban dichotomy has become less crucial to explaining how these territories are structured. This shift leaves open the question of how to overcome tensions and conflicts among actors at a regional scale. At the same time, innovative modalities of cooperation deserve greater attention.

If the contemporary relevance of democracy and democratizing processes is reflected in the theoretical and practical challenges currently posed by right- and left-wing populism (Muller, 2017), it is also strongly reflected in urban and suburban social practices. The authors of the previous chapters all either directly or indirectly raise the issue of democracy when they discuss the interdependency of social practices within metropolitan regions. The experience of cooperation through suburban practices, as examined in the preceding chapters, raises at least three main issues.

First, the way that sociability is understood as a "way of life" in suburban contexts concurs with everyday politics (Walks, 2013). The case studies presented in this book provide a good illustration of how the challenges associated with suburban governance are place-bounded. Individual and collective preferences in terms of life-style or cultural values are affirmed in relation to both agencies of governance and the ability of actors to challenge them through various modalities of interpersonal relations and mobilization. However, governance agencies are largely configured according to past decisions. The existing empirical configuration of metropolitan governance will therefore need to adapt in the face of future challenges and as new demands for coordination emerge. This need is why looking beyond the urban/suburban dichotomy in metropolitan governance and considering "the strong interdependencies within urban areas" (Storper, 2014, p. 115) can be described as "the governance problem *par excellence*" (p. 116). It highlights the need to closely examine the definition of collective action on which governance theory is usually based, a definition that tends to emphasize cooperation and minimize conflict, including conflict arising from class struggle or from new forms of protest that challenge the foundations of cultural domination.

To some degree, the second issue echoes the governance issues discussed above. Thus, the processes that foster the emergence of new urban settlements also face challenges in the form of social demands related to the democratization of planning practices and public spaces. As spatial divisions and segregation remain highly visible, the city or urban space defined as a "collective good" becomes less accessible to everyone. Saskia Sassen (2017) therefore argues that the question of "who owns the city" needs to be raised anew in light of the threat currently posed to urbanity by the "surge in large-scale corporate redevelopment and privatizing of urban space" (p. 125). Does it mean that insurgent collective action seeking improved public services and opposing urban discrimination is less likely to be effective? Under what conditions can existing metropolitan governance institutions provide the tools necessary for citizens to deliberate and take action, in an inclusive and effective manner, with the aim of improving the conditions of everyone's social, cultural, and material life?

Granted, the notions of "participatory governance" (Baiocchi, 2003), "deliberative governance" (Andersen & Loftager, 2014), and "urban assemblages" (Farias, 2011, 2016) have helped to understand the conditions under which hybrid forums can emerge in terms of the social, technical, and political requirements for expanding and democratizing public deliberation. However, positive empirical results have proven difficult to achieve and ambivalent at best. Doubts regarding the possibility of success reflect a larger uncertainty regarding democracy itself. The idea that democracy needs to be constantly reinvented (Lefort, 1981) should be applied to suburban and metropolitan governance while paying careful attention to the theoretical implications of this perspective, which places special emphasis on the uncertainty of social life.

The third and final issue relates to the rise of "city networks" (Davidson et al., 2019). Along with intra-regional relationships (Belinda & Lehrer, 2017), cross-national networking among cities is by no means a recent feature of suburban globality. Planners, civic activists, and promoters have always been inspired by achievements elsewhere, not to mention enamoured with the idea of exporting their own innovations. However, it is important to recognize that, in the era of the internet and social networks, exchanges and cooperation between cities now serve to enhance their status, with important implications for urban governance: "As the landscape of city networks changes, so do the pressures that it puts on urban governance ... From the city-to-city partnering of 'sister cities' movements of the Cold War, and early efforts at transnational urban campaigns like ICLEI [International Council for Local Environmental Initiatives], we are now witnessing the emergence of complex networked urban governance structures that involve extensive engagement by multilateral and private actors" (Davidson et al., 2019, pp. 3544–5; see also Miraftab, 2011).

Transnational suburban governance gives local governments a larger role in the formation of local states, thereby strengthening their legitimacy – democratic or other. This phenomenon has been observed in several metropolitan regions, and all the case studies discussed in this book address it to some extent. On the other hand, the mobilization efforts of local actors on the ground – an increasingly important aspect of suburban and metropolitan development everywhere (Savini & Bertolini, 2019) – cannot be understood without reference to national history and local culture. Anyone attempting to analyse decisions taken in Shanghai to address global competitiveness, while also considering the conflicts and uncertainty surrounding planning practices and metropolitan governance in Johannesburg, will inevitably find themselves comparing apples and oranges. Nevertheless, processes of democratization are clearly at stake in the political debates occurring in both contexts.

Coda

The contributions to this book point out how issues of suburban governance are becoming more pressing in various peripheral urban areas around the world. In many cases, suburban governance involves a range of political modalities including state policy, capitalist accumulation, and/or private management (Ekers et al., 2012). The lesson is that these diverse modalities are operating within national and local contexts – through a system of multilevel governance where national boundaries are under pressures from both above and below (Piattoni, 2010) – which set limits on the potential for collective action while also sometimes allowing new opportunities to emerge.

However, this finding does not mean that the issue of suburban governance has been resolved. Clearly, no prescriptive and operational framework for suburban governance has been established, which reflects not only the diversity of venues where social and political actors deliberate on the future of metropolitan regions but especially the need to better explore the forms of cooperation that these actors have successfully defined in diverse countries, across different political and institutional contexts, and through interactions between states and civil society actors.

Finally, the study of suburban politics draws attention to the overarching question of democracy. The current crisis of the political has served to highlight the indeterminate nature of public choices about living together. Suburban governance is multifaceted and therefore evolves in response to a wide range of local and global demands. Cities have been described as the places "which are the greatest challenges to democracy" (Massey, 2005, p. 155). But what about suburban landscapes and metropolitan regions, where most of the world's population now lives? Although the contingent practices of suburban governance can, in some instances, challenge the authority of the state, they do not necessarily foster citizen empowerment and/or local self-determination.

But one thing is certain: governing suburbia has become a critical element for planning metropolitan regions in the twenty-first century. Thus, two outcomes are worth mentioning: First, despite the differences in historical, geographical, cultural, and political terms characterizing metropolitan regions in diverse national contexts, local actors are directly or indirectly confronted with democratic challenges. Second, if the suburban contribution to the restructuring of urban regions can no longer be ignored, it remains difficult to build a viable path for cooperation among those actors at various scales. Overcoming economic and territorial conflicts to improve suburban governance remains at stake, and this task must be undertaken considering not only the diversity of socio-economic realities that suburbs are experiencing but also their role in the development and redevelopment of metropolitan regions.

NOTES

1 Here is how Araujo and Martuccelli (2017) have described the situation in their work on Latin America, and Chile in particular: "In no society do individual actors invent subject ideals. These ideals are offered and put at their disposal. They are part of the culture and society in which an individual is forged. The specificity of occidental modernity and institutional individualism is that the individual is interpellated to constitute her- or himself as an individual-subject by institutions. Institutions are the ones that offer representation and support" (p. 27).
2 Here, I refer explicitly to metropolitan regions in the United States, keeping in mind that the suburban experience in Canada, and especially in Toronto and Montreal (see the case studies in this book), has been rather different than in American cities (Taylor, 2019). City life in Canada is certainly influenced by American culture, but it also draws on the European urban tradition. As a result, "Canada is situated between the urban experiences of more market-oriented urban development of the United States and the more state-led developments in European cities" (Keil et al., 2017, p. 15).

REFERENCES

Addie, J.-P., & Keil, R. (2015). Real existing regionalism: The region between talk, territory and technology. *International Journal of Urban and Regional Research, 39*(2), 407–17. https://doi.org/10.1111/1468-2427.12179
Amin, A., & Thrift, N. (2017). *Seeing like a city*. Polity Press.
Andersen, S.C., & Loftager, J. (2014). Deliberative democratic governance. *Administrative Theory & Praxis, 36*(4), 510–29. https://doi.org/10.2753/ATP1084-1806360404

Araujo, K., & Martuccelli, D. (2017). Beyond institutional individualism: Agentic individualism and individuation process in Chilean society. *Current Sociology, 62*(1), 24–40. https://doi.org/10.1177/0011392113512496

Bailey, D., Clark, J., Colombelli, A., Corradini, C., De Propris, L., Derudder, B., Fratesi, U., Fritsch, M., Harrison, J., Hatfield, M., Kemeny, T., Kogler, D., Lagendijk, A., Lawton, P., Ortega-Argilés, R., & Usai, S. (2020). Rethinking regions in turbulent times. *Regional Studies, 54*(1), 1–4. https://doi.org/10.1080/00343404.2019.1698837

Baiocchi, G. (2003). Emergent public spheres: Talking politics in participatory governance. *American Sociological Review, 68*(1), 52–74. https://doi.org/10.2307/3088902

Bauman, Z. (2001). *The individualized society*. Polity Press.

Beauregard, R.A. (2015). *Planning matter: Acting with things*. University of Chicago Press.

Beck, U., & Beck-Gernsheim, E. (2002). *Individualization: Institutionalized individualism and its social and political consequences*. Sage.

Belinda, B., & Lehrer, U. (2017). The global city-region: A constantly emerging scalar fix. In R. Keil, P. Hamel, J.-A. Boudreau, & S. Kipfer (Eds.), *Governing cities through regions: Canadian and European perspectives* (pp. 83–97). Wilfrid Laurier University Press.

Bevir, M., & Rhodes, R.A.W. (2010). *The state as cultural practice*. Oxford University Press.

Booth, P., & Jouve, B. (2005). *Metropolitan democracies: Transformation of the state and urban policy in Canada, France and Great Britain*. Ashgate.

Brenner, N. (2019). *New urban spaces: Urban theory and the scale question*. Oxford University Press.

Cockburn, C. (1977). *The local state: Management of cities and people*. Pluto Press.

Crouch, C. (2004). *Post-democracy*. Polity Press.

Damay, L. (2018). Effets de milieu et ressource spatiale dans les scènes participatives. In E. Lenel (Ed.), *L'espace des sociologues: Recherches contemporaines en compagnie de Jean Rémy* (pp. 247–74). Éditions Érès.

Davidson, K., Coenen, L., Acuto, M., & Gleeson, B. (2019). Reconfiguring urban governance in an age of rising city networks: A research agenda. *Urban Studies, 56*(16), 3540–55. https://doi.org/10.1177/0042098018816010

de Singly, F. (2017). *Double Je: Identité personnelle et identité statutaire*. Armand Colin.

Dubet, F. (2009). *Le travail des sociétés*. Seuil.

Dubet, F. (2016). *Ce qui nous unit: Discriminations, égalité et reconnaissance*. Seuil.

Dubet, F. (2017). Peut-on se passer de l'idée moderne de société? *Revue internationale de philosophie, 281*(3), 241–58. https://www.cairn.info/revue-internationale-de-philosophie-2017-3-page-241.htm

Eatwell, R., & Goodwin, M. (2018). *National populism: The revolt against liberal democracy*. Pelican Book.

Ekers, M., Hamel, P., & Keil, R. (2012). Governing suburbia: Modalities and mechanisms of suburban governance. *Regional Studies, 46*(3), 405–22. https://doi.org/10.1080/00343404.2012.658036

Farias, I. (2011). The politics of urban assemblages. *City, 15*(3–4), 365–74. https://doi.org/10.1080/13604813.2011.595110

Farias, I. (2016). Divising hybrid forums: Technical democracy in a dangerous world. *City, 20*(4), 549–62. https://doi.org/10.1080/13604813 .2016.1193998

Fishman, R. (1987). *Bourgeois utopias: The rise and fall of suburbia.* Basic Books.

Flyvbjerg, B. (1998). *Rationality and power: Democracy in practice.* University of Chicago Press.

Hamel, P. (2018). Débat public et enjeux urbains: La contribution des mouvements sociaux. In L. Guay & P. Hamel (Eds.), *Les aléas du débat public: Action collective, expertise et démocratie* (pp. 293–313). Les Presses de l'Université Laval.

Hamel, P., Lustiger-Thaler, H., & Maheu, L. (1999). Is there a role for social movements? In J.L. Abu-Lughod (Ed.), *Sociology for the twenty-first century: Continuities and cutting edges* (pp. 165–80). University of Chicago Press.

Hanlon, B., & Vicino, T. (Eds.). (2019). *The Routledge companion to the suburbs.* Routledge.

Harris, R. (2013). How land markets make and change suburbs. In R. Keil (Ed.), *Suburban constellations* (pp. 33–8). Jovis Verlag.

Harrison, J., Delgado, M., Derudder, B., Anguelovski, I., Montero, S., Bailey, D., & De Propris, L. (2019). Pushing regional studies beyond its borders. *Regional Studies, 54*(1), 125–39. https://doi.org/10.1080/00343404.2019 .1672146

Hayden, D. (2003). *Building suburbia: Green fields and urban growth, 1820–2000.* Pantheon Books.

Heinelt, H., Razin, E., & Zimmermann, K. (Eds.). (2011). *Metropolitan governance: Different paths in contrasting contexts: Germany and Israel.* Campus Verlag.

Jones, K.E., Lord, A., & Shields, R. (Eds). (2015). *City-regions in prospect? Exploring points between place and practice.* McGill-Queen's University Press.

Keil, R. (1998). Globalization makes states: Perspectives of local governance in the age of the world city. *Review of International Political Economy, 5*(4), 616–46. https://doi.org/10.1080/096922998347408

Keil, R. (2018). *Suburban planet.* Polity Press.

Keil, R., Hamel, P., Boudreau, J.-A., Kipfer, S., & Allahwala, A. (2017). Regional governance revisited: Political space, collective agency, and identity. In R. Keil, P. Hamel, J.-A. Boudreau, & S. Kipfer (Eds.), *Governing cities through regions: Canadian and European perspectives* (pp. 3–26). Wilfrid Laurier University Press.

Leca, J. (1996). La démocratie à l'épreuve des pluralismes. *Revue française de science politique*, *46*(2), 225–79. https://doi.org/10.3406/rfsp.1996.395052

Lefebvre, H. (1974). *La production de l'espace*. Éditions Anthropos.

Lefèvre, C., Roseau, N., & Vitale, T. (2013*). De la ville à la métropole: Les défis de la gouvernance*. L'œil d'or.

Lefort, C. (1981). *L'invention démocratique*. Fayard.

Le Galès, P. (2002). *European cities: Social conflicts and governance*. Oxford University Press.

Le Galès, P. (2021). The rise of local politics: A global review. *Annual Review of Political Science*, *24*, 345–63. https://doi.org/10.1146/annurev-polisci -041719-102158

Lukas, M. (2019). Urban governance. In A. Orum (Ed.), *The Wiley Blackwell encyclopedia of urban and regional studies* (pp. 1–11). John Wiley.

Magnusson, W. (1985). The local state in Canada: Theoretical perspectives. *Canadian Public Administration*, *28*(4), 575–99. https://doi.org/10.1111 /j.1754-7121.1985.tb00385.x

Magnusson, W. (2015). *Local self-government and the right to the city*. McGill-Queen's University Press.

Martuccelli, D. (2017a). *La condition sociale moderne: L'avenir d'une inquiétude*. Gallimard.

Martuccelli, D. (2017b). Les deux modernités occidentales et la géo-modernité actuelle. *Revue internationale de philosophie*, *281*(3), 349–67. https://doi.org /10.3917/rip.281.0349

Massey, D. (1996). Politicising space and place. *Scottish Geographical Magazine*, *112*(2), 117–23. https://doi.org/10.1080/14702549608554458

Massey, D. (2005). *For space*. Sage.

Massey, D. (2013). Doreen Massey on space. *Social Science Bites in association with Sage*: https://www.socialsciencespace.com/2013/02/podcastdoreen -massey-on-space/

Miraftab, F. (2011). Symposium introduction: Immigration and transnationalities of planning. *Journal of Planning Education and Research*, *31*(4), 375–78. https://doi.org/10.1177/0739456X11425001

Morales, A.J., Dong, X., Bar-Yam, Y., & Pentland, A.S. (2019). Segregation and polarization in urban areas. *Royal Society Open Science*, *6*(10), Article 190573. https://doi.org/10.1098/rsos.190573

Mouffe, C. (2018). *Pour un populisme de gauche*. Albin Michel.

Mounk, Y. (2018). *People vs democracy: Why our freedom is in danger and how to save it*. Harvard University Press.

Muller, J.-W. (2017). *Qu'est-ce que le populisme?* Gallimard.

Nijman, J., & Clery, T. (2020). Searching for suburbia in Metropolitan Miami. In J. Nijman (Ed.), *The life of North American suburbs: Imagined utopias and transitional spaces* (pp. 65–87). University of Toronto Press.

Ong, A. (2011). Introduction: Worlding cities, or the art of being global. In A. Roy & A. Ong (Eds.), *Worlding cities: Asian experiments and the art of being global* (pp. 1–26). Wiley-Blackwell.

Paasi, A., & Metzger, J. (2017). Foregrounding the region. *Regional Studies, 51*(1), 19–30. https://doi.org/10.1080/00343404.2016.1239818

Phelps, N.A., & Wu, F. (Eds.). (2011). *International perspectives on suburbanization: A post-suburban world?* Palgrave Macmillan.

Piattoni, S. (2010). *The theory of multi-level governance: Conceptual, empirical, and normative challenges.* Oxford University Press.

Pinson, G. (2015). Gouvernance et sociologie de l'action organisée: Action publique, coordination et théorie de l'État. *L'année sociologique, 65*(2): 483–516. https://doi.org/10.3917/anso.152.0483

Robinson, J. (2016). Thinking cities through elsewhere: Comparative tactics for a more global urban studies. *Progress in Human Geography, 40*(1), 3–29. https://doi.org/10.1177/0309132515598025

Rosanvallon, P. (2020). *Le siècle du populisme: Histoire, théorie, critique.* Seuil.

Rothstein, B. (2012). Good governance. In D. Levi-Faur (Ed.), *Oxford handbook of governance* (pp. 143–54). Oxford University Press.

Sassen, S. (2004). Local actors in global politics. *Current Sociology, 52*(4), 649–70. https://doi.org/10.1177/0011392104043495

Sassen, S. (2017). The city: A collective good? *Brown Journal of World Affairs, 23*(2), 119–26. https://www.jstor.org/stable/27119058

Savini, F., & Bertolini, L. (2019). Urban experimentation as a politics of niches. *Environment and Planning A: Economy and Space, 51*(4), 831–48. https://doi.org/10.1177/0308518X19826085

Savitch, H.V., & Vogel, R.K. (2000). Introduction: Paths to new regionalism. *State and Local Government Review, 32*(3), 158–68. https://doi.org/10.1177/0160323X0003200301

Savoie, D.J. (2019). *La démocratie au Canada: L'effritement de nos institutions.* McGill-Queen's University Press.

Schmid, C., Karaman, O., Hanakata, N.C., Kallenberger, P., Kockelkorn, A., Sawyer, L., Streule, M., & Wong, K.P. (2018). Towards a new vocabulary of urbanisation processes: A comparative approach. *Urban Studies, 55*(1), 19–52. https://doi.org/10.1177/0042098017739750

Scott, A.J. (2019). City-regions reconsidered. *Environment and Planning A: Economy and Space, 51*(3), 554–80. https://doi.org/10.1177/0308518X19831591

Stoker, G. (1998). Governance as theory: Five propositions. *International Social Science Journal, 50*(155), 17–28. https://doi.org/10.1111/1468-2451.00106

Storper, M. (2014). Governing the large metropolis. *Territory, Politics, Governance, 2*(2), 115–34. https://doi.org/10.1080/21622671.2014.919874

Swanstrom, T. (2001). What we argue about when we argue about regionalism. *Journal of Urban Affairs, 23*(5), 479–96. https://doi.org/10.1111/0735-2166.00102

Taylor, Z. (2019). *Shaping the metropolis: Institutions and urbanization in the United States and Canada*. McGill-Queen's University Press.

Teaford, J.C. (2006). *The metropolitan revolution: The rise of post-urban America*. Columbia University Press.

Touraine, A. (2018). *Défense de la modernité*. Seuil.

Tzaninis, Y., & Boterman, W. (2018). Beyond the urban–suburban dichotomy: Shifting mobilities and the transformation of suburbia. *City*, *22*(1), 43–62. https://doi.org/10.1080/13604813.2018.1432143

Walks, A. (2013). Suburbanism as a way of life, slight return. *Urban Studies*, *50*(8), 1471–88. https://doi.org/10.1177/0042098012462610

Weiss, T.G. (2013). *Global governance: Why? What? Whither?* Polity Press.

Contributors

Marie-Hélène Bacqué is a professor of urban studies at the French university Paris Nanterre. She is also a member of the research unit Lavue (UMR 7218) and of the Institut universitaire de France. Her research interests focus on the transformation of neighbourhoods in France and in North America, looking at social mobilization as well as public policies. She has published several books, including *Retour à Roissy: Voyage sur le RER B* (with photographs by André Mérian; Seuil, 2019) and *Banlieues populaires: Territoires, sociétés, politiques* (with Emmanuel Bellanger and Henri Rey; l'Aube, 2018).

Fernando Burga is an assistant professor at the University of Minnesota's Humphrey School of Public Affairs in the Master of Urban and Regional Planning Program. His research, teaching, and service focus on the impacts of Latinx immigration on urban planning, planning history, and urban food systems. He is currently finalizing a book on the impacts of Cuban immigration regarding comprehensive planning in Miami, under contract by the University of Toronto Press.

Éric Charmes is a research director at ENTPE (Vaulx-en-Velin). He does research in urban studies, urbanism, and planning. He works with the Laboratory of Interdisciplinary Research on City, Space and Society (RIVES, University of Lyon, UMR CNRS 5600). He has published several books, including *Métropoles et éloignement résidentiel* (Autrement, 2021); *La Revanche des villages* (Seuil, 2019); *Quitter Paris? Les classes moyennes entre centres et périphéries* (with Stéphanie Vermeersch, Lydie Launay, and Marie-Hélène Bacqué; Créaphis, 2019); *The Middle Classes and the City: A Study of Paris and London* (with Marie-Hélène Bacqué, Gary Bridge et al.; Palgrave, 2015); and *La Ville émiettée: Essai sur la clubbisation de la vie urbaine* (Presses Universitaires de France, 2011).

Michael Collens holds a master's degree in environmental studies (planning) and a bachelor's degree in environmental studies specializing in urban and regional environments from York University. His professional interests focus on regional transportation infrastructure, governance, and land-use development patterns. He is particularly concerned with how they intersect and impact residents' quality of life and social equity. Michael works for the government of Ontario, focusing on long-range planning policy, implementation, and data analysis to help coordinate planning for growth. Michael lives in Toronto with his wife and son.

Pierre Filion is a professor emeritus at the School of Planning, University of Waterloo. His recent research focuses on the obstacles to a smart growth–inspired transformation of cities, as well as on metropolitan-scale planning models put forth in the plans of large North American metropolitan regions. More generally, his research projects have dealt with the relationship between transportation and land use, and with the impact of societal change on cities, with a particular focus on values, the economy, and institutions.

K. Murat Güney is a social scientist and an urban researcher. He received his PhD degree in anthropology from Columbia University. His research interests include urban resilience, earthquakes, urban transformation, housing problems, and wealth and income inequality. Previously, he taught in the anthropology department at Boston University and worked as a postdoctoral researcher in the City Institute at York University. Güney is the editor of the books *Massive Suburbanization: (Re)Building the Global Periphery* (co-edited with Roger Keil and Murat Üçoğlu; University of Toronto Press, 2019); *Başka Dünyalar Mümkün* (Other Worlds Are Possible; Varlık, 2007); *Türkiye'de İktidar'ı Yeniden Düşünmek* (Rethinking Power Relations in Turkey; Varlık, 2009); and the political and cultural criticism journal *Davetsiz Misafir* (The Uninvited Guest).

Pierre Hamel is a professor emeritus of sociology, Université de Montréal, and the former editor of the sociology journal *Sociologie et Sociétés*. He is also a former chair of Canadian studies at Paris 3, Sorbonne Nouvelle (2010–11). His research focuses on collective action and issues of democratization around urban issues. Among his publications are *Les aléas du débat public: Action collective, expertise et démocratie* (co-edited with Louis Guay; Presses de l'Université Laval and Hermann Éditeurs, 2018) and *Handbook on Urban Social Movements* (co-edited with Anna Domaradzka; Edward Elgar, 2024).

Roger Keil is a professor in the Faculty of Environmental and Urban Change, York University. He researches global suburbanization, urban political ecology, cities and infectious disease, infrastructure, and regional governance. Among his recent publications are *Suburban Planet* (Polity, 2018) and *After Suburbia* (co-edited with Fulong Wu; University of Toronto Press, 2022), as well as *Pandemic Urbanism* (with S. Harris Ali and Creighton Connolly; Polity, 2023) and *Turning Up the Heat: Urban Political Ecology for a Climate Emergency* (co-edited with Maria Kaika, Tait Mandler, and Yannis Tzaninis; Manchester University Press, 2023). Keil is a Fellow of CIFAR's Humanity's Urban Future program.

Alan Mabin lives in Cape Town and is an emeritus professor at the School of Architecture and Planning, University of the Witwatersrand, Johannesburg, which he directed from 2005 to 2010. Alan has research experience in Brazil, France, Tanzania, and South Africa, as well as NGO, post-apartheid government, and consulting experience. He co-led the Africa cluster for the Global Suburbanisms project; his recent work addresses both large city-regions and small towns.

Valentin Meilinger holds a PhD in spatial planning from the Department of Human Geography and Spatial Planning at Utrecht University and currently works as a research fellow in the field of urban climate change adaptation at the German Environment Agency. Drawing from science and technology studies, urban studies, and debates in critical geography, his research revolves around the shifting relations between infrastructure, water, and landscapes in cities under climate change. In particular, Valentin focuses on the political role of infrastructure in the creation and remaking of urban nature to analyse contemporary technological cultures of urban nature. His PhD research analysed these questions in the city of Los Angeles, California, while his current research focuses on German cities.

Jochen Monstadt holds the Chair for Governance of Urban Transitions and Dynamics in the Department of Human Geography and Spatial Planning at Utrecht University. His research interests are at the interface of urban studies and social studies of technology. He has conducted and coordinated extensive research on the urban governance of socioecological and sociotechnical change in the Global North and South. His current research projects and interests involve the governance of urban and infrastructural vulnerability and resilience, urban and infrastructural transformations in East and South Africa, and low-carbon transformations in European cities.

Margot Rubin is a lecturer in spatial planning at the School of Geography and Planning, Cardiff University and guest lecturer at the School of Architecture and Planning, as well as a research associate with the Gauteng City Region Observatory. Recently, she co-edited the volumes *Densifying the City? Global Cases and Johannesburg*; and *Housing in African Cities: A Lens on Urban Governance.* Her research focuses on housing and urban governance in the Global South. She has been writing about inner-city regeneration and housing policy, and is currently engaged in work around mega housing projects and issues of gender and the city.

Alison Todes is a professor of urban and regional planning in the School of Architecture and Planning, University of Witwatersrand. She was previously a research director at the Human Sciences Research Council and a professor of planning in the School of Architecture, Planning and Housing at the University of KwaZulu-Natal, Durban. She has researched and published extensively on urban and regional development and planning. Recent books include the co-edited volumes *Densifying the City? Global Cases and Johannesburg* (2020); and *Changing Space, Changing City: Johannesburg after Apartheid* (2014). She is currently working on co-authored books on urban peripheries and on planning in South Africa.

Murat Üçoğlu is a Mitacs Accelerate postdoc researcher at York University. He works on the discussion of missing-middle housing in Toronto. He received his PhD in environmental studies from York University in 2021. He co-edited the book *Massive Suburbanization: (Re)Building the Global Periphery* (together with K. Murat Güney and Roger Keil), published by the University of Toronto Press. His research interests include the financialization of housing, massive suburban expansion, urban political economy, and political ecology. He teaches courses in urban sustainability, land and urban development and urban sociology.

Fulong Wu is Bartlett Professor of Planning at University College London. His research interests include urban development in China and its social and sustainable challenges. He is the author of *Planning for Growth: Urban and Regional Planning in China* (Routledge, 2015), *Creating Chinese Urbanism: Urban Revolution and Governance Changes* (UCL Press, 2022, free downloadable from the publisher website), and co-editor (with Roger Keil) of *After Suburbia: Urbanization in the 21st Century* (Toronto University Press, 2022). He is currently working on a European Research Council (ERC) advanced grant – Rethinking China's Model of Governance (ChinaUrban).

Index

GLOBAL SUBURBANISMS

Series Editor: Roger Keil, York University

Published to date:

Milton Keynes UK
Ingram Content Group UK Ltd.
UKHW042012210924
448480UK00002B/29/J